Non-Distinct Arguments in Uto-Aztecan

By Ronald W. Langacker

University of California Publications
Linguistics 82

NON-DISTINCT ARGUMENTS IN UTO-AZTECAN

TO MY PARENTS

NON-DISTINCT ARGUMENTS IN UTO-AZTECAN

BY
RONALD W. LANGACKER

UNIVERSITY OF CALIFORNIA PRESS
BERKELEY • LOS ANGELES • LONDON

UNIVERSITY OF CALIFORNIA PUBLICATIONS IN LINGUISTICS

Volume 82
Approved for publication February 21, 1975

Issued January 5, 1976

University of California Press
Berkeley and Los Angeles
California

University of California Press, Ltd.
London, England

ISBN: 0-520-09539-1

Library of Congress Catalog Card Number: 75-620019

PREFACE

This monograph reports on one facet of a wide-ranging program of research on comparative Uto-Aztecan historical grammar. A Senior Fellowship granted by the National Endowment for the Humanities for the academic year 1973-1974 enabled me to lay the groundwork for this research program, and the present monograph was written in preliminary form during the tenure of this fellowship.

Uto-Aztecan is one of the largest and better described families of American Indian languages. It occupies much of the western United States and Mexico, ranging from Oregon and Idaho to the area of Mexico City, with isolated outposts farther south. Uto-Aztecan and Kiowa-Tanoan are thought to be related in a larger family called Aztec-Tanoan, but I will confine my attention here to Uto-Aztecan proper. Within Uto-Aztecan I have limited my primary consideration to twenty daughter languages, chosen on the basis of availability of information and fullest possible representation of subfamilies. More than twenty other languages and dialects have been examined to some degree (in most cases only fragmentary data is available), but they will not figure prominently in the discussion.

Various alternative schemes have been suggested for grouping the Uto-Aztecan languages into subfamilies. The most conservative classification posits eight major subfamilies (leaving aside the extinct and barely attested Giamina), and this is the classification I will adopt as a working hypothesis. The twenty languages under primary consideration are listed and classified in Appendix A; none of the subfamilies shown there is considered controversial, though their degree of substantiation varies. I believe further subgroupings can be justified, but I prefer to treat this as a possible ultimate outcome of comparative research and not as a working assumption.

While Uto-Aztecan is fairly well described as American Indian language

[v]

families go, published information leaves much to be desired, particularly
in the domain of morphology and syntax. I have examined virtually all significant published sources of information, but it has been necessary to tap
an unusually wide variety of other sources as well. These include elicitation from native speakers; personal communications (both oral and written);
doctoral dissertations; unpublished manuscripts; student term papers; and
informal written notes of all kinds, ranging from extensive, well-organized
descriptions to handouts and other scraps of paper. Some sources are naturally more trustworthy than others, and one must deal with many instances
of spurious, fragmentary, or conflicting information. It is therefore essential to note the origin of one's data so that it may be properly evaluated and
checked for accuracy. To this end I have assembled all my sources of information in the Bibliography. Each is assigned a simple code designation
for convenient reference, and every example cited in the monograph (apart
from citations of individual morphemes) is accompanied by the code designation indicating its source together with the page number (where appropriate).

Because of the large number of languages being considered, and more
importantly because of the wide variety of sources from which I have drawn
information, it has been helpful if not essential to normalize transcriptions.
For example, I consistently use the symbol i̱ for a high, non-front, un-
rounded vowel, while the writers from whom I have taken data have variously represented such sounds as i̱, ï, ǝ, e̱, u̱, ü, ʌ, and y̱. The symbols I have
chosen are all established ones and are used with approximately the phonetic
values normally understood. The level of representation is basically phonemic but may on occasion be more or less abstract; such variation is un-
avoidable in the absence of homogeneous pools of data based on careful and
extensive phonological analyses of each daughter language. Information on
stress and other suprasegmental phenomena is in so many instances either
absent or untrustworthy that I have not attempted to write these features. No
doubt I have made some mistakes in standardizing the transcriptions. Hopefully these will not affect the validity of the analysis, and in any case the
reader will be able to find the original transcription by virtue of the reference codes.

The material offered in the Appendices and Bibliography transcends the

present work, in that it was formulated and collected for the overall research project of which this monograph represents only a small part. Not
all of the language abbreviations cited in Appendix B are used here, nor all
of the abbreviations for grammatical terms listed in Appendix C; the full
sets are offered to make the overall system of notation apparent, for possible convenience of reference in future works, and for whatever utility they
may have for other scholars. Likewise, relatively few of the references
listed in the Bibliography are cited directly in the text, but the usefulness
of an up-to-date and reasonably comprehensive bibliography of Uto-Aztecan
hardly needs comment.

Finally, I wish to acknowledge the many people who have contributed to
this work in one way or another. These include the many previous scholars
whose efforts have facilitated my own; the native speakers who have provided the linguistic community with the precious resource of their languages;
the students who have sat through my courses on Uto-Aztecan, given me
helpful comments on my work, carried out valuable fieldwork, and provided
me with extensive data and insights in the form of dissertations, manuscripts, and personal discussions; the linguists who have taken the time to
read a preliminary version of this monograph and provide constructive crit-
icism; and the family, colleagues, acquaintances, and secretarial staff who
have contributed or suffered in numerous and sundry ways in the process of
research, writing, and publication.

R. W. L.

CONTENTS

Tables

INTRODUCTION

In this monograph I will examine a class of syntactic constructions in
the large Uto-Aztecan family of American Indian languages. I will present pertinent data from twenty representative languages for which information is available; offer and justify reconstructions for Proto Uto-
Aztecan; trace the evolution of the proto forms, step by step, through the
intermediate proto language stages to the ultimate daughter forms; and
explore the implications of the analysis for Uto-Aztecan studies and for
linguistic theory, both synchronic and diachronic.

Four basic types of syntactic constructions will be examined: passive,
impersonal, reflexive (including reciprocal), and unspecified argument
constructions. These four are not chosen arbitrarily, but rather because
they bear extensive and significant relations to one another, both in terms
of historical Uto-Aztecan grammar and in terms of linguistic theory and
analysis. The precise nature of this relationship has not previously been
established, so we will begin by characterizing the four kinds of constructions, noting their manifestation in Uto-Aztecan, and elucidating their
common properties.

The four types of constructions can be defined by reference to clause
structure at the surface and semantic levels. In discussing semantic
representations, it is helpful to view a clause (or proposition) as consisting of a predicate together with its associated arguments. I will assume
that at most two arguments (N_1 and N_2) can be associated with a given
predicate (V), and that these arguments are ordered, in the sense that a
proposition of the form $N_1 V N_2$ will not always be semantically equivalent
to one of the form $N_2 V N_1$ (where N_1, N_2, and V are held constant). Surface clauses tend to be considerably more complex, but to some degree

they can be described in the same terms. The basic elements of a surface clause are typically a verb and its non-oblique complements (i.e. its subject and direct object); these are the respective surface counterparts of semantic predicates and arguments.

Most commonly, the subject and direct object of a transitive clause are both lexically specified and referentially distinct, as in sentence (1).

(1) My cat caught a lizard.

Of course this is not always the case, for one of the arguments of a clause may be left unspecified, as in (2), or the subject and direct object may be coreferential, as in (3).

(2) My cat ate.

(3) My cat bit itself.

The notion of coreference is problematic in various ways, but not in any way that affects the present discussion, so I will take this notion for granted. The notion of unspecified arguments may require some clarification, however.

It is important to distinguish between unspecified arguments and deleted arguments. The direct object of ate in (2) is unspecified, since it is not identified in any way. By contrast, the object of ate in (4) is specified, though it fails to surface, for it is clearly identified as the cake.

(4) Kevin baked, and Martha ate, the cake.

Similarly, the subject of the Spanish sentence (5) is uniquely identified by inflection as the speaker even though yo (like other subject pronouns) is omitted when not emphasized.

(5) Trabajo. 'I work.'

The verb in (6) lacks an object, but here we cannot felicitously speak of the object being unspecified, since no object is semantically implied.

(6) Kevin snores.

An unspecified argument, then, is one that is semantically implied but is not identified in any way, either by reference or by lexical content.

Three of the four kinds of syntactic constructions under consideration involve unspecified arguments. A number of Uto-Aztecan languages have verb prefixes which are used to indicate that a subject or direct object is unspecified, and three such prefixes can be reconstructed for the proto language. In addition, various Uto-Aztecan languages have passive and impersonal constructions marked by verb suffixes, the same suffix commonly being used for both. Impersonal sentences, as I will define the term here, are those with an unspecified underlying subject; impersonal constructions are thus a special case of unspecified argument constructions. Passives will in turn be defined as a special kind of impersonal construction. A passive sentence is one with an unspecified underlying subject in which the underlying direct object is moved into surface subject position.[1]

Let us sketch abstractly the typical structure of (non-reflexive) passives and impersonals in Uto-Aztecan. Three basic features can be noted. First, the same verb suffix is often used for both transitive and intransitive clauses. With transitive clauses, the underlying direct object becomes the surface subject, yielding passive sentences analogous to (7).

(7) The villages were bombed.

With intransitive clauses, there is no direct object to become the surface subject, so surface subject position remains vacant and the sentence qualifies as impersonal but not as passive. (English has no direct counterpart to such sentences.) Second, the various verb suffixes used to indicate passive and impersonal sentences in Uto-Aztecan are all relatable in some way to an element meaning 'be'. Third, the underlying (or semantic) subject of these sentences is unspecified. This is true of course by definition, but it is more than simply a matter of definition, for behind it lies a substantive issue liable to controversy. English passive sentences like (8) have almost invariably been analyzed as deriving from underlying structures with specified subjects; this subject is said to become the by-phrase object by transformation.

(8) The charges were denied by the defendant.

The correctness of this analysis for English is a matter of contention (see UA-LM-PM for some discussion), but such an analysis must clearly be rejected for Uto-Aztecan. Agentive phrases (the equivalent of English by-phrases) are seldom encountered in Uto-Aztecan passives (in some

---

[1]More precisely, we should say that the underlying object is moved into derived subject position. The derived passive subject may fail to appear in surface subject position due to the operation of other rules extraneous to the present discussion, deletion rules for example.

languages they are not permitted at all), and intransitive impersonal sentences never allow them.

On the basis of these observations, I posit Figure I as the synchronic underlying structure of passive and impersonal sentences in various daughter languages and in the proto language. N_1 here is the underlying

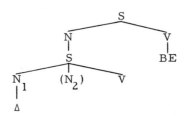

Figure I

subject, indicated by the symbol Δ to be unspecified, and N_2 is the direct object. If the direct object is absent, or if it is present and remains as a direct object, the result is an impersonal sentence. If the direct object is present and is substituted for N_1 as the surface subject, the result is a passive sentence. BE is attached to the lower V as a suffix to derive the surface form of the sentence. When an agentive phrase is present, it is presumed to derive from a conjoined (or juxtaposed) clause in which the agentive postposition functions as the underlying predicate.

The subsequent discussion should amply support the plausibility of Figure I as the underlying representation of non-reflexive passives and impersonals in Uto-Aztecan. In terms of this structure the relationship among passive, impersonal, and unspecified argument constructions is readily apparent. We must examine now the connection between these three constructions and reflexive sentences. Reflexives would seem at first blush to be quite different, since they involve coreferential rather than unspecified arguments. Some kind of relationship must be assumed, however, if only because reflexive prefixes in many Uto-Aztecan languages have come to be used to express passive sense. What is the nature of this relationship?

Reflexive clauses are those in which the subject and object are coreferential. If we compare a representation of reflexive clauses with the lower clause of Figure I, we can begin to perceive the similarity between passive/ impersonal and reflexive structures. The two kinds of structures are shown in Figure II. In reflexive clauses, the subject and object are coreferential, as indicated by the common variable symbol, x. The unspecified

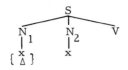

Figure II

subject, marked by Δ , is characteristic of passive and impersonal clauses. The crucial similarity, I suggest, is that in both cases the subject and direct object are referentially non-distinct. Naturally they are non-distinct in the case of coreference. When the subject is unspecified, it is not thereby coreferential to the object, but neither can it contrast with the object in reference or lexical content. The concept of non-distinctness is familiar from phonology, but little use of it has been made in syntactic studies. To be sure, the relevance of non-distinctness to syntax cannot be taken for granted but must be demonstrated empirically.

Succeeding chapters will provide a number of instances where the concept of non-distinct arguments proves useful in accounting for diachronic developments. For the moment we will content ourselves with two observations that support the notion of non-distinct arguments, though they may not in themselves establish the necessity for defining this concept in linguistic theory. Both observations suggest that coreferential arguments and unspecified arguments can insightfully be viewed as special cases of the more general category of non-distinct arguments.

The first observation is only suggestive. It is well known that certain English transitive verbs permit their direct object to remain unspecified, as illustrated in (2) and (9) - (10).

(9) George smokes.

(10) Roger drank quickly.

With other predicates, objects may optionally be omitted when they are reflexive, giving rise to synonymous sentence pairs like those in (11) and (12).

(11) The girl washed (herself).

(12) Jacob shaved (himself).

Although these constructions and their cross-linguistic analogs merit closer scrutiny than they have received, it should be apparent that the notion of non-distinct arguments makes it possible to regard the two as special cases of a more general phenomenon--in both instances the object is non-distinct from the subject and fails to surface. The concept thus allows us to subsume the two phenomena under a single generalization and makes the implicit prediction, which can now be tested cross-linguistically, that languages which display one of these constructions should show some (at least statistical) tendency to have the other as well.

The second observation is that reflexive markers show a strong diachronic and cross-linguistic tendency to take on passive/impersonal sense in addition to their basic reflexive use. This has happened in various Uto-Aztecan languages, as noted above; in Spanish, as shown by the ambiguity of (13); and in so many other languages that the phenomenon is clearly non-accidental and requires explanation.

> (13) Se vendió el esclavo.
> 'The slave sold itself.' / 'The slave was sold.'

The concept of non-distinct arguments makes such an explanation available. If this notion is valid and is defined in linguistic theory as a category to which statements characterizing the distribution of grammatical elements can directly refer, it is easy to see how an affix used to mark coreference could be extended to passive/impersonal use. The extension is a minimal one, from marking clauses with coreferential arguments to marking clauses with non-distinct arguments. This represents a generalization in function, since coreference is a special case of non-distinctness.[2]

It might be objected that many languages in which reflexive morphemes are used to mark passives do not allow intransitive impersonal clauses to be so marked, despite the fact that I have posited an intimate connection between the two, treating passives as a special case of impersonals. For

---

[2] This account of the extension of reflexive marking to passive use is preferable to the one I proposed for Spanish in my review of Mark G. Goldin, Spanish Case and Function, Language 46.167-185, 1970. There I proposed deriving reflexive passive sentences by copying (as opposed to simply moving) the underlying object into surface subject position; this results in a derived structure with coreferential subject and object that meets the conditions for regular reflexivization. The non-distinct argument analysis is preferable because it can be extended to cases (like object omission in English-- cf. (9) - (12)) that involve no movement, so that the copying mechanism is not available to capture the relation between coreferential and unspecified arguments.

example, while Spanish tolerates use of the reflexive markers for intransitive impersonal sentences as well as for passives, as (14) demonstrates, French does not, nor do the Uto-Aztecan languages.

> (14) Se trabaja.
>   'One works.'

In actuality, however, this asymmetry is predicted by the non-distinct argument hypothesis and thus further supports it. Recall that an unspecified argument is one that is semantically implied but is in no way identified. With a true intransitive predicate like the one in (6), therefore, we cannot properly refer to the subject and object as being non-distinct, for there is no object, unspecified or otherwise. For this reason, the extension of a grammatical element from marking coreferential subject and object to marking non-distinct subject and object is restricted to transitive clauses; the concept of non-distinct arguments is simply inapplicable with intransitive predicates.

What do we say, then, about those languages like Spanish in which a reflexive marker has been extended both to passive and to intransitive impersonal sentences? I would claim that this situation results from an additional change, hence we would expect it to obtain in only a subset of those languages with reflexive-marked passives. Specifically, a language which uses a reflexive marker for sentences with non-distinct arguments, as in Figure II, is subject to possible reanalysis whereby the existence of an unspecified subject comes to be the criterion (or one of the alternative criteria) for using the marker. Once this reanalysis has occurred, extending the marker to intransitive clauses is a natural generalization.

Granted that the concept of non-distinct arguments has a certain amount of utility for both synchronic and diachronic description and merits incorporation in linguistic theory, we might now ask why human language employs this category. Why should languages tend to treat alike the two conceptually distinct situations depicted in Figure II? Questions like this often cannot be answered, and inability to answer them satisfactorily does not itself invalidate the theoretical constructs to which they refer. Nevertheless, a plausible characterization of the function of the constructs may help them gain acceptance, however informal and exploratory the characterization might be.

One factor is the well-known tendency for languages to extend existing lexical or grammatical devices to new uses rather than inventing entirely new devices for these uses. Another, related factor is the tendency for overly subtle semantic distinctions to be blurred and ultimately lost. It is apparently natural for speakers to perceive semantic similarities between two situations and to mark them linguistically by the same lexical or grammatical device. In this way numerous concepts can be expressed without the unlimited proliferation of markers, and in exchange non-essential semantic distinctions are neutralized.

When the subject and direct object of a transitive clause are both specified and referentially distinct, each one must be separately identified in some way, must be differentiated from all the other members of the class of potential subjects or objects for the sentence. What the two situations of Figure II have in common is that separate identification of the two arguments is unnecessary. Only one lexical-referential identification need be made in these situations, so only one overt nominal constituent is required in the sentences expressing these situations. What a non-distinct argument marker actually means in structures like Figure II, then, is that only one lexical-referential identification is necessary even though two arguments are semantically implied. One identification can be omitted, either because the two arguments are coreferential or because one of them is unspecified, but the non-distinct argument marking does not distinguish between the two possibilities. Just as some languages do without an overt distinction between reflexive and reciprocal relations, or fail to mark a visible-invisible distinction with their demonstratives, so some languages manage to get along without indicating whether transitive clauses having only one lexical-referential identification lack the second one due to coreference or due to unspecificity. There is no strong need for this information,[3] hence the tendency for reflexive markers to be extended to passive use.

[3] Context or internal semantic factors will leave little doubt in most instances whether the reflexive or the passive sense is intended. Languages also have the option of favoring one interpretation over the other by convention when both are plausible. In Spanish, for instance, reflexive-marked sentences with human subjects are normally interpreted as reflexive or reciprocal rather than passive. (The special pragmatic relationship (or "collocation") between 'sell' and 'slave' overrides this convention in (13) and renders the sentence ambiguous.)

I. DATA

1.1. Northern Paiute

Pertinent Northern Paiute data is somewhat sparse. However, two relevant verb prefixes have been described, an unspecified object prefix <u>ti</u>-, and the reflexive prefix <u>na</u>-. These are illustrated in (1) and (2) respectively.[1]

    (1) ti-$^{\textrm{?}}$acuna-'ya'k$^{\textrm{w}}$i
        UNSPEC- sew- REPET
        OBJ
        'She is sewing.'   (NP-L-M)

    (2) na-yaka-'ya'k$^{\textrm{w}}$i
        REFL- cry- REPET
        'She is crying (to) herself (i.e. mourning).'   (NP-L-M)

To see the function of <u>ti</u>-, contrast (1) with (3), which has a specified object.

    (3) ma'sato$^{\textrm{?}}$a $^{\textrm{?}}$a'cuna-'ya'k$^{\textrm{w}}$i
        glove   sew-REPET
        'She is sewing gloves.'   (NP-L-M)

The reflexive prefix has several additional uses. First, it may have reciprocal value:

    (4) ta'mi na-ata$^{\textrm{?}}$a
        we   REFL-sit
        INCL   PL
        'We sit together.'   (NP-L-PL-69)

Next, it combines with nouns to form derived nouns designating the members of a reciprocal relationship, as in (5) and (6).

---

[1]The Numic "final features" (see section 5.2.3 for discussion) will be indicated by superscripts preceding the affected consonant. ['] stands for the fortis or geminating feature, [$^{\textrm{n}}$] for prenasalization, and [$^{\textrm{h}}$] for preaspiration; unmarked medial consonants undergo lenition. Due to limited information, I cannot claim to represent these final features with full accuracy in all cases. Normally I will omit them in word-final position, where they have no effect, and write them after the hyphens marking morpheme boundaries (since it is the following consonant they affect) regardless of whether the feature is contributed by the preceding morpheme or is intrinsic to the affected consonant. See Appendix B for a list of the abbreviations used for grammatical terms, and the Bibliography for the reference codes.

(5) na-wa'ŋaʔa
    REFL-younger
        brother
    '(two) brothers'   (NP-L-M)

(6) na-notɨ'k^{w}a
    REFL-wife
    'married couple'   (NP-L-M)

Finally, it is used for the passive:

(7) nopi na-a'taa-'kɨ-'ti   yaʔa
    house REFL-sit-CAUS-PRES here
            PL
    'Houses are put up here.'   (NP-L-M)

The reduplicated na'na- may sometimes be used in the plural; nai- has also
been cited as a variant (NP-M-LO-176).

(8) na'na-wa'ŋa-mɨ
    REFL-younger-PL
        brother
    '(several) brothers'   (NP-L-PL-70)

Several reflexive pronouns and similar elements have been cited for
Northern Paiute, including pɨɨ='su 'EMPH',[2] pɨɨ-'sɨʔmɨ 'alone', pɨɨ-'noo
'with/also', na-ma 'together', na-noo 'together', and nahoy='su 'RCPR'.

(9) pɨɨ='su mia-u   ʔisaʔa
    REFL   go-PNCT coyote
    'Coyote went.'   (NP-AF-N-335)

(10) pɨɨ-'sɨʔmɨ manai
    alone   be
    'be alone'   (NP-L-M)

(11) nɨ'mɨ pɨ-'noʔo
    we   also
    EXCL
    'we too'   (NP-L-M)

(12) su wɨta ka tɨhɨ'ya-nu na-ma   nopi-kaʔyu
    ART bear ART deer-with together house-have
              ACC
    'Bear was living with Deer.'   (NP-N-HG-206)

(13) na-noo mi-mia-u   tawni-waitu delia 'ste'la-noo
    together RDP-go-PNCT town-to   PN   PN-with
    'Delia and Stella went to town together.'   (NP-L-M)

(14) nahoy='su na'na-'notɨ'k^{w}a-tuʔ-yak^{w}i
    RCPR   REFL-wife-make-REPET
    'They used to marry into each other's tribes.'   (NP-L-M)

---

[2] The equal sign is used for clitic boundaries; hyphens mark other morpheme boundaries (not all morpheme boundaries are indicated).

1.2.   Mono

The Mono data is quite similar to that in Northern Paiute. The prefix
tɨ- basically indicates an unspecified object, as shown by (1) and (2). (3)
indicates that tɨ- can also serve a partitive function; presumably this represents a Mono innovation.

    (1) tɨ-'tɨwɨ
        UNSPEC-ask
        OBJ
        'ask (for something)'   (M-L-G-189)

    (2) tɨ-poo-'tɨ?ɨ
        UNSPEC-shear-AG
        OBJ
        'barber'   (M-L-G-188)

    (3) ?i-?a'po-na   nɨɨ tɨ-weni-tɨhɨ
        my-basket-ACC I   UNSPEC-sell-PRES
                     OBJ
        'I'm selling some of my baskets.'   (M-L-G-189)

The reflexive prefix na-is used with either reflexive or passive value:

    (4) na?-wahaci
        REFL-hide
        'hide oneself'   (M-L-G-180)

    (5) na-pu-'maaci
        REFL-eye-know
        'be recognized'   (M-L-G-180)

Mono allows the expression of a passive agent by means of a postpositional
phrase with the postposition -paa'tu; -paa' by itself has locative value.

    (6) ?etɨ nɨ-paa'tu na-ca'tɨ'kɨ?i-'tɨ
        gun me-by   REFL-fire-TNS
        'The gun was fired by me.'   (M-L-G-212)

As in Northern Paiute, na- also occurs in the reduplicated form na'na-.
Apparently either na'na- or a shorter third variant na'- marks a reciprocal
relationship, either on verbs or with nouns and postpositions.

    (7) na'na-'waqa
        RCPR-talk
        'talk to each other'   (M-L-G-181)

    (8) na'na-petɨ
        RCPR-daughter
        'parent and daughter'   (M-L-G-181)

    (9) na-'pi-'pi-'naha
        RCPR-RDP-back-at
                  behind
        'one after another'   (M-L-G-182)

There are two reflexive pronouns based on piɨ. piɨ='su reinforces the reflexive prefix na-, as shown in (10), while piɨ-'siʔɨ translates as 'alone'.

(10) piɨ='su   na-yawi-'ti
     REFL-precisely REFL-laugh-TNS
     'He's laughing at himself.'   (M-L-G-180)

(11) piɨ-'siʔɨ-'ki'ma-'ti
     REFL-one-come-TNS
        alone
     'came alone'   (M-L-G-69)

1.3.   Shoshoni

In Shoshoni we find two unspecified argument prefixes, tɨ- for unspecified objects and ta- for unspecified subjects. The latter is used in certain types of subordinate or nominalized clauses, one of which is illustrated in (4), as well as in finite main clauses.

(1) tɨɨ-poo-'nu
    UNSPEC-write-PERF
    OBJ
    'He wrote.'   (SH-D-PMS-59)

(2) nɨ tɨ-pe'ka-'nu
    I UNSPEC-kill-PERF
       OBJ
    'I killed (something).'   (SH-M-IN-14)

(3) ta-ka^{h}ni-pai
    UNSPEC-house-have
    SUBJ
    'One has a house.'   (SH-M-IN-14)

(4) huu-'pi   [ta-^{n}ko'too-na]
    stick-ABS UNSPEC-make-NR
             SUBJ   fire
    'stick with which to make a fire'   (SH-M-IN-14)

Similarly, Shoshoni has two reflexive prefixes, na- and nɨɨ'-, each of which can be used as well to express passive sense.

(5) nɨ na-pui-^{h}ka
    I REFL-see-RSLTV
    'I see myself.'   (SH-M-IN-14)

(6) ta'mɨ na-pui-ka
    we   REFL-see-RSLTV
    INCL
    'We are seen.'   (SH-D-PMS-111)

(7) te^{n}k^{w}a'pɨ nɨɨ-'pe'ka-^{h}k^{w}a
    man   REFL-kill-PERF
    'The man killed himself.'   (SH-M-IN-15)

(8) tɨ-^{n}pi   nɨɨ-'nua
    rock-ABS REFL-push
    'The rock got pushed.'   (SH-M-IN-15)

Notice that in (6) the subject form of the inclusive pronoun is used; the object form would be ta'm(a)i rather than ta'mɨ. This indicates that sentences such as (6) are passive in the sense defined in the Introduction, not merely impersonal. That is, the semantic object has taken over surface subject position.

Like Mono, Shoshoni permits reflexives with na- to be reinforced by a reflexive pronoun. Unlike Mono, however, Shoshoni displays a full paradigm of such pronouns, inflected for person, number, and case (SH-D-PMS-82, 83). Here we will be content to illustrate the phenomenon with a single example:

(9) nɨɨ nɨsɨsɨ na-pui-ka
    I   myself REFL-see-RSLTV
    'I see myself.'   (SH-D-PMS-83)

na- has a variety of other uses. With a nominalizer, it forms expressions equivalent to English -able forms; this no doubt stems from its passive use:

(10) tu'ku na-tɨ'ka-'na
     meat REFL-eat-NR
     'The meat is edible.'   (SH-M-IN-14)

It has been reanalyzed in various forms as an obligatory derivational prefix, for instance na-peni 'be tired' and na-pui 'be light' (cf. pui 'see') (SH-D-PMS-111). Finally, it is used as a reciprocal marker on either verbs or nouns, in either its basic or reduplicated form (the reduplicated nana is a proclitic rather than a prefix (SH-D-PMS-63)).

(11) na-k^{w}ihɨ
     REFL-fight
     'fight with one another'   (SH-D-PMS-111)

(12) nana ʔu-ha'ni-tɨ
     REFL it-fix-PROG
     'fixed it together'   (SH-D-PMS-63)

(13) na-nɨmɨ
     REFL-person
     'relative'   (SH-D-PMS-112)

(14) nana ʔa-'pɨʔɨ
     REFL father-ABS
     'father and child'   (SH-D-PMS-112)

1.4. Southern Paiute

The verb prefix <u>na-</u> is used for the reflexive and the reciprocal (but not for the passive).

(1) na-uŋ^{w}ai-'pɨkai
REFL-hang-PAST
'hung himself'   (SP-S-G-108)

(2) na-patɨkɨ-yɨ
REFL-wash-PRES
'washes himself'   (SP-S-G-108)

(3) na-ku'k^{w}i-^{n}kɨ
REFL-shoot-APPLIC
'shoot at each other/fight'   (SP-S-G-109)

(4) na-tɨpiŋu-'ka-kai
REFL-ask-PL-while
'(while) asking one another'   (SP-S-G-277)

With certain verbs, such as <u>na-kaa</u> 'wear (clothing)' and <u>na-pa'kɨ</u> 'bathe', this prefix is obligatory (SP-S-G-108, 109). Reduplicated as <u>nana-</u>, it has repetitive or distributive sense:

(5) nana-too'k^{w}a-yɨ
REPET-stretch-PRES
REFL
'stretches oneself several times'   (SP-S-G-109)

<u>na-</u> occurs with nouns and postpositions:

(6) na-papi-ŋ^{w}ɨ
REFL-older-PL
      brother
'(two) brothers'   (SP-S-G-110)

(7) na-pi-na^{n}k^{w}a-'p$^?$a='k^{w}a^3 yuna-'pɨkai
REFL-<u>back-direction-at-</u>them put-PAST
      behind   down
'He put them down behind himself.'   (SP-S-G-212)

It is also to be found in <u>na-pai</u> 'six' (cf. <u>pai</u> 'three') (SP-S-G-110).

Southern Paiute also displays a series of emphatic or reflexive pronouns built on the base <u>na'noo</u>; they include at least the subject form <u>na'noo='su</u>, the object form <u>na'noo-tia='su</u>, and the oblique form <u>na'noo-p(a)</u>, incorporating the postposition <u>-pa</u> 'at' (SP-S-G-212). The verb prefix <u>na-</u> apparently does not co-occur with these pronouns.

---

[3] $_?$...'k^{w}a is a discontinuous clitic indicating a third person inanimate invisible subject or object.

(8) na'noo='su$^?$u='k^{w}a $^?$uŋ^{w}a-tuk^{w}a-'pɨka$^?$ai='k^{w}a
self-NOM-it   him-to-PAST-it
'He himself gave it to him.'   (SP-S-G-212)

(9) na'noo-p $^?$uni-^{n}kɨ-'pɨkai
self-at   make-APPLIC-PAST
'He made it for himself.'   (SP-S-G-212)

Evidently the element ='su has gained reflexive value through contamina-
tion. Sapir cites ninia='su as 'myself ACC'; contrast this with nɨ'nia 'me
ACC' (SP-S-G-212, 177).

    Passives and impersonals are marked in Southern Paiute by verb suf-
fixes. The impersonal suffix is -'tu$^?$a; it may occur with either transitive
or intransitive verbs.

(10) pa'ka-ŋu-'tu$^?$a-yɨ=aŋa
kill-PNCT-IMPRS-PRES-him
'One is killing him.'   (SP-S-G-148)

(11) nɨ$^?$ pɨni-'ka-yɨ   [$^?$ipi-'tu$^?$a]
I   see-RSLTV-PRES drink-IMPRS
'I see (someone) drinking.'   (SP-S-G-148)

Sapir states that this suffix may be preceded by the plural subject suffix
-'ka when the unspecified subject is understood to be "people in general"
(SP-S-G-147).

(12) tɨ'ka-'ka-'tu$^?$a-yɨ
eat-PL-IMPRS-PRES
'People are eating.'   (SP-S-G-148)

   The passive suffix is -'tɨɨ.

(13) taŋa-'tɨɨ-'ka='ca=taŋ^{w}a
kick-PASS-PL-PAST-we
                      INCL
'We were all kicked.'   (SP-S-G-147)

(14) sa'pika-'tɨ-tɨ
overcome-PASS-PRTC
'one who is overcome'   (SP-S-G-147)

(15) maai-'t$^?$ui-^{n}kɨ-'tɨ-pa=aŋa=taŋ^{w}a
catch-CAUS-APPLIC-PASS-FUT-he-us
                         INCL
'He will cause us to be caught.'   (SP-S-G-147, 278)

(16) pa'ka-ŋu-'tɨɨ=ca=aŋa   k^{w}iyaci-ŋ^{w}ana^{n}k^{w}a
kill-PNCT-PASS-PAST-he bear-by
'He was killed by the bear.'   (SP-S-G-221)

Examples (13) and (14) both indicate that the construction is passive rather
than impersonal, i.e. that the underlying object functions as derived

subject. In (13) this is shown by the occurrence of the plural subject marker -'ka (the semantic subject can hardly be "people in general"). Participles in -ti are identical in reference to the subject of the clause from which they derive, not the object; hence true passivization must be involved in the derivation of (14), since the referent of the participle corresponds to the underlying object of 'overcome'. The passive suffix always follows the causative suffix when both occur, regardless of semantic scope. Thus the passive suffix -'ti follows the causative -'t?ui in (15), even though we might anticipate the opposite due to the fact that the passive relationship is semantically in the scope of causation. Agentive phrases are attested for Southern Paiute passives, as in (16).

1.5.   Kawaiisu

Relatively little information is available from Kawaiisu, but attestation has been found for many of the elements of concern to us. The passive suffix has been cited as -'to?o:

(1)   ka?a-'to?o
      eat- PASS
      'be eaten'   (K- Z- D- 96)

There are two reflexive prefixes, na- and ni-. (2) shows na- with a verb that Munro suggests is inherently reflexive (K-M-SPO-16); it is also used with reciprocal kinship terms.

(2)   na- pa'ka
      REFL-bathe
      'bathe (oneself)'   (K- Z- D- 49)

(3)   nimi na-papi-wi
      we   REFL-older-PL
      DL   brother
      'We are brothers. '   (K- M- SPO- 16)

ni- is apparently more common as a verb prefix:

(4)   ni -pi 'kee-ti   ni?i
      REFL- see- TNS I
      'I looked at myself. '   (K- M- SPO- 16)

Several reflexive pronouns have been reported. niwayi, which has the variant nawayi, is used with reflexive and reciprocal value; it is accompanied by the appropriate possessor clitic.

(5) ni̱wayi̱=ni pi̱'kee-ti̱ po?o-'paana
    self-my   see-TNS water-in
    'I saw myself in the water.'   (K-M-SPO-16)

In addition, nano'so has locative and emphatic value, while ='su has emphatic value.

(6) nano'so kati̱-t   ni̱?
    self   live-TNS I
    'I live by myself.'   (K-M-SPO-17)

(7) ni̱?i̱='su sa?a'kata=a'ka
    I-self   cooked-it
    'I cooked it myself.'   (K-M-SPO-18)

1.6.   Tubatulabal

Voegelin treats the suffix -iw(a) as impersonal with intransitive verbs and passive with transitive verbs.[4]

(1) ?anaŋ-iiwa-t
    cry-IMPRS-PRES
    'There is crying.'   (TU-V-G-99)

(2) ?aašin-iiwa-t
    bathe-IMPRS-PRES
    'He is being bathed.'   (TU-V-G-99)

Scope inversion occurs with the desiderative suffix (which translates as 'got ready to' in perfective forms); that is, the passive/impersonal suffix follows the desiderative suffix even when the desiderative has broader semantic scope. This is illustrated in (3).

(3) taŋ-iiba?-iu
    kick-DESID-IMPRS
    'He got ready to be kicked.'   (TU-V-G-117)

Voegelin cites three forms of an emphatic or reflexive pronoun: ?omoix 'himself', ?omohic 'each other', and ?omoixp 'by himself' (TU-V-G-181). Evidently these all involve a pronoun base that we can write as ?omo(h)i(x). The third form no doubt incorporates the postposition -p 'to/in/on', but -c does not occur by itself as a postposition.

(4) ?oo-noo?o-la ?omoix
    RDP-back-go self
    PERF
    'He went back himself.'   (TU-V-G-83)

(5) piš=kič   ?omox-pa ?aa?a-wa
    then-QUOT self-to   RDP-broil
                PERF meat
    'Then, it is said, he cooked by himself.'   (TU-V-T-194)

[4] When the vowel a is absent, w vocalizes to u by means of a regular phonological process to yield the variant -iu.

1.7.   Hopi

The Hopi reflexive prefix is <u>naa-</u>.

(1) nɨ naa-tɨhota
    I REFL-hurt
    'I hurt myself.'   (H-VV-H-200)

(2) tɨwat   sok naa-wiiwakna
    instead only REFL-rope
    'I roped myself instead.'   (H-VV-H-199)

This prefix can also be used in reciprocal sentences:

(3) pɨma naa-paʔaŋ^wa-ya
    they REFL-help-PL
    'They helped each other.'   (H- L- EN)

One source has cited an apparent reciprocal pronoun <u>nahoy</u>, but this has also been glossed as 'apart' or 'across'.

(4) nahoy naawakna
    RCPR want
    'wanted each other'   (H- K- LA- 36)

(5) pɨma naahoy nak^wsɨ
    they apart   set
                 out
    'They walked in opposite directions.'   (H- M- INO)

(6) kiison- va naahoy yɨɨtɨ
    plaza- on across run
                      PL
    'They ran across the plaza.'   (H- M- INO)

There is in addition an emphatic reflexive <u>naap</u> (sometimes <u>naav</u>):

(7) pay ʔas   son   ʔiʔ ʔɨɨ-wɨɨti ʔɨŋ naap   ʔasna-ni
    now IMPOT EXHRT this your-wife you herself wash-FUT
                                      ACC   hair
    'Let this wife of yours wash your hair herself.'   (H-VV-H-198)

(8) pam naav   pɨt coocona
    he himself her kiss
    'He himself kissed her.'   (H- L- EN)

Passives in Hopi present a complicated picture that must await detailed work in synchronic and diachronic Hopi verb morphology for clarification. Apparently there are three basic types of passive suffix.[5]
-<u>(i)lti</u> is evidently the commonest and most productive of the three presently and is sometimes translated with 'got'. A second passive suffix is

---

[5]Whorf also cites a resultative passive suffix -<u>(i)wta</u> and a cessative passive -<u>viwa</u>
(H- W- L- 34), but their status as true passive suffixes is much in doubt. In any case
they clearly derive from the basic passive suffix -<u>(i)wa</u>.

-i, which replaces the final vowel of the stem, and the third is -(i)wa,
which Whorf calls a distributive passive and describes (rightly or wrongly)
as being used "when the influence converges on the subject from all a-
round, or from different people, or accumulates from successive acts,
etc." (H-W-L-34).

(9) tɨk-i
    tɨkɨ
    cut-PASS
    'is cut'   (H-W-L-33)

(10) tɨk-ilti
     cut-PASS
     'It got cut.'   (H-M-INO)

(11) nɨ? pö?-i-ni
     I   pö?a
         beat-PASS-FUT
     'I'll be beaten.'   (H-M-INO)

(12) paasa ?ɨɨy-ilti-ni
     field plant-PASS-FUT
     'The field will be planted.'   (H-L-EN)

(13) kɨɨyi-?am hiik^w-iwa
     water-their hiiko
               drink-PASS
     'Their water is being drunk up.'   (H-W-L-34)

Since all three versions of the passive suffix can change the final stem
vowel to i, it would of course be possible to analyze the passive morpheme
as consisting of three allomorphs, $\emptyset$, -lti, and -wa, each of which causes
i-ablaut of the preceding vowel (cf. UA-H-MP2-15). Some speakers apparently reject passive sentences with agentive phrases, or accept them
only in restricted circumstances (perhaps as a semantic extension of instrumental phrases), but such sentences are attested with -(i)wa:

(14) nɨ? ?itaa-so-y   ?a-ŋq^w piiki-t   mak-iwa
     I   our-grandmother-ACC her-from piki-ACC maqa
                                           give-PASS
     'I was given piki bread by our grandmother.'   (H-M-INO)

(15) taaqa talwivtaqa-t   ?a-k^w mɨ?-iwa
     man lightning-ACC it-with strike-PASS .
     'The man was struck by lightning.'   (H-L-EN)

Such locutions need further study. In addition, Ekkehart Malotki reports a
rare impersonal use of -(i)wa, one that allows either a fully unspecified
subject or a minimally specified one:

(16) yaw   ʔoray-ve yees-iwa
     QUOT PN-at   sit-IMPRS
                      PL
     'They (people) were living at Oraibi, it is said.'   (H-M-INO)

(17) naat paaqavi-t ʔe-p sino-m   yees-iwa
     still PN-ACC it-at person-PL sit-IMPRS
                            PL
     'People were still living at Bakabi.'   (H-M-INO)

Finally, Hopi displays a verbal prefix <u>tɨɨ</u>- that marks unspecified objects. At present this prefix is used productively to indicate indefinite (plural) or unspecified human objects:

(18) nɨ̵ʔ ʔaŋ   tɨɨ-ʔaʔawna
     I   there UNSPEC-tell
                H OBJ
     'I told them there.'   (H-M-INO)

(19) pam panis tɨɨ-caʔaʔa-toyna
     he   only   UNSPEC-cry-CAUS
                  H OBJ   REPET
     'He only makes others cry.'   (H-M-INO)

The human sense of <u>tɨɨ</u>- probably represents a recent specialization from an earlier general unspecified object sense. A segmentable <u>tɨɨ</u>- is found with certain verb stems in frozen combinations that imply or allow a non-human object. For example, we find <u>tɨɨ vahoma</u> 'wash (e.g. clothes)' alongside <u>naavahoma</u> 'wash oneself/take a bath' with the reflexive prefix <u>naa</u>- (H-L-EN); the fact that <u>tɨɨ vahoma</u> can occur with specified objects indicates that <u>tɨɨ</u>- has been reanalyzed as part of the stem. Also note the nominalization in (21).

(20) nɨ̵ʔ ʔi-hɨmita-y   tɨɨ vahoma
     I   my-shelled-ACC wash
             corn
     'I washed my shelled corn.'   (H-M-INO)

(21) tɨ-cvalan-pi
     tɨɨ-covalan
     UNSPEC-gather-INSTR
     OBJ
     'rake'   (H-M-INO)

1.8.   Serrano

In Serrano, reflexives are not formed through verbal inflection, but rather periphrastically with a possessed form of the noun <u>taqa</u> 'self' (< 'man/person'; cf. UA-VVH-TCG-143, UA-M-CS-45).

(1) ni-taqa=n čikịn wihaa-n
my-self-I poke thorn-with
'I pricked myself with a thorn.'   (SR-H-G-120)

(2) hih? mɨ-taq
see your-self
'Look at yourself!'   (SR-C-IO-2)

The same device is used for reciprocal expressions.[6]

(3) kʷɨnɨ pɨɨ-tax̣   piiha?n
QUOT their-self love
they
'They loved each other.'   (SR-H-G-120)

(4) kʷɨnɨ=mɨ=?   pɨɨ-tax̣a-ika ?ɨnaaç vɨraa-vɨra-?n
QUOT-they-PAST their-self-to nicely RDP-talk-STAT
'They talked together nicely.'   (SR-H-G-120)

As (4) shows, the reflexive noun may be oblique.

In (1) - (4) **taqa** takes the appropriate possessor prefix. (5) and (6), on the other hand, involve the postposition -**nuk** 'alone/by oneself' preceded by the appropriate postpositional prefix.[7]

(5) pɨ-nukʷ   t   yeii?-v
him-alone DUB take-FUT
'He'll take it with him.'   (SR-H-G-121)

(6) ?ama? pɨ-nuk miy ča-?aači?
it   it-alone go   our-horse
'Our horse went on by itself.'   (SR-H-D2-5)

Serrano evidently has no passive construction.

1.9.   Cahuilla

Reflexives in Cahuilla are marked by the verb prefix **tax-**, which also serves for reciprocals.

(1) tax-tiŋ?ay-qal
REFL-treat-DUR
'He treats himself.'   (CA-F-MV-17)

---

[6] When not followed by a clitic, the quotative particle kʷɨnɨ normally shortens to kʷɨn by a regular rule truncating final short vowels. When this truncation fails to apply, as in (3), it marks the subject as third person plural. The third person plural subject clitic can be regarded phonologically as vowel length or ɨ when it occurs alone with the quotative, and the vowel truncation rule shortens final ɨɨ to ɨ.

[7] -**nuk** shows some variation for forms other than the third person singular; this variation will be discussed in Chapter 3. The third person singular possessor prefix in Serrano is ?a-, while the corresponding postposition base is pɨ-; the examples cited thus establish the postpositional status of -**nuk**. The kʷ of -**nuk**ʷ in (5) presumably shows non-distinctive rounding of k after u.

(2) tax- wayni- yam
REFL- call- IMP
              PL
'Call each other!'   (CUP-J-SC-49)

The incorporation of tax- as a verb prefix is clearly recent; note, for example, that this element can function as a postpositional object:

(3) pe?i-y   pe tax-ŋa čeq pe-m-yaxi-wen
this-ACC and self-on just it-they- put- DUR
                                          PL
'They put this on.'   (CA-H-BSK-46)

Certain other uses of tax-must be presented more tentatively. (4) suggests
a plural variant taxam- (-m or -am is a plural noun suffix).

(4) piš-taxam-tewa-p
SUBR-REFL-care- UNR
          PL
'to take care of themselves'   (CA-B-IN)

The form taxat is supposedly a variant of the emphatic particle ta? (CA-H-
BSK-57); however, the following example suggests that it may better be
viewed (diachronically at least) as an absolutive form of tax- (-t is an absolutive suffix).

(5) pe? taxat mu pipl^{y}em-qal taxat ñišxi- š pa
he EMPH still roll-DUR   EMPH ash-ABS it-in
'He rolled himself in the ashes.'   (CA-H-BSK-39)

These constructions strongly corroborate the recent nominal origin of tax-.

Bright has recorded a series of emphatic reflexive pronouns occurring
in the following construction:

(6) ne-qi?   tax-wika ne-kuktaš-qa
my-self self-to   I-talk- DUR
'I'm talking to myself.'   (CA-B-IN)

(7) ?emem ?eme-qi? tax-wika ?em-kuktaš-we
you   your-self self-to   you-talk- DUR
PL   PL   PL   PL
'You are talking to yourselves.'   (CA-B-IN)

It is not readily apparent whether -qi? is attached to the possessor or postpositional form of the pronoun. The postposition -wika is also puzzling,
since -ika is the expected form. The form heme-qi?i 'by themselves' (CA-
B-IN) is clearly related.

While Cahuilla has no passive construction per se, it does allow the expression of passive notions.

(8) kiki-t-am   qʷaʔi-ve-l-em
    child-ABS-PL eat-R-ABS-PL
    'The children have been eaten.'   (CUP-J-SC-55)

(9) ʔaya nanvanek [qʷaʔa-pi-š]
    now ready   eat-UNR-ABS
    'They are ready to be eaten now.'   (CUP-J-SC-55)

The realized and unrealized suffixes, -ve and -pi respectively, most commonly occur in subordinate clauses. (8) shows that they can however be
used in main clauses as well (at least in surface structure), and they lend
passive force. The semantic subject of (8) is unspecified, and the semantic object 'children' functions as the surface subject, as indicated by the
plural suffix on the predicate.

1. 10.   Cupeno

   Cupeno reflexives are formed with the reflexive noun tax, which is preceded by a possessor prefix and followed by the suffix -wi, supposedly a
rare suffix attached to possessed nouns (CU-HN-M-124). Reciprocals are
formed in the same way.[8]

(1) naʔa=n na-tax-wi   qaʔ-ni-qat   kuka-t   pa-či
    I-I   my-self-POSSD bite-CAUS-gonna spider-ABS it-with
    'I'm gonna get myself bitten by a spider.'   (CU-H-VN-354)

(2) ča=pa   čam-tax-wi   taw
    we-UNR our-self-POSSD see
    'We shall see one another.'   (CUP-H-SCD-50)

Emphatic reflexives involve the element -qi preceded by a pronominal
morpheme which could be either possessive or postpositional; the vowels
of this pronoun have obviously been colored by that of -qi.

(3) pimi-qi   mal=pa   pam-tax-wi   kʷa-wana
    their-self they-UNR their-self-POSSD eat-FUT
                                       DUR
                                       PL
    'They will eat their own bodies.'   (CU-HN-M-122)

(4) paʔ haši-pa-ya-qal   pi-qi
    he go-he-STAT-PAST his-self
                   DUR
    'He was going by himself.'   (CUP-H-SCD-50)

---

[8]The suffix -ni in (1) may be the manifestation of the underlying sequence -ni-in
(CAUS-ACT) (CU-H-VN-354).

Example (3) indicates that the basic sense of <u>tax</u>, namely 'man/person/ body', has not been lost entirely in its adaptation to reflexive use.

There is a passive construction in Cupeno. A verb which normally takes the active suffix -<u>in</u> can be made passive by changing this to the stative suffix -<u>yax</u>. The underlying subject of a passive sentence is un-specified, and the underlying object becomes the surface subject. The tense-aspect marker occurs in its plural form.

(5) wamki-š   yut-pə-yəx-wən
     ceremonial-ABS build-it-STAT-PAST
     enclosure   DUR
                                  PL
     'A ceremonial enclosure was built.'   (CU-H-G-79)

(6) gəyiinə təm-pə-yəx-wə
     chicken enclose-it-STAT-DUR
                            PL
     'A chicken was cooped up.'   (CU-H-G-79)

The subject marker -<u>pə</u> in these examples agrees with the derived subject, indicating that these sentences are passive rather than just impersonal.

Additional ways are available to mark passive relationships. Sentence (1) presumably derives from a complex underlying structure with a passive clause subordinated to a causative predicate; the details of this construction must await further data. (7) and (8) employ the realized and unrealized suffixes -<u>və</u> and -<u>pi</u> respectively; normally these occur in subordinate clauses, as in (9).

(7) hunwə-t mamayəw-və-l
     bear-ABS help-R-ABS
     'The bear was helped.'   (CUP-J-SR-11)

(8) hunwə-t mamayəw-pi-š
     bear-ABS help-UNR-ABS
     'The bear will be helped.'   (CUP-J-SR-11)

(9) tuku-t   [pə' hal-və-l]
     wildcat-ABS SUBR look-R-ABS
                         for
     'the wildcat that was looked for'   (CUP-J-SC-92)

1.11.   Luiseno

Reflexive locutions are formed in Luiseno with a possessor prefix plus -<u>taax</u>. Reciprocals are formed in the same manner.

(1) noo no-taax toow-q
     I   my-self see-PRES
     'I see myself.'   (L-L-FN)

(2) wunaalum wok-ax   pom-taax
     they   cut-PAST their-self
     'They cut themselves.'   (L-L-FN)

(3) pom-taax ʔaaʔaya-wun
     their-self look-PRES
                    PL
     'They are looking at each other.'   (L-L-FN)

(4) qay pom-taax kaytu-wun
     NEG their-self fight-PRES
                         PL
     'They do not fight with one another.'   (L-H-I-101)

The reflexive noun has also been recorded in the expanded form -taxaw:

(5) supul=up čam-taxaw loʔxa-lut
     one-he   our-self   do-gonna
     'One of ourselves is gonna do it.'   (L-KG-SG-101)

There is an emphatic reflexive pronoun, also taking a pronominal prefix, which has been variously recorded as -xay, -xa, and -ha. It has a variety of syntactic uses, partially illustrated in (6) - (9).

(6) noo=n=il te-tiŋal   no-taax no-ha
     I-I-PAST RDP-doctor my-self my-self
                PAST
     'I doctored myself.'   (L-KG-SG-102)

(7) noo=n=il lo-loʔxa   no-ha
     I-I-PAST RDP-make my-self
                PAST
     'I made it by myself.'   (L-KG-SG-102)

(8) no-naawi no-xa
     my-write my-self
     'my own writing'   (L-KG-SG-156)

(9) noo no-xay ʔaaʔ-ma
     I   my-self live-DUR
     'I live alone.'   (L-L-FN)

Luiseno has no well-established passive construction. However, the effect of a passive can be achieved by using the nominalized form of a verb, as in (10) and (11).

(10) ʔawaal xeč-aa-t
      dog   hit-NR-ABS
      'The dog is being beaten.'   (CUP-J-SC-178)

(11) ʔawaal xeč-i-š
      dog   hit-NR-ABS
      'The dogs are beaten.'   (CUP-J-SC-178)

Little can be said about this construction without a better understanding of Luiseno noun morphology. The subject form of 'dog' is used in both sentences;[9] verbs nominalized with -aa apparently refer to ongoing activity, while those with -i refer to the state resulting from previous activity (CUP-J-SC-179). Passive sense can also be conveyed by verb forms in -vo and -pi. These indicate realization and non-realization respectively and are normally used in subordinate clauses, as in (14).

(12) ṣahovi-t tanʔi-vo-l
    war-ABS dance-R-ABS
    dance
    'The war dance was done.'   (CUP-J-SC-121)

(13) ʔivi=p hilaʔi-pi-š
    this-it eat-UNR-ABS
    'This will be eaten.'   (CUP-J-SC-121)

(14) tukwu-t   [po   no-nonomi-qal-vo]
    mountain-ABS SUBR my-follow-DUR-R
    lion
    'the mountain lion that I was following'   (CUP-J-SC-120)

1.12.   Papago

A passive suffix -ĵid has been cited for Papago (P-SS-D-140), but apart from the two verb forms quoted, muʔa-ĵid 'be killed' and bɨhi-ĵid 'be taken', I have no information. (Some additional passive constructions for Papago will be discussed in Chapter 5.)

Although they have very limited distribution, Papago does have something resembling unspecified argument prefixes. These are ču- and ta-, which Hale refers to as "indefinite object" and "indefinite agent" prefixes respectively (P-H-G-75). They are found in adjectives or adverbs derived by means of the suffix -m or -ma:

(1) s-ču-ʔɨɨbida-m
    AFF-UNSPEC-fear-ADJR
        OBJ
    'fearful'   (P-H-G-75)

(2) s-ta-ʔɨɨbida-m
    AFF-UNSPEC-fear-ADJR
        SUBJ
    'frightening'   (P-H-G-75)

---

[9] I have found one example in which an accusative noun is apparently used instead for the semantic object of an -i form (CUP-J-SC-178).

(3) s-ču-hɨhɨmi-m
AFF-UNSPEC-laugh-ADJR
      OBJ
'full of laughter'   (P-H-G-132)

(4) s-ta-hɨhɨm-ma
AFF-UNSPEC-laugh-ADJR
      SUBJ
'funny/laughter-inducing'   (P-H-G-132)

The contrast between unspecified agent and object is far from straight-forward, as these examples indicate; we will discuss it later in more detail.

Papago has three reflexive prefixes, ñi- and t- for first person singular and plural, and ʔɨ- for non-first person.[10]

(5) n=t   o   ñ-hii
I-PERF FUT myself-shear
                   PERF
'I'm gonna cut my hair.'   (P-H-P-205)

(6) ʔɨ   g   wakon
REFL IMP wash
'Wash yourself!'   (P-M-LPA-46)

These prefixes are commonly reinforced by the reflexive pronoun hɨǰɨl, which has the plural variant hɨhɨ ʔɨǰɨl.[11]

(7) hɨǰɨl ʔa=ñ   ñi-ñɨid   ʔaañi
self AUX-I myself-see I
'I see myself.'   (P-SS-D-123)

(8) hɨhɨ ʔɨǰɨl ʔa=č   t-ñɨid   ʔaačim
selves AUX-we ourselves-see we
'We see ourselves.'   (P-SS-D-123)

The reflexive prefixes are used for reciprocals and may be reinforced by the reciprocal particle ʔaʔay.

(9) ʔɨ-kawañ
REFL-quarrel
'quarreled with each other'   (P-M-LPA-47)

---

[10] ʔɨ- is not as closely tied to the verb phonologically as the other prefixes; it may be better viewed as a particle with proclitic tendencies. Mason cites ʔɨʔɨm- as a variant for the second person plural and analyzes it as ʔɨ- followed by the second person plural object prefix ʔɨm- (P-M-LPA-46).

[11] In the following examples, ʔa is a base, apparently meaningless in itself, to which various auxiliary elements are suffixed or cliticized. The variant ʔo is used when nothing is attached.

(10) ʔaʔay ʔa=m   ʔɨ   ñɨid ʔaapim
    RCPR AUX-you REFL see you
            PL   PL
    'You see each other.'   (P-SS-D-123)

Some verbs, such as <u>wayla</u> 'dance' (< Spanish <u>baile</u>), occur only with a reflexive prefix.

(11) čioǰ ʔo   ʔɨ-wayla
    man AUX REFL-dance
    'The man is dancing.'   (P-L-FN)

Finally, we note that reflexives may be used with passive force.

(12) ǰɨwɨd   ʔa=t   ʔɨ-moihu
    ground AUX-PERF REFL-plow
                    PERF
    'The ground was plowed.'   (P-H-NP-25)

An agentive phrase involving the preposition <u>ʔamjɨd</u> can be used in this
construction:

(13) haiwañ ʔa=t   ʔɨ-wuu   ʔab ʔamjɨd g   huan
    cow   AUX-PERF REFL-rope there from ART PN
                    PERF
    'The cow got roped by Juan.'   (P-H-PC)

1.13.   Northern Tepehuan

I have found only one relevant example in the very sparse information
available on Northern Tepehuan. It points to the existence of a passive
suffix -<u>gi</u>.

(1) dai koko-tu-gi   ʔanɨ
   and sick-CAUS-PASS I
   'And I was being made sick.'   (NT-B-T-86)

1.14.   Tepecano

Tepecano has a reflexive prefix (u)m-, which may also be used for the
passive.

(1) m-a-i-ši-m-nagia
   away-COMPL-VERT-INTNS-REFL-hang
   'Lower yourself!'   (TO-M-PL-379)

(2) n-a-t-um-aargi
   CONN-he-PAST-REFL-form
   'He was formed.'   (TO-M-PL-346)

(3) has-si̱-pu-m-kka?
how-Q-thus-REFL-eat
'How is it eaten?'   (TO-M-PL-346, 379)

The following statement by Mason seems to indicate that there are other reflexive prefixes as well: "For the average reflexive the pronominal object is used without variation, but in the case of the third person singular reflexive where there is no object pronoun, the deficiency is supplied by the passive sign" (TO-M-PL-346). Unfortunately he gives no non-third person singular examples. The pronominal object prefixes he describes as occurring in reflexives are as follows:

(i)n-	(i)t-
(u)m-	am-
∅	a-

From this I conclude that the reflexive prefixes in Tepecano are much like those in Papago. The first person singular reflexive prefix is basically n-, and that of the first person plural is t-. All of the non-first person reflexive forms involve m-, with the exception of the third person plural a-, which I take to be reduced from an earlier form *am-. For comparative purposes, then, we can posit the three prefixes n-, t-, and m-, the latter corresponding to Papago ?i̱- in function (non-first person) but not in form; the vowels result from resegmentation in the strings of prefixes typical of Tepecano. The paradigm is quite similar to that of the non-reflexive object prefixes, and this led to Mason's somewhat confusing description.

Tepecano also has an unspecified object prefix, tu-.

(4) ?an-ti-ki-tu-hu
I-PAST-just-UNSPEC-eat
                OBJ
'I'm gonna eat in a moment.'   (TO-M-PL-348)

It is interesting to note that this prefix can also occur with a specified object, perhaps with partitive value.

(5) yam-haštu   n-iš-tu-ka?   ga-hoovit
NEG-something I-AFF-UNSPEC-eat ART-zapote
     nothing   OBJ
'I have never eaten zapotes.'   (TO-M-PL-379)

(6) hi̱ga-imaai n-a-pu-haban-tu-hidoor
that-squash CONN-he-EMPH-with-UNSPEC-cook
                              it   OBJ
'to cook the squash'   (TO-M-PL-387)

1.15.   Tarahumara

Tarahumara has two primary ways of expressing the reciprocal, with the verb prefix <u>na-</u> or with the reciprocal particle <u>ʔanagu</u>.

(1) tabire tumu na-šuri-ši   wasarara
     NEG   you RCPR-take-IMP hoe
          PL   PL
     'Don't go taking each other's hoes!'   (TA-B-G-410)

(2) tabire tumu ʔanagu čigo-ši
     NEG   you RCPR rob-IMP
          PL   PL
     'Don't rob each other!'   (TA-B-G-410)

Sometimes the reciprocal particle occurs in the longer form <u>ʔanagupu</u> (TA-B-G-410).

There are two reflexive pronouns in Tarahumara, the singular <u>binoy</u> and the plural <u>ʔaboy</u>. Both allow the ending -<u>po</u>, which I take to be the same as the -<u>pu</u> found on the reciprocal particle. These reflexive pronouns can co-occur with an explicit object pronoun, but more commonly they do not. The plural form may be reciprocal, bringing to three the number of distinct reciprocal constructions.

(3) nehe ke-niči   binoy pago
     I   ACC-me self   wash
     'I wash myself.'   (TA-T-TED-38)

(4) binoy-po kutahiwa-re
     self   rope-PAST
     'He roped himself.'   (TA-B-G-409)

(5) kaca ta ʔaboy-po goʔi-boo
     NEG we selves   kill-FUT
     'so that we won't have to kill ourselves'   (TA-B-G-409)

(6) ʔaboy-po goya-re
     selves   kill-PAST
     'They killed each other.'   (TA-B-G-410)

The reflexive pronouns can also be used as emphatic pronouns and to express possession.

(7) muhe binoy
     you   self
     'you yourself'   (TA-B-G-54)

(8) binoy kučiwa-ra
     self   son-POSSD
     'his own son ACC'   (TA-B-G-54)

The passive/impersonal suffix has a multiplicity of forms. Basically
there are three sets. One set consists of the variants -riwa, -ria, and
-wa; the latter two are clearly reduced forms of the former. The second
set consists of -tu and -ru; since r is a common intervocalic reflex of t,
these can also be equated. Also attested are the obviously related variants
-kia, -gia, and -giwa, which Brambila regards as derivatives of the first
set by virtue of random interchange of r and g/k (TA-B-G-92). These are
only the present tense forms. The -tu and -riwa sets combine with following tense, modal, and aspect suffixes to form non-present passive endings
with varying degrees of morphological transparency. We will not be concerned with these combinations here.

These suffixes are impersonal with intransitive verbs and passive with
transitives. In addition, -tu may be used as a reflexive.

> (9) taši goči-ru
> NEG sleep-IMPRS
> 'One doesn't sleep.'   (TA-B-G-429)

> (10) we   ce noca-ria   ʔenay
> much then work-IMPRS here
> 'Here one works a lot.'   (TA-B-G-425)

> (11) gao   ne ʔa-ru
> horse I   give-IMPRS
> 'I was given a horse.'   (TA-B-G-429)

> (12) ke   ne co   ruwe-riwa
> NEG I   either inform-IMPRS
> 'I'm not even informed.'   (TA-B-G-426)

> (13) muhe pago-ru
> you   wash-IMPRS
> 'You wash yourself.'   (TA-T-TED-38)

Notice that the subject form of the pronoun is used in (11) - (12), showing
that we are dealing with a true passive construction. Brambila intimates
that the -tu passive contrasts with the -riwa passive in being stative,
focusing on the result of the verbal action (TA-B-G-95). There may be
such a contrast, perhaps only an incipient one, but the examples make it
evident that this difference, if it exists, is far from clear-cut.

1.16.   Yaqui

The suffix -wa marks passive and impersonal verbs in Yaqui; with a
specified object, the construction is apparently always passive.

(1) tuisi yi?i-wa-k
much dance-IMPRS-PAST
'There was much dancing.'　(Y-L-TG-19)

(2) mesa-m ?ama ho-hoa-wa
table-PL there RDP-put-IMPRS
'The tables are put there.'　(Y-F-YP-10)

(3) nok-wa-me
say-IMPRS-PRTC
'things that are being said'　(Y-J-I-19)

(4) hu kuču b^{w}a?a-wa-k　　?im ?usi-m-mea
that fish eat-IMPRS-PAST my child-PL-with
'The fish was eaten by my children.'　(Y-L-TG-147)

(3) and (4) show that the construction is passive with transitive verbs and
not simply impersonal. In (3) this is apparent because participles are
identical in reference to the subject of the clause from which they derive,
not the object. It is evident from (4) because hu and kuču lack the accusative suffix; contrast (4) with its active counterpart (5).

(5) ?im ?usi-m hu-ka kuču-ta b^{w}a?a-ka
my child-PL that-ACC fish-ACC eat-PAST
'My children ate the fish.'　(Y-L-TG-147)

The agent of a passive sentence can be expressed by means of a postpositional phrase. With plural agents, the postposition is -mea, illustrated in
(4); it is -e with singular agents:

(6) hu maaso wepul ?o?oo-ta-e　　me?e-wa-k
this deer one man-ACC-with kill-IMPRS-PAST
'The deer was killed by one man.'　(Y-L-S-38)

Johnson reports three reflexive prefixes for Yaqui, ?ino- for first person singular, ?emo- for second person (singular and plural), and ?ama-
for third person singular; he does not cite a first or third person plural
form. Their occurrence apparently precludes the appearance of a subject
prefix on the verb, and they are said to be rare (Y-J-I-22).

(7) ?ino-bekta-bae
myself-reassure-DESID
'I want to reassure myself.'　(Y-J-I-22)

(8) ?emo-wo?oke
yourself-scratch
'You are scratching yourself.'　(Y-J-I-22)

(9) ?ama-hi?ika-k
himself-involve-PAST
'He involved himself.'　(Y-J-I-22)

Lindenfeld (Y-L-PC) reports a full paradigm that differs in certain details:

?ino	?ito
?omo	?omo
?aw	?omo

She treats these as independent elements rather than as prefixes, and the position of the clitic =ne in (10) would tend to confirm their autonomy.

(10) ?ino=ne wooke
myself-I scratch
'I am scratching myself.'   (Y-L-PC)

(11) ?itepo ?ito   wooke
we   ourselves scratch
'We are scratching ourselves.'   (Y-L-PC)

(12) ?eme?e ?omo   mee-bae
you   yourselves kill-DESID
PL
'You want to kill yourselves.'   (Y-L-PC)

(13) ?aapo ?aw   mee-bae
he   himself kill-DESID
'He wants to kill himself.'   (Y-L-PC)

Several unspecified argument prefixes are found in Yaqui, though data is somewhat limited. Buelna and Mason cite a prefix ne- which they call an "indefinite personal object" marker and state that it occurs only with the verb sawe 'command' (CAH-B-A-34; Y-M-PS-206). They describe yore- the same way, Buelna noting that yore- is used with all other verbs and that it does not occur when the object is specified (CAH-B-A-34). Johnson cites the variants yoe-, yoo-, and yee-, all obviously reductions from yore-, which is clearly related to the (participial?) noun yoe-me 'person/ Indian' (Y-J-I-11, 12).

(14) yoe-yo?ore
UNSPEC-respect
H OBJ
'respect (someone)'   (Y-J-I-12)

In addition, we find hi- (cf. hita 'something'--I take this prefix to be of recent origin), naw- 'together', and na-, which Johnson describes simply as "objeto" (Y-J-I-11, 12):

(15) hi-pona
UNSPEC-play
NH OBJ
'play (something)'   (Y-J-I-12)

(16)   naw-te-b^{w}ika
       together-?-sing
       'sing together'   (Y-J-I-12)

(17)   na-biču-k
       UNSPEC-see-PAST
       OBJ
       'He saw it.'   (Y-J-I-12)

(18)   ?a-na-wiite-k
       him-UNSPEC-hit-PAST
            OBJ
       'hit him (with something?)'   (Y-J-I-12)

The prefix te- in (16) is unidentified. The function of na- in (17) and (18)
is unclear; notice, however, that the object prefix for third person singular specified objects is ?a-.

1.17.   Cora

    Passive and impersonal sentences in Cora are marked by the verb suf-
fix -riwa, which also occurs in the shorter versions -iwa and -wa.

(1)   yest-iwa
      do-IMPRS
      wedding
      'A wedding takes place.'   (CR-P-G-55)

(2)   nakamu-riwa
      hear-IMPRS
      'be heard'   (CR-P-G-54)

(3)   tui-wa
      give-IMPRS
      'be sacrificed'   (CR-P-G-54)

A verb can also be passivized by changing its final vowel to i; thus we find
pairs such as tape 'tie' and tapi (also tapiwa) 'be tied', raste 'carry out'
and rasti 'be carried out' (CR-P-G-54). Preuss suggests that -me and -če
have passive force as well; however, the only seemingly clear case he
cites is moaite 'defeat' versus moaiti-če 'be defeated' (CR-P-G-55).

    The reflexive prefixes of Cora are as follows (CR-P-G-27; CR-MM-
CE-x):

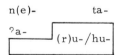

The hu- form is no doubt a phonetically strengthened variant of the u-
which results from the loss of r in ru-. These reflexive prefixes follow

the subject prefix, which is usually zero in the third person singular, and they may be used for reciprocals. The non-reflexive glosses of some of the examples suggest that the verbs may be inherent reflexives.

(4) ta-ta-tebi?ira?a
we-ourselves-ashamed
'We are ashamed.'   (CR-MM-CE-x)

(5) pa-?a-saupe
you-yourself-rest
'You rest!'   (CR-P-G-28)

(6) mu-ru-tam^{w}ave
they-REFL-happy
'They are happy.'   (CR-P-G-28)

(7) ha?ine sa-u-ruure
what   you-REFL-do
        PL
'What are you doing to each other?'   (CR-MM-CE-x)

1.18.   Huichol

Grimes states that Huichol has four passive suffixes, -ri, -ya, -wa, and -ki, and that the choice among them depends on the verb stem (HU-G-S-97). However, in the examples he cites elsewhere the most common passive suffix appears to be -riwa, and -rie (presumably from -ri-ya) is also attested.

(1) nunuuci p-a-nu-k^{w}ei-yaa-ni
child   ASSR-toward-other-carry-PASS-FUT
                    side
'The child will get carried away.'   (HU-G-S-55)

(2) mpai ti-ni-kihiawa-riwa   tewi
thus DISTR-NARR-tell-PASS man
'The man got told this.'   (HU-G-S-56)

(3) temaiki kuciira   kani-u-k^{w}ei-tia-rie-ni
boy   machete NARR-RESTR-carry-CAUS-PASS-NARR
'The boy was given a machete.'   (HU-G-S-55)

(4) p-u-wewi-ya
ASSR-RESTR-make-PASS
'It is made.'   (HU-M-HP-32)

From the consistent lack of object prefixes, it is clear that with transitive verbs the construction is passive rather than impersonal.

The reflexive prefixes of Huichol are much like those of Cora:

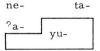

The plural prefixes can express reciprocal as well as reflexive relationships, and some verbs, such as temaawi 'be happy', take the reflexive
form obligatorily (HU-G-S-95).

(5) pɨ-yuu-temaawi
     ASSR-REFL-happy
     'He is happy.'   (HU-G-S-95)

(6) taame te-n-ta-ku-naakiku-ni
     we   we-NARR-ourselves-back-meet-FUT
                               and
                               forth
     'We shall meet each other.'   (HU-G-S-48)

(7) we-pɨ-yuu-naaki?eeri
     they-ASSR-REFL-love
     'They love one another.'   (HU-G-S-96)

With some stems, reflexive prefixes can be used to indicate an unspecified
object:

(8) we-p-te-yu-ka-naaki?eeri
     they-ASSR-DISTR-REFL-down-love
             PL
     'They love.'   (HU-G-S-96)

In this construction, a directional prefix is employed that ordinarily would
not be with the stem in question (e.g. ka- in (8)--cf. (7)), and a distributive
prefix is frequently found (HU-G-S-96).

1.19.   Pochutla[12]

     Little pertinent information is available from Pochutla. However, an

_____

[12] Pochutla, now presumably extinct, is by far the most divergent of the many
Aztec dialects. Compared to Pochutla, even Pipil, spoken far to the south, appears to
differ from Classical Nahuatl and closely related dialects only in relatively minor ways.
Pochutla is the only Aztecan dialect I have found which can lay some claim to being a
true sister to Classical Nahuatl rather than a descendant of the classical language or a
close dialect thereof. In particular, Pochutla has apparently failed to undergo at least
two sound changes characteristic of all other Aztec. First, general Aztec i̱ corresponds to Pochutla o̱ in many cases (e.g. A mičin 'fish', PO mičom), suggesting that
Pochutla did not undergo the *u > i sound change. Second, general Aztec e̱ corresponds
to Pochutla o̱ (e.g. A teX 'rock', PO tot), indicating that Pochutla did not undergo the
*ɨ > e change, at least not in all environments (PO-B-PML-108; PO-B-DMP-12, 13).
More precisely, we may suppose the common Aztecan development *ɨ > *ə, followed
by *ə > e in Aztec and *ə > o in Pochutla. (For similar developments in Cupan, cf. UA-
L-VP.)

unspecified object prefix <u>ta</u>- is attested, at least for non-human objects:

(1) š-ta-k^wa-ti
IMP-UNSPEC-eat-go
      OBJ   IMP
'Go eat!'   (PO-B-DMP-22)

Also attested are four subject prefix and reflexive object prefix combinations (PO-B-DMP-17):

n-(m)o-	t-mo-
t-o-	?
∅-mo	?

(2) ʔe-n-mo-teke-k
PERF-I-REFL-lie-PAST
            down
'I lay down.'   (PO-B-DMP-19)

When compared with Classical Nahuatl, this data leaves little doubt that <u>mo</u>- may be considered the basic Pochutla reflexive prefix for all persons. The phonetically awkward sequences <u>nmo</u> and <u>tmo</u> are in the process of simplification, and the loss of <u>m</u> from the latter has been seized upon as a basis for distinguishing the second person singular (now <u>to</u>-) from the previously homophonous first person plural (<u>tmo</u>-).

1.20.   Classical Nahuatl

Classical Nahuatl has three reflexive prefixes, <u>no</u>- for first person singular, <u>to</u>- for first person plural, and <u>mo</u>- for non-first person. They may be employed for reciprocals and passives as well as true reflexives, and used in conjunction with a causative suffix they have honorific value. Certain stems, such as <u>sawa</u> 'fast', take reflexive prefixes obligatorily.

(1) ʔan-mo-sawa-ʔ
you-REFL-fast-PL
PL
'You PL fast.'   (A-B-NA-21)

(2) ʔon-m-iš-keca   ʔin tek^wsistekaλ
away-REFL-face-stand ART PN
            present
'Tecuciztecatl presents himself.'   (A-G-L-131)

(3) ki-mo-lwi-ʔ-keʔ
      ilwia
it-REFL-say-PAST-PL
'They said (it) to one another.'   (A-G-L-131)

(4) mo-tesi
     REFL-grind
     'They are ground.'   (A-DA-FC10-161)

(5) ni-mic-on-no-pie-li-li
     I-you-away-myself-have-CAUS-APPLIC
                                   PAST
     '(which) I have guarded for you HON'   (A-G-L-156)

In addition, Aztec has a series of emphatic pronouns consisting of a possessor prefix and the base -no?ma:

(6) to-no?ma
     our-REFL
     'we ourselves'   (A-R-AM-18)

The forms -no?matka and -ne?wiyaan have been cited as variants (A-M-IN).

   There are three unspecified argument prefixes, te-, χa-, and ne-. te-
and χa- indicate unspecified human and non-human objects respectively:

(7) ni-te-noca
     I-UNSPEC-call
       H   OBJ
     'I call (someone).'   (A-G-L-37)

(8) ni-χa-k^{w}a
     I-UNSPEC-eat
       NH OBJ
     'I eat (something).'   (A-G-L-37)

(9) ni-te-χa-k^{w}epi-lia
     I-UNSPEC-UNSPEC-restore-APPLIC
       H   OBJ   NH OBJ
     'I restore (something to someone).'   (A-M-V1-26)

The function of ne- is not so immediately obvious. Siméon states that it is
a special reflexive prefix used with impersonal verbs and derived nominals
(A-S-DLN-272). But while this appears to be true, ne- is also used in certain instances where a reflexive prefix would not be expected. Consider the
following examples:

(10) ne-sawa-lo
     UNSPEC-fast-IMPRS
     REFL
     'There is fasting.'   (A-A-RL-34)

(11) ne-χalo-lo
     UNSPEC-run-IMPRS
     REFL
     'One runs.'   (A-S-DLN-272; A-A-RL-34)

(12) ne- toti- lis- ne- mač- ti- lo- yaan
       itotia
      UNSPEC- dance- NR- UNSPEC- know- CAUS- IMPRS- place
      <u>REFL   REFL   teach   of</u>
      <u>   dancing   one is taught</u>
                 one is taught dancing
      'dancing school'   (A-S-DLN-305)

(13) ne-k^wa-lo
      UNSPEC- eat- IMPRS
      REFL
      'One eats.'   (A-G-L-35, 46)

(14) ne- no- noca- lo
      UNSPEC- RDP- call- IMPRS
      REFL   <u>RCPR</u>
              deliberate
      'There was deliberation.'   (A-G-L-134)

(15) te-ƛa?so?ƛa-lo
      UNSPEC- love- IMPRS
      H   OBJ
      'One is loved.'   (A-R-AM-30)

(16) ne-ƛa?so?ƛa-lo
      UNSPEC- love- IMPRS
      REFL
      'There is loving of one another.'   (A-R-AM-30)

Since the verbs 'fast', 'run', and 'dance' in (10) - (12) are inherent reflexive verbs, Siméon's characterization of <u>ne-</u> as reflexive seems appropriate.
However, the remaining verbs in (12) - (14) are problematic; 'teach' and
'eat' are not inherently reflexive, and the reduplication could be taken as
responsible for the reciprocal sense of 'deliberate'. The contrast between
(15) and (16) is instructive; it suggests that <u>ne-</u> itself has reciprocal force,
at least when contrasted with <u>te-</u>. Since reflexive or reciprocal uses do
seem to predominate, we might conjecture that these are basic, and that the
apparent use of <u>ne-</u> as unspecified subject (e.g. in (13)) represents an extension. It should further be noted that the argument which <u>ne-</u> stands for
is always human.

    The passive/impersonal suffix appears variously as -<u>lo</u>, -<u>o</u>, -<u>oa</u>, -<u>wa</u>,
and -<u>l</u>. It is impersonal with intransitive verbs and passive with transitives. It is quite common in derived nouns, and when it is used with the
agentive suffix -<u>ni</u> the resulting noun is instrumental.

(17) mik- oa- ya
     die- IMPRS- PAST
               DUR
     'There was dying.'   (A-G-L-146)

(18) koko- l- li
     be- IMPRS- ABS
     sick
     'sickness'   (A-G-L-143)

(19) pano- wa- ni
     cross- IMPRS- AG
     'bridge'   (A-G-L-145)

(20) ʔoo- ni- mak- o- k   ʔome šoči-ƛ
     PERF- I- give- IMPRS- PAST two   flower- ABS
     'I was given two flowers.'   (A-S-DLN-lxiii)

(21) ʔoo- ni- kʷawi- lo- k
     PERF- I- beat- IMPRS- PAST
     'I was beaten.'   (A-S-DLN-372)

The use of subject prefixes rather than object prefixes in (20) and (21) demonstrates that the construction is passive rather than impersonal with transitive verbs.

II. REFLEXIVE PREFIXES

2.0. Introduction

Most of the languages examined in Chapter 1 have one or more reflexive prefixes that occur on verbs. Those which do not, such as Tubatulabal and most of the Takic languages, express reflexive relationships by means of special reflexive pronouns, which are also found in languages that do have reflexive prefixes. We will examine reflexive prefixes in this chapter, and reflexive pronouns in Chapter 3.

2.1 will deal with the form of reflexive prefixes, and 2.2 with their syntactic function. We will trace their evolution step by step in 2.3.

2.1. Form

Let us begin by summarizing the reflexive prefixes found in the various daughter languages. This summary is presented in Table I.

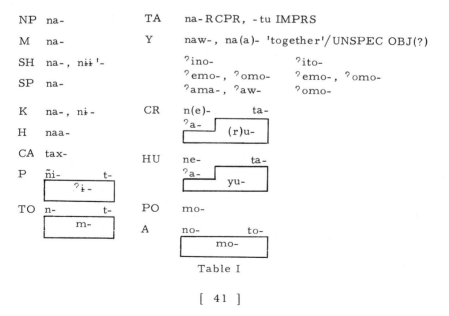

<table>
<tr><td>NP</td><td>na-</td><td>TA</td><td colspan="2">na-RCPR, -tu IMPRS</td></tr>
<tr><td>M</td><td>na-</td><td>Y</td><td colspan="2">naw-, na(a)- 'together'/UNSPEC OBJ(?)</td></tr>
<tr><td>SH</td><td>na-, nɨɨ'-</td><td></td><td>ʔino-</td><td>ʔito-</td></tr>
<tr><td>SP</td><td>na-</td><td></td><td>ʔemo-, ʔomo-
ʔama-, ʔaw-</td><td>ʔemo-, ʔomo-
ʔomo-</td></tr>
<tr><td>K</td><td>na-, nɨ-</td><td>CR</td><td>n(e)-   ta-</td><td></td></tr>
<tr><td>H</td><td>naa-</td><td></td><td>ʔa- (r)u-</td><td></td></tr>
<tr><td>CA</td><td>tax-</td><td>HU</td><td>ne-   ta-</td><td></td></tr>
<tr><td>P</td><td>ñi-   t-
ʔɨ-</td><td></td><td>ʔa- yu-</td><td></td></tr>
<tr><td>TO</td><td>n-   t-
m-</td><td>PO</td><td>mo-</td><td></td></tr>
<tr><td></td><td></td><td>A</td><td>no-   to-
mo-</td><td></td></tr>
</table>

Table I

[41]

Several of these elements require preliminary comment. Discussion of
Shoshoni nɨɨ'- and Kawaiisu nɨ- will be postponed until Chapter 4. Cahuilla
tax- originated as a reflexive noun, and its incorporation was quite recent,
as noted earlier;[1] thus it will be discussed with the reflexive pronouns in
Chapter 3. Tarahumara na- is reciprocal rather than reflexive, but it is
included because of its obvious similarity to the reflexive prefix in Numic
and Hopi; Yaqui naw- and na(a)- are included for the same reason. Reflexives in Tarahumara are marked by the passive/impersonal suffix -tu,
which will be dealt with in Chapter 5.

The most striking aspect of Table I is the split between the northern
languages and the southern languages. The predominant pattern in the
northern languages is for a single prefix, roughly na-, to be used for the
reflexive in all persons. In the southern languages, on the other hand,
there is a strong tendency toward a set of distinct prefixes for different
persons, and na- is not attested for any person in a specifically reflexive
use. It would be most difficult to derive either type of system from the
other. Clearly it would be implausible to suppose that a single prefix na-
would split into a differentiated system such as that of Papago or Huichol,
especially since these systems do not even contain na- as a member.[2] It
is less implausible to suppose that one member of a differentiated system,
nV-, could generalize to all persons, but then the Taracahitic data would
be unexplained. Yaqui in particular suggests that na- and a differentiated
system of reflexive prefixes coexisted in the proto language, and that neither derives historically from the other.

To begin the task of reconstructing the proto system, it will be helpful
to do preliminary reconstruction for each major subfamily. The subfamilies cannot be viewed in total isolation from one another, however. In

---

[1] The recentness of this incorporation, as attested by the independent status of tax in
other Takic languages, rules out one initially plausible hypothesis concerning the origin
of na-, namely that *taka 'man' was incorporated as a reflexive prefix at an early stage
of development and has been eroded to na- or lost in all daughters but Cahuilla. (*t
could possibly be reflected as n through lenition of non-fortis t to l followed by the
sound change *l > n characteristic of the northern Uto-Aztecan languages.) Besides being unable to account for the other Takic languages, in which tax is unincorporated despite its use as a reflexive, this hypothesis fails to handle na- in Tarahumara and
Yaqui; the sound change *l > n did not take place in these languages.

[2] The first person singular form must be reconstructed as *nɨ- rather than *na-, as
shown below.

some instances the proper reconstruction for an intermediate proto language is problematic when only its daughters are examined but reasonably clear when other subfamilies are taken into account.

The reconstruction of *na- for Proto Numic is transparent and requires no comment.

In Pimic, information is available only for Papago and Tepecano. *t- is easily reconstructed for the first person plural reflexive prefix, and the first person singular clearly involves n, but the rest is problematic.

Consider first the first person singular. The palatalization of n to ñ in Papago is quite recent,[3] so n rather than ñ must be reconstructed. The next question is whether to reconstruct *nV- or simply *n- for Proto Pimic. The proper reconstruction is most probably *nV-, both because vowel loss is more common than epenthesis and because Yaqui ?ino-, Corachol ne-, and Aztec no- point to *nV- for Proto Uto-Aztecan. Now we must ask which particular vowel to reconstruct. Papago ñi- makes i the most obvious choice since Tepecano is non-committal, but I believe in this instance the most obvious choice is not the correct one; I will reconstruct *nɨ- instead. *nɨ- will account for the palatalization of n in Papago, since n palatalizes to ñ before any high vowel. Once *nɨ- > *ñɨ- has occurred, ɨ changes to i by assimilation to the preceding ñ, a natural and not unexpected development. Several kinds of evidence support this choice. *nɨ- is more likely than *ni- to give rise to Tepecano n-, since i is a highly stable vowel in Uto-Aztecan which tends not to be lost, in marked contrast to ɨ. *nɨ- also corresponds regularly to ne- in Cora and Huichol, while *ni- is not corroborated in any other language. Finally, *nɨ- has the advantage of reflecting directly the independent pronoun *nɨ 'I' which must be reconstructed for Proto Uto-Aztecan (cf. NT ?a-nɨ 'I', P ?aa-ñi 'I' through assimilation of ɨ to ñ).

For non-first person reflexives, Papago has ?ɨ- and Tepecano has m-. Obviously neither of these derives from the other. Moreover, both can be connected to reflexive prefixes attested in other languages, ?ɨ- to the second person singular ?a- in Cora and Huichol, and m- to mo- in Yaqui, Pochutla, and Classical Nahuatl. This, together with the fact that am(u)-

---

[3] The palatalization is restricted to Papago, in fact to certain dialects of Papago, and clearly functions as a synchronic rule (cf. P-H-PO).

has been cited as a reflexive prefix for Pima Bajo (TO-M-PL-346), suggests that both *ʔɨ- and *m(u)- occurred as reflexive prefixes in Proto
Pimic, with one or the other having been generalized to all non-first person forms in each daughter. The problem now is to determine their distribution. Here again comparative evidence allows a principled choice. Outside of Papago, ʔV- occurs as a reflexive prefix only in Corachol, where it
is restricted to second person singular, while mV- in Yaqui and Aztecan
shows a tendency to generalize to several or all persons. The most plausible reconstruction is therefore the following, which is quite similar to the
pattern attested in Cora and Huichol:

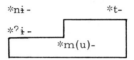

On the basis of Tarahumara na- 'RCPR' and Yaqui naw-/na(a) 'together'
(which in some forms apparently pertains to objects in some way but with
uncertain function), it is reasonable to reconstruct *na- 'RCPR' for Proto
Taracahitic. This prefix is reflected unchanged in Tarahumara; in Yaqui
there has been some remodeling, but the paucity of information makes it
difficult to trace the details. The key to the Yaqui development may lie in
a series of dative prefixes ending in w; compare these with the subject/
object prefixes (Y-J-I-21):[4]

	Dative		Subject/Object	
new-	ʔitow-	ne-	ʔitom-
ʔew-	ʔemow-	ʔenči-	ʔeme-
ʔaw-	(ʔa)mew-	ʔa-	ʔam-

Johnson claims that the dative prefixes incorporate the postposition -w(i)
'at/in/to' and speculates quite plausibly that they may have developed under
Spanish influence, since they are not mentioned in the earliest Yaqui grammar (Y-J-I-22). If we posit a pre-Yaqui reciprocal prefix *na-, then, the
following developments can be proposed. First, na- was expanded to naw-
to express the reciprocal in at least some occurrences after the model of
the new dative prefixes; note that reciprocal constructions often translate

---

[4] Lindenfeld (Y-L-TG; Y-L-S) treats these as independent particles rather than prefixes; similarly for the reflexive elements she cites. Weak cliticization is probably
indicated, but the difference is not crucial for present purposes.

naturally as 'V with one another' or 'V to one another'. At this stage naw-
and na- coexisted in Yaqui as complementary reciprocal prefixes, the
former probably used when the postposition -w(i) was semantically appropriate. Next, this fine semantic distinction between dative and non-dative
reciprocals became blurred, and the two forms began competing for general reciprocal use. For some dialects (or verbs perhaps), naw- eventually
won out, leaving na- as a relic; this explains why na- appears to have no
clear function in some instances. For others, na(a)- is retained as a reciprocal, normally translated as 'together'.

The reflexive prefixes in Yaqui are also archaic, but they correspond
quite well to those in the other southern Uto-Aztecan languages. We may
suppose that they were already obsolescent in Proto Taracahitic, since
they disappeared in Tarahumara and are said to be "rare" in Yaqui. We
may disregard the form ʔaw- for the third person singular, as it represents a likely extension of the dative prefix having the same shape. The
remaining forms are all bisyllabic and have ʔV for their first syllable.
Actually, these forms are not, strictly speaking, reflexive prefixes (at
least not diachronically), but rather frozen combinations of subject prefix
plus reflexive prefix (recall that they occur without the regular subject
prefixes). The first syllable of each may be taken as the remnant of a subject prefix (compare the subject prefixes ʔitom- 'we', ʔenči- 'you', ʔeme-
'you PL', and ʔa- 'he'), leaving no-, to-, mo-, and ma- as the reflexive
prefixes per se. Thus we have the following array:

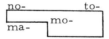

We may push the internal reconstruction a bit further. ʔama- very probably derives from *ʔa-mo- through vowel harmonization, which is a per-
vasive though largely irregular phenomenon throughout Uto-Aztecan (cf.
UA-S-SPN1-402-406); the ʔemo-/ʔomo- variation came about in similar
fashion. We thus arrive at the system below:

The reflexive prefixes in Cora and Huichol are so similar that only two questions arise. First, should we reconstruct (r)u- as in Cora or yu- as in Huichol? Second, whichever one we reconstruct, how did it come to replace the prefix mo- found in the other southern languages?

Let us begin with the second question. The ru-/yu- prefix evidently derives from the reflexive possessor prefix used with nouns; this also is ru- in Cora and yu- in Huichol: CR ru-či?i 'his own house' (CR-MM-CE-vi); HU yu-?iwa 'his own brother' (HU-G-S-50). I have little information on these constructions, but it does appear that ru- and yu-, like the reflexive verb prefix ru-/yu-, can both be plural as well as singular: CR ru-k^{w}inari 'their (own) violin performance' (CR-P-G-26); HU yu-ki-epai (own-house-to) 'to their (own) house' (SON-K-V-285). We may suppose, then, that the reflexive possessor prefix ru- or yu- supplanted the reflexive verb prefix mo-, which it resembled in meaning and function.

As for the choice between *ru- and *yu-, we may begin by noting that the same r/y discrepancy between Cora and Huichol is shown by the third person singular non-reflexive noun suffixes, -ra and -ya: CR huya-ra-hece (path-his-on) 'on his path' (CR-P-NE-2); HU haca-ya 'his axe' (NT-MNR-LM-30). Cora and Huichol share with Pimic the peculiarity of marking possession by means of a suffix for the third person singular and by means of a prefix for all other persons. The Pimic possessor suffix is clearly cognate with Corachol -ra/-ya and possibly ru-/yu-; only the quality of the vowel is problematic. Hence Pimic can tell us whether the r-forms or the y-forms are more primitive, and it turns out that the y-forms are. The third person singular possessor suffix is -ǰ in Papago, -dɨ in Northern Tepehuan, and -d in Tepecano. These reconstruct to Proto Pimic *-d(ɨ), and Proto Pimic *d descends from Proto Uto-Aztecan *y.[5] Consequently the reflexive prefixes reconstructable for Proto Corachol are exactly the same as those of Huichol.

[5] The precise relationship between *-ya and *yu- in Corachol requires further investigation. Possibly these both go back to *-yo (-yo marks inalienable possession in Aztec). P-UA *o becomes P-CCH *u, which would account for yu, and the ya variant could be by analogy to other possessor affixes, in which a predominates. The change of yu from a suffix to a prefix could conceivably be due to its adoption as a reflexive prefix--it became a prefix on verbs, since it replaced the prefix *mo-, and the subsequent change from nominal suffix to nominal prefix status would thus constitute a regularization. For now this analysis is only speculative, however.

Finally we come to Aztecan. Here <u>mo</u>- has evidently generalized to all persons in Pochutla; Classical Nahuatl retains distinct singular and plural first person forms consistent with those in the other southern Uto-Aztecan languages. The reconstructed system for Proto Aztecan will consequently be the same as that of Classical Nahuatl.

The results of these various reconstructions are summarized in Table II.

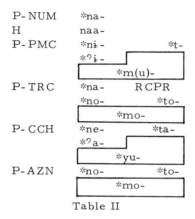

Table II

Once these intermediate reconstructions have been made, the reconstruction of the Proto Uto-Aztecan system is reasonably straightforward.[6] *<u>na</u>- can be reconstructed on the basis of Numic, Hopi, and Taracahitic. Taracahitic suggests clearly that *<u>na</u>- was reciprocal and coexisted with a set of reflexive prefixes. The most probable reconstruction for the reflexive prefixes is as follows:

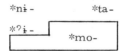

This system is retained virtually unchanged in Proto Pimic. In Proto Taracahitic and Proto Aztecan, *<u>mo</u>- has been generalized to all non-first person forms at the expense of the phonologically weak *ʔɨ-, and the system has further been simplified by the extension of <u>o</u> to all forms in the paradigm. In Proto Corachol, *<u>mo</u>- was replaced by the reflexive

---

[6]Possibly some or all of these reconstructed elements were proclitics to the verb rather than verbal prefixes. This is apparently the case in Yaqui (footnote 4) and with Papago ʔɨ (Chapter 1, footnote 10). The reflexive prefix <u>naa</u>- in Hopi may also be proclitic rather than prefixal.

possessor affix *yu, and *ʔɨ- changed to *ʔa-. This second change also
occurred under the influence of the possessor affixes; the second person
singular possessor prefix in Proto Corachol reconstructs as *ʔa- (CR
m^waʔa-, ʔaʔa-, ʔa-; HU ʔa-). For the first person singular, Proto Pimic
*nɨ- and Proto Corachol *ne- correspond directly via the regular sound
change *ɨ > e.

Reflexive and reciprocal constructions are semantically very similar,
especially in the plural (singular reciprocals are a contradiction in terms).
Both involve coreference of subject and object, and they differ only in the
way in which the verbal relationship is distributed among the members of
the set designated by these arguments. With reflexives, the members of
the set act collectively on the set as a whole, as in Figure III, or each
member acts upon himself, as in Figure IV. With reciprocals, the relations are skewed, as shown in Figure V, despite the identity of the overall
sets involved.

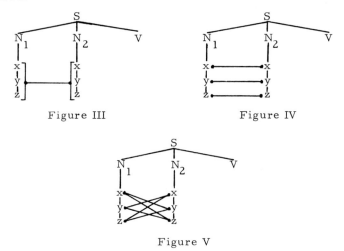

Figure III   Figure IV

Figure V

Languages can get by without these subtle semantic distinctions if need be,
or can mark them in some other manner (e. g. with reflexive pronouns);
thus many languages use the same verbal affixes to mark reflexive and reciprocal relationships.

Consequently, a language which has both a reciprocal prefix and a paradigm of reflexive prefixes is, if not unstable, at least quite subject to diachronic modification. The Proto Uto-Aztecan system survived reasonably
intact only in Proto Taracahitic, but even here we found reason to suppose

that the reflexives were obsolescent. In the other southern languages, the
reciprocal prefix has been lost, and the reflexive has taken on reciprocal
sense. In the northern languages, the reflexive prefixes have been lost,
and in Numic and Hopi the reciprocal has taken on reflexive sense. The
two developments are parallel responses to a common potential for change.

2.2. Syntax

We have posited a reciprocal prefix and a series of reflexive prefixes
for Proto Uto-Aztecan. Both are well-attested among the daughter languages, but only in Yaqui are both retained as such, and even here there
are complications. Consequently a closer examination of the function of
reflexive prefixes and related elements is in order, both to corroborate
the reconstruction and to render more precise our conception of their evolution. Besides their specifically reflexive use, reflexive affixes are commonly used with reciprocal and passive value, and in at least one instance
with impersonal value. In Numic, moreover, the reflexive prefix also
occurs with nouns and postpositions.

Initially we will restrict our attention to the reflexive, reciprocal,
passive, and impersonal uses of reflexive affixes; their occurrence with
nouns and postpositions will be dealt with subsequently. The pertinent
data is summarized in Table III, which also includes non-affixal reflexive
markers. Note that the absence of + in a slot does not invariably imply
non-existence of the phenomenon, but only its non-attestation in the sources
I have been able to examine. For example, the incidence of inherently reflexive verbs must be somewhat higher than Table III would indicate, since
grammatical descriptions tend not to mention their existence, which cannot
be confirmed simply by examining a few individual examples. Indeed, the
tendency for the reflexive to be obligatory with at least a few verbs in a
language makes it difficult to believe that Proto Uto-Aztecan, with both reflexive and reciprocal prefixes, did not have inherent reflexives, but I
will leave this matter for future research.

Several interesting facts emerge from the distribution of properties in
Table III. Notice first that the reflexive marker is almost always used for
reciprocal relations as well. This is probably also the case in Tepecano

and Pochutla, where the relevant data is quite limited. It may also be the case with Shoshoni n<u>ɨɨ</u>'-, but here it would not be surprising to find that the reciprocal use was not permitted, since n<u>ɨɨ</u>'- has a non-reciprocal origin (treated later) and the coexisting prefix <u>na</u>- can express this concept. In Kawaiisu, a reflexive pronoun is apparently used for reciprocal sentences rather than <u>na</u>-/<u>nɨ</u>-, but <u>na</u>- does have reciprocal value when used with nouns. The only other instances where the reflexive marker does not also serve for reciprocals are Tarahumara and Yaqui, and these are the only two languages which have retained a reciprocal prefix distinct from the reflexive prefixes. Observe also that <u>na</u>- tolerates reciprocal use in every language in which it is attested (with the partial exception of Kawaiisu), while this is not invariably true of other reflexive markers.

	REFLEXIVE MARKER	RECIPROCAL USE	PASSIVE USE	IMPERSONAL USE	INHERENT REFLEXIVES	PASSIVE SUFFIX
NP	na-	+	+			
M	na-	+	+			
SH	na-	+	+		+	
	nɨɨ'-		+			
SP	na-	+			+	+
K	na-, nɨ-				+	+
TU	ʔomo(h)i(x)	+				+
H	naa-	+				+
SR	taqa	+				
CA	tax-	+				
CU	tax	+				+
L	taax	+				
P	ñi-, t-, ʔɨ-	+	+		+	+
TO	n-, t-, m-		+			
TA	na- RCPR	+				
	-tu		+	+		+
Y	no-, to-, mo-					+
	naw-, na(a)- RCPR	+				
CR	ne-, ta-, ʔa-, ru-	+			+	+
HU	ne-, ta-, ʔa-, yu-	+			+	+
PO	mo-					
A	no-, to-, mo-	+	+		+	+

Table III

These facts directly corroborate the proposed reconstruction of both a reciprocal prefix *na- and a distinct series of non-reciprocal reflexive prefixes. As long as the reciprocal prefix is retained, there is no need to extend the reflexive prefixes into this domain. Once the reciprocal prefix is lost, on the other hand, some means must be found to express this concept, and the reflexive prefixes are one obvious choice. Similarly, the reciprocal prefix can take over reflexive function once the reflexive prefixes are lost, and if both are lost, as in Tubatulabal and Takic, some other device such as a reflexive pronoun must assume both roles. Of course, it is probably misleading to view the processes of losing one marker and extending the role of another as sequential. In a system like that of Proto Uto-Aztecan, with distinct markers for very similar concepts, there is naturally a tendency for one to invade the domain of the other and eventually displace it. In the northern languages, the reciprocal prefix won out; the reflexive prefixes generally won out in the southern languages. Only in Taracahitic did the two remain on equal terms.

With the single exception of Tarahumara, reflexive affixes in Uto-Aztecan do not mark impersonal sentences, although Table III shows it is not uncommon for them to mark passives. The hypotheses advanced in the Introduction explain these facts and derive further support from them. First we will consider the extension of reflexive markers to passive use; next the non-extension of reflexive markers to impersonal use; and finally the exceptional case of Tarahumara.

A reflexive prefix marks the subject and object of a sentence as being coreferential. Granted the underlying structure of passive sentences discussed in the Introduction (it will be further motivated in Chapter 5), these have unspecified underlying subjects and specified underlying objects. In both cases the underlying subject and object are non-distinct, and for this reason the same affix can come to mark them both. In particular, the extension of a reflexive prefix to passive use represents a generalization in function, from marking coreferential arguments to marking non-distinct arguments.

Table III gives some indication that passive use does in fact constitute an innovation, i.e. that passives were not marked by reflexive prefixes in Proto Uto-Aztecan. First observe that a passive or passive/impersonal

suffix is found in the majority of the daughter languages; it will be reconstructed in Chapter 5. Thus there was no real need for the reflexive prefix to play this role. Observe next that there is a tendency for reflexive
prefixes to mark passives in just those languages where the passive suffix
has disappeared. In four of the six languages (not counting TA) where a
reflexive prefix is used for passives there is no passive suffix (NP, M, SH,
TO); in eight of the eleven languages with a passive suffix, passive use of a
reflexive marker is unattested (SP, K, TU, H, CU, Y, CR, HU). These
figures strongly suggest that reflexive markers in Uto-Aztecan came to assume passive function only as the passive suffixes disappeared. Papago
and Aztec, in which we have both a passive suffix and passive use of reflexive prefixes, hint that the extension in function of the reflexive markers
may have facilitated the loss of the passive suffix (rather than the converse), but either way it seems evident that there are no grounds for attri-
buting passive use to the reflexive prefixes at the P-UA level.

Why are the reflexive markers not extended to mark impersonal sentences as well? The crucial factor here is that impersonal sentences in
Uto-Aztecan are virtually always intransitive (Southern Paiute affords the
only clear exception). When a transitive clause has an unspecified subject,
the underlying object almost always becomes the surface subject, making
the clause passive rather than impersonal. Since impersonal sentences
are normally intransitive, the generalization in function that extends reflexive prefixes to passives is simply inapplicable with respect to impersonals; in an intransitive sentence, it is simply not meaningful to speak of
the subject and object as being non-distinct, for there is no object. A reflexive prefix could occasionally be extended to intransitive impersonal
clauses, but this would require a further round of reanalysis and extension,
one which has not taken place in Uto-Aztecan.

The case of Tarahumara is particularly interesting, for here the extension has gone in the opposite direction. The suffix -tu was originally a
passive/impersonal suffix (cf. Chapter 5), and its reflexive use is innovative, presumably brought about by the loss of the earlier reflexive prefixes.
The possibility of this development is predicted by the notion of non-distinct
arguments and hence supports this notion. In its original passive/imper-
sonal role, -tu marked configurations like those in Figure I, with

unspecified subject. In regard to transitive clauses, having an unspecified subject entails having non-distinct subject and object. Thus when the need arose to find a new way to mark reflexives, it was a simple matter to re-analyze -tu as indicating non-distinct arguments. The fact that this type of extension did not happen more frequently may be attributed to two factors. First, this extension is not fully compatible with the role of -tu as an impersonal suffix, as noted above. Second, the availability of *na- to assume reflexive function (through a somewhat simpler change) made it unnecessary to resort to the passive/impersonal suffix.

Let us now turn to non-verbal uses of *na-. One of these uses is as a noun prefix (often reduplicated) to form a derived noun designating the members of a reciprocal relationship, e.g. M na'na-peti̱ (RCPR-daughter) 'pareꞛt and daughter' (M-L-G-181). This function is observed only in Numic, though Shimkin intimates that the relation (if not the marking) may be basic to Uto-Aztecan (UA-S-KT-227). If so, this use of *na- confirms our decision to reconstruct it as a reciprocal rather than a reflexive prefix, since the kinship relations designated by na-N are reciprocal in character and not reflexive (they hold between two or more individuals, not between one individual and himself). There is no indication that the reconstructed reflexive prefixes could ever be used in this manner.

A second use of *na- is in the formation of numerals, e.g. SP pai 'three', na-pai 'six' (SP-S-G-110). Both Miller (UA-M-CS-69) and Sapir (UA-S-SPN2-313) reconstruct this function for Proto Uto-Aztecan, and I will not repeat the details here. Sapir explicitly equates this *na- with the reflexive prefix na- of Southern Paiute; Miller reserves judgment, simply reconstructing the senses 'twice/double/half'. In view of the close semantic relation[7] and the evidence that the reciprocal *na- did indeed have non-verbal uses, it seems apparent that Sapir was correct.

There is good reason to believe that the reciprocal *na- could occur with postpositions in Proto Uto-Aztecan. This construction is directly attested in Mono and Southern Paiute, e.g. M na-'pi-'pi'naha (RCPR-RDP-

---

[7] Eric Hamp has observed that the use of na- in numerals is almost directly parallel semantically to its use in kinship terms. In both cases, two entities treated as being equivalent (parent and daughter; three and three) additively and exhaustively define a set. The set thus implies reciprocity for its defining members.

behind) 'one after another' (M-L-G-182).[8]   It is somewhat less directly

attested in the Hopi emphatic reflexive pronoun naap (cf. examples (7) and

(8) of section 1.7), which can be analyzed as naa- (which is both reflexive

and reciprocal in Hopi) plus a locative postposition (cf. -pe 'at/in', -pa

'on'). The discussion of reflexive pronouns in Chapter 3 will enhance the

plausibility of this analysis of Hopi naap, and it will provide additional

motivation, from a variety of Uto-Aztecan languages (including southern

languages), for positing the na-P construction at the proto level.

Let me conclude this section by offering one somewhat more speculative

piece of evidence to support the reconstruction of P-UA *na-P. Northern

Paiute has a postposition -noo 'with', illustrated in (1).[9]

NP (1) nɨmi-noo
         people-with
         'together with the people'   (NP-L-M)

This postposition is suspiciously similar to Cahuilla -new/-niw 'with' and

Cupeno -nəw 'with', which reconstruct to P-CAC *-nəw.

CA (2) čeme-new
         us-with
         'with us'   (CA-H-BSK-45)

CU (3) pəmə-nəw
         them-with
         'with them'   (CU-H-G-52)

*-nəw could easily derive from unstressed *-naw, which could also under-

lie NP -noo. *-naw in turn can be decomposed into the reciprocal *na-

plus the postposition *-w(i) (cf. Y -w(i) 'at/in/to', already discussed in

conjunction with the dative prefixes, and A -wi-k 'toward/against'[10]). Not

only does this make sense semantically, but it may also explain the

Cahuilla variant -niw (-new is the regular correspondent of Cupeno -nəw).

The vowel of -niw may be a vestige of vowel harmonization to the vowel of

*-wi, which is not otherwise retained in Cahuilla-Cupeno but is in Yaqui.

---

[8] Also pertinent is Northern Paiute nama 'together' (NP-N-HG-206), from na- plus
the postposition -ma 'with'.

[9] This postposition, which has also been transcribed as -no, -noʔ, -noʔo, -noko,
-na, and -nu, has come to function as a conjunction with nouns. Two or more historically distinct postpositions may be involved here; clearer data and more detailed examination are needed. All that matters for present purposes is the existence of -no or
-noo as a valid transcription, and we will find Southern Numic corroboration of this in
Chapter 3.

[10] Aztec -naawak 'near/with' is also suggestive here. Possibly it derives from
*na-wi-k through vowel harmonization.

That is, alongside the development *-na-w(i) > *-na-w > *-nə-w> CA -new,
we have the alternative development, retained only in Cahuilla, of
*-na-wi > *-nə-wi > *-ni-wi > -niw.

This analysis receives some corroboration from the fact that -noo in
Northern Paiute tends to be reinforced by means of a particle or emphatic
pronoun based on na- and translatable as 'together':

NP (4) su   wɨta ka   tɨhɨ'ya-nu na-ma   nopi-ka?yu
       ART bear ART deer-with RCPR-with house-have
                ACC   together
       'Bear was living with Deer.'   (NP-N-HG-206)

NP (5) na-noo   mi-mia-u   tawni-waitu delia 'ste'la-noo
       RCPR-with RDP-go-PNCT town-to   PN   PN-with
        together
       'Delia and Stella went to town together.'   (NP-L-M)

I hypothesize the following course of development for NP -noo. Originally,
*na-w was an independent particle meaning 'with one another/together'. At
this stage, we may suppose sentences such as (6).

(6) N_1 N_2 na-w V   'N_1 (and) N_2 V together.'

Next, *naw changes phonetically to noo. Perhaps because the reciprocal
base na- is then no longer phonetically apparent, this sequence is reanalyzed as a monomorphemic postposition meaning '(together) with' and is
attached to N_2 like any other postposition. This yields sentences like (7).

(7) N_1 N_2 -noo V   'N_1 V with N_2.'

Finally, to emphasize the reciprocity of a relationship, sentences like (7)
are reinforced by new expressions consisting of the reciprocal na- plus a
postposition; (4) exemplifies na-ma in this reinforcing role, and (5) exemplifies na-noo, which can arise (despite the etymological redundancy)
once -noo has become a postposition and speakers are no longer aware of
its relation to na-.

2.3.   Evolution

2.3.0.   Introduction

Once the proto system has been reconstructed, one might suppose that
tracing its evolution in the various daughter languages and justifying subgroupings by means of shared innovations would be a straightforward

matter. In fact it is not, even granting the correctness of the reconstruction. Every step in the process involves non-trivial issues and hypotheses. For example, what are the causes and mechanisms of morphosyntactic change? At each stage, what are the abstract structures that underlie the surface structures whose evolution we are trying to determine?

We will be more directly concerned with another class of problems, those pertaining to language subclassification and the concept of shared innovations. The traditional source of difficulty in this domain, the conflict between the "family tree" model of linguistic relationship and the "wave" model, is largely a red herring and should not bother us here. Some daughter languages are so similar to one another in comparison to other daughters that the tree metaphor is plainly justified, but in using it we are not at all compelled to follow it to the ends of the earth. For instance, we can perfectly well view Northern Paiute and Mono as a genetic unit and posit an entity called Proto Western Numic without believing or pretending that this was a uniform dialect or that it split off definitively from the rest of Numic before Northern Paiute and Mono started to differentiate, thereby precluding an innovation connecting one of these but not the other to some other Numic language. Our problem is to trace the history of these languages and reconstruct the linguistic situation at earlier stages, and this can be done whether the transitions were abrupt or gradual.

However, having a realistic conception of the tree model does not in itself resolve the descriptive problems that arise in particular instances. For example, the reflexive prefix *mo- generalized to all non-first person forms in Tepecano, Taracahitic, and Aztecan, but not in Papago or Corachol. No one would seriously propose a Tepecano-Taracahitic-Aztecan subfamily on this basis, but agreement on this point leaves various other questions still to be resolved. Did the change originate in one group and spread by diffusion or did it originate independently on two or more occasions? Should we consider the change as evidence for the Aztecan subfamily when the shared innovation is not restricted to Aztecan? What should we say about Proto Tepehuan, since we have no information about reflexive prefixes in Northern Tepehuan to compare with the Tepecano data?

Let us consider another example. The reciprocal verb prefix *na- was
lost everywhere except in Numic, Hopi, and Taracahitic. What does this
tell us about subclassification and the criterion of shared innovations? I
think it tells us two things. First, the distribution of a linguistic feature
in itself has no definite implications for subclassification; it takes on significance only in relation to a previously formulated hypothesis of genetic
relationship. No one would take the distribution of *na- as evidence for a
subfamily consisting of Numic, Hopi, and Taracahitic (or the complement
of this set), but a Numic-Hopi subgrouping is not totally out of the question, and we would be derelict in closing our eyes to this similarity between them. However, we can think in these terms only because we
already have a fairly good idea of the genetic relationships within Uto-
Aztecan. This previous conception allows us to interpret the distribution
of *na- as possible evidence for a Numic-Hopi subfamily without wasting
our time tracking down Proto Numic-Hopi-Taracahitic.

Second, the term "shared innovation" is not very precise, and if we
interpret it strictly and narrowly in the sense usually intended (as a
change occurring in all the members of a putative subfamily but in no
daughter outside that subfamily), we find that it in no way constitutes a
mechanical or criterial device for determining subclassification. For instance, I would take the fact that Tarahumara and Yaqui alone retain *na-
among the southern languages to be valid evidence, however weak in itself,
for the claim that they derive from a common source; yet the retention of
*na- is not a change--it is the loss of *na- which represents the change--
and it is not unique, since Numic and Hopi show the same property. Similarly, the generalization of *mo- beyond its original domain might be tak-
en as supporting the Aztecan subfamily even though the change was not
limited to this subfamily.

Let us pursue this critique of the notion of shared innovations in somewhat greater detail. At least three classes of shared historical developments can be distinguished, classes that differ as to the strength of the
possible conclusions one can draw from them in regard to subclassification. One class, which we might call "positive innovations", consists of
additions to the grammatical devices or repertoire of the language; examples might be the addition of a phonological rule, the adoption of a new

lexical item, or the extension of a suffix to a new meaning.[11] Shared positive innovations constitute the clearest evidence for subclassification, but even here we must be wary due to the frequency of parallel innovations.

The second class might be called "negative innovations", or "shared loss"; the loss of rules, affixes, and lexical items are the obvious examples. If two languages both lose the same suffix, we must regard this as a shared innovation, but it is not at all obvious that this shared negative innovation should be given the same weight as a positive one for purposes of subgrouping. For one thing, the loss of an element is a very non-specific kind of change--there are many different kinds of positive innovations that corresponding elements in two daughters can undergo, so an identical positive innovation affecting them carries some weight, but the disappearance of an element has no comparable variety of possible outcomes. Moreover, the loss of linguistic units or constructions is a process that is not well understood and may involve special considerations that bear on its evidential value for classification. Linguistic units normally become disfavored long before their total disappearance, often being regarded as highly formal or archaic. Speakers of a language are sensitive to their marginality, and children learning the language also learn this marginality. It is not out of the question, then, for two or even several languages that do not constitute a subfamily to lose independently an element whose status was marginal in their nearest common ancestor.

Let us now consider the third class, "shared retentions", in light of these tentative observations. Normally, of course, nothing whatever can be deduced about subclassification from the fact that two daughters retain a given trait; if Cahuilla and Luiseno retain a Proto Cupan suffix that Cupeno has lost, we can deduce only that Cupeno has undergone a negative innovation, not that Cahuilla and Luiseno likely form a subfamily. Suppose, however, that a given trait is lost quite consistently over a large area with the exception of just two languages for which a subfamily relationship is not implausible; the retention of *na- in Tarahumara and Yaqui alone out of all the southern Uto-Aztecan languages is an example. On the basis of the foregoing observations, I would be more inclined under these special

[11]This class can also include modifications (without loss) in existing grammatical devices, e.g. a change in the quality of the vowel in a suffix.

circumstances to take the distribution of *na- as (weakly) supporting subfamily status for Tarahumara and Yaqui than as supporting subfamily
status for all of the southern languages exclusive of Tarahumara and Yaqui.
We cannot overlook the (likely) possibility of parallel loss of an element
that was marginal at an early stage before the divergence of the southern
languages, nor can we exclude the possibility that the retention of this
marginal element in Tarahumara and Yaqui reflects a shared positive innovation of sorts, namely a comeback in popularity of the reciprocal prefix *na- in Proto Taracahitic.

These remarks naturally must be taken as only speculative and exploratory. I offer them to demonstrate that the notion of shared innovations is
far more complex and problematic than is commonly realized, as is the
process of evaluating potential evidence for genetic subgrouping. As it is
normally understood, the concept of shared innovations does not embrace
a unified class of phenomena of equal evidential value for subclassification,
nor does it include all phenomena having evidential potential. The different classes of shared historical developments must be weighted appropriately, but the proper weighting is not apparent a priori, and there is no
reason to believe that all examples representing the same class should
carry the same weight. These uncertainties do not prevent us from arriv-
ing at reasonably clear and well-supported hypotheses of genetic subclassification, at least when relatively large numbers of shared historical
developments are taken into consideration (many more than are presented
in this monograph). Nevertheless we will do well to bear in mind the con-
ceptual complexity of the process and the undesirability of trying to reduce it to slogans or to rigid procedures mechanically applied.

It is apparent from all this that the linguist cannot stop thinking when
he has reconstructed the proto system. Carefully tracing the evolution of
the daughter systems is also highly important, both as a check on the
plausibility of the reconstruction and for what we can learn about language
change (and hence about language); but working out the historical changes
step by step itself involves analysis and hypotheses subject to rational de-
bate, and the uncertainties are multiplied when one seeks to reconstruct
the intermediate proto languages and draw conclusions about subclassification.

I will proceed on the assumption that the subfamilies outlined in Appendix A are valid, and that an intermediate proto language can be reconstructed for each. However, this will not prevent us from noting innovations and similarities that conflict with these subfamilies, any more than it will prevent us from noting possible evidence for grouping them into larger subfamilies. Some similarities will be treated as coincidental, others as potential evidence for classification. My procedure here will be highly conservative, in that similar changes affecting two languages will be taken as coincidental only in extreme instances and will be taken as potential evidence for subclassification whenever the possibility of common heritage or mutual influence is within reason. In tracing the historical evolution of the reconstructed proto forms, then, I will try to single out those shared developments that can reasonably be construed as having evidential value for subclassification, though I will make no specific claims about subgrouping here.

In summarizing the historical evolution of reconstructed forms in the final section of each chapter, I will distinguish between "innovations" (I) and "common developments" (CD). An innovation is simply a change, either a positive or a negative innovation in terms of the classes discussed above, and in itself the label is not meant to imply anything about subclassification. A common development is a historical development shared by two or more languages which may reasonably be construed as evidence bearing on subgrouping. Common developments will include all three classes considered above, namely positive innovations, negative innovations, and common retentions in the face of general loss of the element in question. (Ideally these types should be given different weights, but I will not introduce that refinement here.) Both common developments that support the generally accepted scheme of subclassification and those that contradict it are included. When a sufficient number of studies of this kind are completed, the (weighted) number of common developments between two or more languages should correlate directly with the strength of the evidence for grouping them into a subfamily.

2.3.1.   Proto Uto-Aztecan

Proto Uto-Aztecan had the following reflexive prefixes:

Inherent reflexive verbs may be presumed, but these prefixes probably
were not used for passive or reciprocal sentences. The prefix *na-
marked reciprocal verbs. It also marked reciprocal relations with postpositions and occurred in certain numerals, but its use with nouns is uncertain.

The following changes affected the P-UA system as it evolved into its
immediate daughters.[12]

I2.3.1.1. The reflexive prefixes were lost in P-NUM, TU, H, and
P-TAK. This is a common development, i.e. one potentially significant
for classification, hence we may label it CD2.3.1.1.

I2.3.1.2/CD2.3.1.2. *na- was extended to reflexive use in P-NUM
and H.

I2.3.1.3. *na- was lost in TU, P-TAK, P-PMC, P-CCH, and P-AZN.
This verb prefix was retained only in P-NUM, H, and P-TRC. As noted
earlier, the retention of *na- may be considered a development common to
P-NUM and H (CD2.3.1.3), and independently, a development common to
Tarahumara and Yaqui (CD2.3.1.4).

I2.3.1.4/CD2.3.1.5. A reflexive pronoun construction was adopted to
mark reflexives and reciprocals in TU and P-TAK.

I2.3.1.5/CD2.3.1.6. Reflexive prefixes were extended to reciprocal
use in P-PMC, P-CCH, and P-AZN.

I2.3.1.6. The prefix *mo- was extended to all non-first person forms
in P-TRC and P-AZN. This change also affected TO (through P-TEP?), a
non-immediate daughter of P-UA; since mutual influence is not ruled out,
we may designate this CD2.3.1.7.

I2.3.1.7/CD2.3.1.8. The vowel o of *mo- generalized to all the reflexive prefixes in P-TRC and P-AZN.

---

[12] The order in which the changes are listed is not intended to be necessarily chrono-
logical.

I2.3.1.8/CD2.3.1.9. A reduplicated variant of *na-, *nana-, was innovated in P-NUM; this common development is evidence for the Numic subfamily.

I2.3.1.9. The *na-P and *na-N constructions disappeared in most languages, at least as active processes. The *na-N construction is limited to P-NUM (CD2.3.1.10) and may represent either a retention or an innovation. The *na-P construction is attested both in P-NUM and, at least in remnant form, in H. This is almost certainly a retention (CD2.3.1.11).

I2.3.1.10. *ni- > *ne- in P-CCH. This is a regular sound change and hence will not be counted in our tabulation of the morphosyntactic evidence for subgrouping.

I2.3.1.11. The reflexive prefixes were influenced by nominal possessor prefixes in P-CCH. *mo- was replaced by the reflexive possessor prefix *yu- (CD2.3.1.12). Perhaps due to the link between nominal and verbal prefixes established by this development in the reflexives, *ʔi- (> *ʔe-) was replaced by the (non-reflexive) possessor prefix *ʔa- (CD2.3.1.13).

I2.3.1.12/CD2.3.1.14. The reflexive prefixes were extended to passive use in P-PMC and P-AZN.

2.3.2.   Proto Numic

Proto Numic had a verb prefix *na- used for reflexive and reciprocal sentences, but not for passives. The reduplicated variant *nana- indicated general plurality (PL/REPET/DISTR). *na- also occurred with nouns and postpositions to mark reciprocal relationships. This system derives from that of P-UA through innovations 1, 2, and 8 of set I2.3.1 (cf. also I2.3.1.9).

Several fairly minor changes affected this system as it evolved to P-WNM, SH, and P-SNM.

I2.3.2.1/CD2.3.2.1. *nana- was extended to nouns in P-WNM and SH.

I2.3.2.2/CD2.3.2.2. *na- was extended to passive use in P-WNM and SH.

I2.3.2.3. The *na-P construction was evidently lost in SH.

I2.3.2.4. *nana- came to mark reciprocal verbs in SH. This change also took place in M, a non-immediate daughter of P-NUM (CD2.3.2.3).

2.3.3. Proto Western Numic

The prefix *na- of Proto Western Numic was used for reflexives, reciprocals, and passives. It occurred with postpositions, and both *na- and the reduplicated *nana-, indicating plurality, could be used with nouns. This system derives from that of P-NUM through changes I2.3.2.1 and I2.3.2.2.

This is essentially the system of Northern Paiute. In Mono, apparently, na'na- has taken on reciprocal value with verbs, na- being retained for reflexives and passives (cf. CD2.3.2.3).

2.3.4. Proto Southern Numic

The Proto Southern Numic system is essentially the same as that of Proto Numic. Possibly *nana- narrowed to REPET/DISTR sense, no longer indicating general plurality; this seems to be the case in Southern Paiute.

I2.3.4.1. *nana- was evidently lost in K. A reflexive pronoun assumed reciprocal function in K; the reciprocal use of na- with verbs may have been lost, and possibly also the *na-P construction (cf. I2.3.2.3).

2.3.5. Proto Pimic

Proto Pimic had the following reflexive prefixes:

$$
\begin{array}{cc}
\text{*n\textsubscript{i}-} & \text{*t-} \\
\end{array}
$$

*Ɂᵻ- *m(u)-

These prefixes were used as well for reciprocals and passives. This system derives from that of P-UA by means of innovations 3, 5, 9, and 12 of set I2.3.1. Vowel loss or resegmentation also affected the plural prefixes.

I2.3.5.1. *nᵻ- palatalized to *ñᵻ- in P in accordance with a regular sound change; this palatalization then colored the vowel, yielding ñi-.

I2.3.5.2. *Ɂᵻ- displaced *m- in P and generalized to all non-first person forms.

Since no pertinent information is available concerning Northern Tepehuan, we can only speculate that the P-TEP system was the same as that attested in TO. The only significant change affecting P-PMC in the evolution of the TO reflexives is the generalization of the prefix *m(u)- to all non-first person forms (cf. I2.3.1.6).

2.3.6.   Proto Taracahitic

Proto Taracahitic had a reciprocal verb prefix *na- and three reflexive prefixes, *no- for first person singular, *to- for first person plural, and *mo- for non-first person. The P-UA system evolved to the P-TRC system through changes 6, 7, and 9 of set I2.3.1.

I2.3.6.1. The reflexive prefixes were lost in TA.

I2.3.6.2. *na- changed to naw- in Y through the influence of (or as part of) a series of dative prefixes.

I2.3.6.3. In Y, *mo- underwent vowel harmonization in combination with the subject prefix ?a-: *?a-mo- > ?a-ma-.

2.3.7.   Proto Corachol

The following verb prefixes were used in Proto Corachol for reflexives and reciprocals:

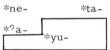

Innovations 3, 5, 9, 10, and 11 of set I2.3.1 derive this system from that of P-UA.

I2.3.7.1. *yu- became (r)u- in CR.

I2.3.7.2. In HU, the reflexive prefixes were extended to marking unspecified objects (cf. Chapter 4).

2.3.8.   Proto Aztecan

The following verb prefixes were used in Proto Aztecan to mark reflexive, reciprocal, and passive relations:

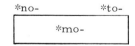

The P-AZN system derives from that of P-UA through changes 3, 5, 6, 7, 9, and 12 of set 12.3.1.

12.3.8.1.   *mo- was extended to all persons in PO.

III. REFLEXIVE PRONOUNS

3.0.   Introduction

Reflexive pronouns have been somewhat neglected in modern linguistics, both theoretical and descriptive. Grammars and structural sketches of the Uto-Aztecan languages typically say little about them or omit them entirely. Yet at least fifteen of the twenty languages under primary consideration here have reflexive pronouns of some kind, and the remainder may appear to lack them only due to limited information.

The term reflexive pronoun is perhaps unfortunate. Morphologically, reflexive pronouns are often nouns, sometimes combined with a possessive pronoun (e.g. myself, herself). Syntactically, they typically differ in various respects from true pronouns, and only in certain uses do they replace a noun. Nevertheless, the term is established and useful, and it emphasizes the similarity in function between these elements and the reflexive prefixes and clitics.

As commonly employed, the term reflexive pronoun is a generic term embracing the forms used in several distinct syntactic constructions. Consider (1) - (8).

(1) The girls bit themselves.   REFLEXIVE
(2) The girls themselves did it.   EMPHATIC
(3) The girls did it themselves.   EMPHATIC
(4) The girls did it by themselves.   LOCATIVE/EMPHATIC
(5) The girls bit each other.   RECIPROCAL
(6) The girls bit one another.   RECIPROCAL
(7) The girls bit their own hands.   REFLEXIVE POSSESSOR
(8) The girls bit each other's hands.   RECIPROCAL POSSESSOR

While retaining the term reflexive pronoun as a generic, it will be helpful

to have more precise terms available to designate specific functions of
these elements. Only in (1) is the pronoun a simple reflexive; in (2) and
(3) it is emphatic, in (5) and (6) it is reciprocal, and in (7) and (8) it is
possessive. (4) is particularly interesting, being ambiguous between a
true locative sense and an emphatic sense. In the locative sense it means
that the girls did it while alone--they were with themselves (or each other)
but with no one else. The emphatic reading of (4)--that it was done by the
girls without help, and by no one else--apparently derives from the locative reading by extension and threatens now to displace it entirely. Finally, the reflexive pronoun in any of these sentences can be rendered emphatic, or doubly emphatic, through contrastive stress.

Several aspects of the English reflexive pronouns are not atypical in
cross-linguistic terms and are worth repeating and bearing in mind as we
examine reflexive pronouns in Uto-Aztecan. First, they are composed of
an object or possessor pronoun plus a noun and are used in sentences of
the type for which a reflexive prefix or clitic is used in certain related
languages. Second, the same forms can be employed with several different syntactic/semantic functions. Third, when combined with a locative
preposition, the resulting expression is semantically equivalent to 'alone';
this locution tends to lose its locative force and become merely emphatic.

3.1. Data

The data on reflexive pronouns is initially quite confusing. We find a
multiplicity of forms with no obvious reconstruction and a multiplicity of
functions having no clear correlation with the forms. The analytical problem is compounded by the sketchiness of the data, particularly with respect
to the possible functions a given form may have. The limitations of the
data place corresponding limitations on the completeness of the reconstruction; this is most notable at the level of fine semantic and syntactic detail.
Nevertheless I believe we can begin to make sense of the Uto-Aztecan reflexive pronouns and uncover the broad outlines of their evolution.

We will begin by summarizing the available data. Table IV lists the
various reflexive pronouns discussed in Chapter 1, and also a few others
which have been or will be introduced subsequently. The second column

lists the attested functions of each pronoun, to the extent that I have been able to determine them, in terms of the categories discussed in section 3.0. The third column notes whether the pronoun is known to co-occur with the basic reflexive or reciprocal markers in the language; in most instances these will be verb prefixes. Note that in Tubatulabal and the Takic languages the basic reflexive and reciprocal markers are themselves reflexive pronouns and are listed in the table. In the case of Shoshoni, the forms cited merely exemplify paradigmatic sets of forms. Various Numic forms are clitics or contain clitics, and Cahuilla <u>tax-</u> is a verb prefix.

It is immediately apparent from Table IV that the reflexive pronouns co-occur rather infrequently with the basic reflexive or reciprocal markers; this is attested only with ten of thirty-eight forms. However, this low figure is somewhat misleading, for two reasons. First, we would not necessarily expect the basic reflexive or reciprocal marker to be used in every instance when two nominals in a clause happen to be coreferential, or when some nominal is emphasized. The criterion for the use of such a prefix might be considerably more restrictive--in particular, such a prefix might be used only when the subject and direct object are coreferential, not when the subject and a possessor are coreferential, when a noun is being emphasized, or when someone is said to be alone. From all indications the reflexive and reciprocal prefixes of Uto-Aztecan do tend to be highly restricted in their use, quite in accord with the spirit of our discussion of non-distinct arguments. If these prefixes are used only under the condition of coreference of subject and direct object, we would expect them to co-occur with reflexive pronouns only when the latter have reflexive or reciprocal function, as in the following examples from Mono and Papago.

M (1) pɨɨ='su na-yawi-'ti
       REFL REFL-laugh-TNS
       PRON
       'He's laughing at himself.'   (M-L-G-180)

P (2) ʔaʔay ʔa=m   ʔɨ   ñɨid ʔaapim
       RCPR AUX-you REFL see you
                  PL   PL
       'You see each other.'   (P-SS-D-123)

In this function, the pronouns serve to reinforce or render more precise

	REFLEXIVE PRONOUN	FUNCTION	CO-OCCURS WITH BASIC MARKER
NP	piɨ='su piɨ-'siʔmɨ piɨ-'noo na-noo na-ma nahoy='su	EMPH 'alone' 'with/also' 'together' 'together' RCPR	 +
M	piɨ='su piɨ-'siʔɨ	EMPH/REFL 'alone'	+
SH	pɨ'nɨ^{n}sɨ pɨ ('nɨ)	REFL POSSR	+ +
SP	=pɨ na'noo='su ='su	POSSR EMPH EMPH(?)	
K	nɨwayɨ=POSSR nɨwayɨ=pɨme nano'so ='su	REFL/RCPR REFL/RCPR LOC/EMPH EMPH	
TU	ʔomoix ʔomohic ʔomoixp	REFL/EMPH RCPR LOC	
H	nahoy	RCPR	
SR	POSSR-taqa PRON-nuk	REFL/RCPR LOC/EMPH/POSSR	
CA	tax- taxat PRON-qiʔ(i)	REFL/RCPR EMPH LOC/EMPH	 +
CU	POSSR-taxwi PRON-qi	REFL/RCPR LOC/POSSR	+
L	POSSR-taax PRON-xay	REFL/RCPR LOC/EMPH/POSSR	+
P	hɨjɨ̆l ʔaʔay	REFL RCPR	+ +
TA	ʔanagu(pu) binoy(po) (SG) ʔaboy(po) (PL)	RCPR REFL/EMPH/POSSR REFL/EMPH/POSSR/RCPR	
CR	ru-itax	POSSR	
A	POSSR-noʔma(tka) POSSR-neʔwiyaan	EMPH EMPH/POSSR	+

Table IV

the sense of the prefix. Second, we must take into account those reflexive pronouns in Table IV which are themselves the basic reflexive or reciprocal marker in the language and hence cannot be said to co-occur with the basic marker. This is true of the Tubatulabal forms as well as the <u>taqa</u>/<u>tax</u> forms in Takic.

When we now examine only those pronouns with reflexive or reciprocal value, and when we further exclude the Tubatulabal and Takic forms just noted, we arrive at a rather different result. Reflexive pronouns are attested with the basic reflexive or reciprocal marker in Northern Paiute, Mono, Shoshoni, and Papago. They are not so attested in Kawaiisu, Hopi, and Tarahumara, but we must discard Kawaiisu, since Northern Paiute, Mono, and Shoshoni establish the co-occurrence as a Numic phenomenon. Thus we have Numic and Papago balanced against Hopi and Tarahumara, leaving the historical picture rather indeterminate. It would not be unreasonable to hypothesize that the co-occurrence was possible in the proto language, but it is dubious on the basis of present data that we can establish this. In any event, such co-occurrence must have been somewhat limited. First, it must have been limited to the reciprocal pronoun, since (as we will see) the non-reciprocal reflexive pronoun in P-UA had locative and emphatic value, but probably not specifically reflexive value. Second, the co-occurrence would not be expected even with the reciprocal pronoun in pre-P-UA in view of the origin posited for this form (see section 3.2.9, and especially Figure VI), though by P-UA times the situation could well have changed.

The forms in Table IV are obviously quite diverse, but not so diverse as they might at first appear to be. They fall into four groups. Most of the Numic forms constitute one group; a second consists of the <u>taqa</u>/<u>tax</u> reflexive pronouns of Takic and the reflexive possessor of Cora; and the Aztec reflexive pronouns comprise a third. Discussion of these three groups will be deferred until section 3.4. Section 3.2 will deal with the fourth group, which is the largest and consists of all the other forms. The Kawaiisu forms based on <u>nɨwayɨ</u>, which belong to this fourth group, merit special attention and will be the subject of section 3.3.

3.2.   The Original Set

3.2.1.   Reconstruction

A substantial number of the reflexive pronouns in Table IV can, I believe, be traced back to a single reflexive pronoun base in Proto Uto-
Aztecan. Two reflexive pronouns formed on this base can be reconstructed. The reflexes of these proto forms are presented in Table V.

NP	nahoy='su	RCPR
TU	ʔomoix	REFL/EMPH
	ʔomohic	RCPR
	ʔomoixp	LOC
H	nahoy	RCPR
SR	PRON-nuk	LOC/EMPH/POSSR
CA	PRON-qiʔ(i)	LOC/EMPH
CU	PRON-qi	LOC/POSSR
L	PRON-xay	LOC/EMPH/POSSR
P	hiǰɨl	REFL
	ʔaʔay	RCPR
TA	ʔanagu(pu)	RCPR
	binoy(po)	(SG) REFL/EMPH/POSSR
	ʔaboy(po)	(PL) REFL/EMPH/POSSR/RCPR

Table V

Although the members of this set are quite varied, certain similarities
are apparent, and more become apparent when we probe a little deeper.
One recurring feature is the sequence of a non-high vowel followed by i or
y: oi, oy, ay; these consistently occur near the end of the word. Another
recurring feature is the sequence of n followed in the next syllable by a
velar or glottal obstruent: n...h, n...k, n...g; these tend to occur earlier in the word. The initial ʔo of the Tubatulabal forms is also interesting
when compared with the initial ʔa in Papago and Tarahumara, and things
get more interesting still when we note that the third person singular pronoun used in the composite Takic forms, the one most frequently exemplified, reconstructs as Proto Takic *pɨ, which is cognate by regular correspondences to Tarahumara bi.

As a first approximation (to be refined in section 3.3), I will claim that
the P-UA reflexive pronoun base was *-nakoyɨ. Reflexive pronouns were

formed from this base by combining it with either *pɨ- or *ʔa-, both of
which are well-attested third person singular pronominal elements in Uto-
Aztecan.[1] I believe we can go further and determine the function of these
reflexive pronouns with reasonable confidence. Specifically, *ʔa-nakoyɨ
was reciprocal, while *pɨ-nakoyɨ was locative and emphatic. Let us now
look more carefully at specific forms and sets of forms to justify this reconstruction.

3.2.2.   Northern Paiute

The reciprocal pronoun nahoy='su consists of the base nahoy, which is
the part that concerns us here, and the clitic ='su, which is found in association with reflexive pronouns in all the Numic languages and is normally
glossed as something like 'just' or 'precisely'. The derivation of nahoy
from *-nakoyɨ is non-problematic, involving only the spirantization of k to
h (which happened in other daughters as well) and loss of the final ɨ. Most
likely the pronominal element was *ʔa- rather than *pɨ-; this choice permits a more straightforward account of its loss, since word-initial ʔ is
largely automatic in Uto-Aztecan and a matches the first vowel of the base.
The prefix na- has both reflexive and reciprocal use in Northern Paiute.
The reciprocal pronoun nahoy='su can co-occur with this prefix and thus
has a disambiguating function. This may have something to do with its
preservation (cf. section 3.2.4).

3.2.3.   Tubatulabal

The three Tubatulabal forms clearly derive from a common base, which
was represented in Chapter 1 as ʔomo(h)i(x). We can actually be somewhat more precise and posit ʔomohy or ʔomohi as the synchronic underlying representation of this form;[2] the surface variants result from independently motivated synchronic rules. Voegelin notes (TU-V-G-83) that h

---

[1]It is possible that *pɨ- alternated with other pronominal elements to mark other
persons, as in Takic; there is no indication of this outside of Takic, however, and I
will not pursue the matter further. Shoshoni provides a relatively clear example of an
instance in which a single reflexive pronominal element was elaborated into a complete
paradigm of such forms (cf. section 3.4.1.3), and I will assume for purposes of exposition that something similar happened in Takic.

[2]y and i may be regarded as equivalent for purposes of this discussion. The difference between them will be considered an automatic consequence of syllable structure.

sometimes becomes x̲ in word-final position. He also posits a metathesis
rule whereby word-final h̲y̲ changes to y̲h̲ (TU-V-G-86). While I have no
fully convincing explanation for the application of these two rules in the locative form (where -p̲ would be expected to block them), the basic situation
seems clear enough. The base ʔomohy occurs alone in a reflexive or emphatic role; word-final h̲y̲ thus metathesizes to y̲h̲, which becomes i̲x̲
through the velarization of h̲, yielding the desired output ʔomoix. The
underlying representation of the reciprocal form is ʔomohy-c. Here h̲y̲ is
not word-final, due to the presence of -c̲, so metathesis is blocked, as is
velarization, and the phonetic result is ʔomohic.

The diachronic consequences of this analysis are as follows. For pre-
Tubatulabal we can posit the reflexive pronoun *ʔomohy, which has reflexive and emphatic function (as does contemporary ʔomoix). Postpositions
were added to this base to form the complex reflexive pronouns *ʔomohy-p
and *ʔomohy-c, with locative and reciprocal function respectively. In the
case of the locative form, the analysis is straightforward, since -p̲ is a
Tubatulabal postposition meaning 'to/in/on'. The reciprocal is less
straightforward, since -c̲ does not exist synchronically as a postposition.
However, several postpositions in the language do involve c̲ (or its voiced
counterpart ẓ), and in each case there is internal or comparative evidence
to justify segmenting c̲V as a probable morpheme: -bacu 'away from',
ʔakaẓiip 'across', wacɨʔaš 'with/by means of' (TU-V-G-150, 151; TU-V-
WD-227). A full examination of these postpositions is beyond the scope of
the present inquiry, but it seems not at all implausible to posit the earlier
existence of a postposition of the form *-c̲V which was suffixed to the reflexive pronoun base to make this base reciprocal and which subsequently
disappeared except in derived forms. The semantic development that this
implies, from something like 'from/with/between themselves' to reciprocal sense, is fully plausible.

It may be possible to relate the phonological difference between the locative and reciprocal pronouns to the difference in status of the two postpositions. Since -p̲ is synchronically still an independent postposition, it
is separated from the reflexive base by at least a morpheme boundary. -c̲,
on the other hand, is no longer identifiable as a separately occurring postposition, and hence it may well have been reanalyzed as part of the base,

entailing the loss of the morpheme boundary. If metathesis and h-velarization can be sensitive to certain morpheme boundaries as well as to word boundaries, their application with the locative but not the reciprocal pronoun will be explained.

By internal reconstruction, we have now posited and justified for pre-Tubatulabal the reflexive and emphatic pronoun *ʔomohy. Now we must relate this form to the hypothesized P-UA system, in which *pɨ-nakoyɨ functions as a locative and emphatic reflexive pronoun and *ʔa-nakoyɨ as a reciprocal pronoun. In most immediate daughters of P-UA, one or both of these forms was lost, and we may suppose that when one was lost the other tended to generalize its function. It was clearly *ʔa-nakoyɨ that survived in Tubatulabal, and no trace of *pɨ-nakoyɨ is left. Once the latter disappeared, the former took on its function and could presumably be used in a variety of syntactic roles of the sort described in section 3.0. Eventually special reciprocal and locative forms were innovated to render reflexive pronoun constructions semantically more precise; quite possibly this greater precision was needed because of the loss of the reflexive and reciprocal prefixes in Tubatulabal.

All that remains is to sketch the derivation of *ʔomohy from *ʔa-nakoyɨ, and while the order of the individual changes cannot be fully determined, the general course of development is fairly clear. P-UA *k backs to *q and ultimately to h in Tubatulabal by regular sound changes (cf. UA-VVH-TCG; UA-L-VP), so *ʔanahoyɨ is expected. Regressive vowel harmonization will derive *ʔanohoyɨ and then *ʔonohoyɨ. The loss of final ɨ over this long period is hardly surprising, nor is there anything implausible about the simplification of the form to two syllables through the loss of o. Finally, we must suppose that n changed to m, a change facilitated by the rounded vowel on either side.[3]

---

[3]Eric Hamp has suggested as an alternative that the mo of *ʔomohy continues the reflexive prefix mo-, attested in various southern Uto-Aztecan languages but in no northern language. I find this derivation slightly less plausible, but one cannot rule it out entirely. Kawaiisu nɨwayɨ, to be discussed in section 3.3, indicates that the consonant reflected as h in the Tubatulabal form may originally have been labial, and this could have influenced the *n > m shift.

3.2.4.   Hopi

The derivation of the Hopi reciprocal pronoun nahoy is considerably less complex. Both ease of derivation and consideration of the overall Hopi system suggest that nahoy descends from *ʔa-nakoyɨ, with *pɨ-nakoyɨ simply being lost. In Hopi, the reflexive verb prefixes were lost, but the reciprocal prefix was retained and assumed both reflexive and reciprocal value. It will be recalled that Hopi also possesses an emphatic pronoun naa-p, which I have claimed to be a remnant of the *na-P construction of P-UA. Hopi thus has retained throughout its history the means to express reflexive and emphatic notions, quite apart from the two reflexive pronouns. All that was really needed was some means to distinguish between reflexive and reciprocal sense once the prefix naa- had come to mark both, and this is precisely the role of nahoy. We may therefore hypothesize that the reciprocal pronoun *ʔa-nakoyɨ has survived as nahoy in order to preserve the reflexive/reciprocal distinction, while *pɨ-nakoyɨ was quite dispensable and eventually disappeared.

I have no particular explanation for the simplification of *ʔa-nakoyɨ to *nakoyɨ. It might be noted, however, that the loss of ʔa before nakoyɨ is more probable than the loss of pɨ, since ʔ is a weak consonant (and is generally predictable before initial vowels in Uto-Aztecan) and a is identical to the first vowel of the base. The backing of *k to *q before a non-high vowel is regular, but the further change of *q to h is not expected in Hopi. The only other modification required is the loss of final ɨ.

While I take this to be approximately correct as the diachronic development, the synchronic picture is slightly more complex. Sentences with only naa- are ambiguous between a reflexive and a reciprocal sense, as noted, and nahoy forces the reciprocal reading; however, naa- is not presently required in sentences marked by nahoy (the naa in (2) no doubt derives from the prefix naa- but has been reanalyzed as part of the verb stem):[4]

---

[4]The failure of naa- and nahoy to co-occur possibly reflects the primitive state of affairs; cf. section 3.1 and section 3.2.9, especially Figure VI.

(1) pɨma taaqa-t   niq pɨma tiyo-t   naa-qö-qya
     those man-DL and those boy-DL REFL-RDP-kill
                                          PL
     'The (two) men and the (two) boys killed themselves/each other.'
     (H-H-IN)

(2) nahoy naawakna
     RCPR want
     'wanted each other'   (H-K-LA-36)

Moreover, nahoy is apparently segmentable synchronically into naa- plus
the particle ʔahoy 'back' (H-K-PC):

(3) ʔahoy nima
     back go
           home
     'returned home'   (H-VV-D-35)

(4) nɨʔ ʔi-napna-y   ʔahoy ʔa-w tɨɨʔiha
     I   my-shirt-ACC back it-to sew
     'I sewed my shirt back up.'   (H-VV-ISNL-27)

I take ʔahoy to be a back formation (pardon the pun) based on the reciprocal
particle nahoy and the reconstructed *na-P pattern posited for pre-Hopi.

However, enough loose ends remain that the status of Hopi nahoy merits
further consideration. For one thing, only Kennard (H-K-LA-36) has cited
nahoy in what appears to be a specifically and narrowly reciprocal use.
Ekkehart Malotki (H-M-INO) glosses this element as 'away from self' or
'apart'; by extension it takes on the meaning 'across', i.e. 'away from self
in two directions':

(5) naahoy nɨʔ ʔi-t   laŋtaqa-t   laŋtoyna
     apart I   this-ACC rubber-ACC pull
                         band
     'I pulled this rubber band apart.'   (H-M-INO)

(6) pɨma naahoy nak^{w}sɨ
     they apart set
                 out
     'They walked in opposite directions.'   (H-M-INO)

(7) kiison-va naahoy yɨɨtɨ
     plaza-on across run
                     PL
     'They ran across the plaza.'   (H-M-INO)

Some notion of reciprocity is clearly involved in these uses, and also in
the derived verb naahoyŋ^{w}a 'exchange' (H-M-INO; H-VV-D-53), but one
would like more extensive attestation of nahoy as an explict reciprocal

pronoun. To further complicate the situation, there is a verb hoyo 'move' from which Malotki suggests nahoy may be derived.

It is conceivable, then, that Hopi nahoy is of recent origin and that the reciprocal use cited by Kennard is only apparent. If so, it is a remarkable coincidence that this form fits so neatly into the cognate set reflecting the P-UA reciprocal pronoun *ʔa-nakoyɨ, from which it could easily have derived; note in particular the Northern Paiute reciprocal pronoun nahoy (discussed in section 3.2.2). A second possibility is that nahoy does in fact descend from *ʔa-nakoyɨ and that the use cited by Kennard is archaic; I will adopt this position for sake of further discussion. Still a third possibility is that the Hopi descendant of *ʔa-nakoyɨ was influenced by similar elements (such as the verb hoyo) and perhaps merged with them.

3.2.5.   Takic

Locative and emphatic value predominate in the Takic reflexive pronouns listed in Table V. I presume that the possessor use is secondary (though most likely reconstructable for Proto Takic), and that fuller data would reveal both locative and emphatic potential for all of these forms. All four reflexive bases (SR -nuk, CA -qiʔ(i), CU -qi, L -xay) can occur with a full series of pronouns; they are not restricted to reflexes of the third person singular *pɨ-. I have no evidence for deciding whether this continues the P-UA situation or whether *pɨ-nakoyɨ was generalized at the Proto Takic stage to all persons. There is no basis for reconstructing any reflex of *ʔa-nakoyɨ at the Proto Takic level, and the daughter languages apparently manage without a special reciprocal marker.

Among the Takic languages under consideration, Cahuilla, Cupeno, and Luiseno clearly form a subfamily, Cupan, with Serrano being quite divergent; the reflexive pronouns illustrate this split quite clearly. The Serrano and Cupan forms nevertheless share at least one important innovation in their evolution from *pɨ-nakoyɨ, in addition to their common property of being used with all persons. The development presented here is only a first approximation; it will be refined in section 3.3 in light of the Kawaiisu data. Let us begin this preliminary analysis with Serrano.

Examples (1) - (3) illustrate the locative, emphatic, and possessor uses of -nuk.

SR (1) ʔamaʔ pu-nuk   qaçɨi
         he   him-REFL be
         'He's all alone.'   (SR-C-PC)

SR (2) pɨ-nuk^w   t   yeiiʔ-v
         him-REFL DUB take-FUT
         'He'll take it with him.'/'He'll take it himself.'
         (SR-H-G-121)

SR (3) x^waan=vɨ=ʔ   pu-nuk   ʔa-ʔaš-ti   hiihi
         PN-he-PAST him-REFL his-pet-ACC see
         'Juan saw his own dog.'   (SR-C-PC)

The rounding of pɨ- to pu- before -nuk is of course a minor phonetic modification due to vowel harmonization and need not detain us. Some comments are however in order concerning the precise form of -nuk, since it
differs somewhat in the other persons.

Below I list the normal pronoun bases used with postpositions in Serrano
and the actually attested forms (SR-C-PC) representing the combination of
these bases with -nuk.[5]

Pronoun Bases		Reflexive Pronouns	
nɨɨ-	ʔačamɨ-	nowk(ɨ)	ʔačamuk
ʔɨmɨ-	ʔɨɨmɨ-	ʔɨmuk	ʔɨɨmuk(ɨ)
pɨ-	pɨmɨ-	pɨnuk	pumuk(ɨ)

Apart from expected modifications of the pronoun base, two changes have
affected the reflexive forms: reduction of -nuk to -uk in certain forms,
and an apparently more drastic change in the first person singular. -nuk
becomes -uk in the second person singular and in all the plural forms.
These are precisely the cases in which the pronoun base contains m, suggesting the fairly obvious hypothesis that -uk derives from -nuk through
the simplification of mn clusters, no doubt a fairly recent development. In
the second person singular, for example, we can posit the development
*ʔɨm(ɨ)-nuk > *ʔɨmnuk > ʔɨmuk.

The explanation for the first person singular is not quite so obvious.
As in other persons, the final ɨ appears only when protected from deletion

---

[5] It was argued previously (cf. Chapter 1, footnote 7) that Serrano -nuk has been reanalyzed as a postposition. For the second person singular, the alternate form mumuk
is attested (SR-C-PC), no doubt reflecting the possessor prefix mɨ- instead of the postposition base ʔɨmɨ-. This partial confusion of the two paradigms is not surprising in
view of the extension of -nuk to possessor use.

by a following clitic, as shown in (4) - (5).[6]

SR   (4)   nowkɨ=n qaç
               REFL-I be
               'I'm all alone.'   (SR-H-G-121)

SR   (5)   nowk nɨ² čaahčo
               REFL I   sing
               'I'm singing by myself.'   (SR-C-PC)

Beyond this, we must account for the special vowel quality (ow versus u) and the apparent lack of a pronoun base. Limitations of the data and our sketchy knowledge of Serrano phonology prevent me from giving a detailed account of the special vowel quality, but the conditioning factor definitely appears to be stress. The vowel ow of nowkɨ is apparently always stressed, while in all the other forms stress is attracted to the pronoun base (e.g. púmukɨ). The lack of a pronoun base is therefore responsible for the special vowel quality in the first person singular; since the pronoun base is absent, stress must fall instead on the reflexive morpheme, thus preserving the full vowel quality ów and preventing its reduction to u. The absence of the pronoun base is probably due to haplology. From something approximating *nɨ-nowkɨ, nowkɨ was innovated to avoid two successive syllables of the form nV. This change did not lead to ambiguity, since the first person singular was still distinct from all the other persons.

To conclude our discussion of Serrano -nuk, more adequately written as -nowkɨ for comparative purposes, we must now consider the relation between *pɨ-nakoyɨ and pre-Serrano *pɨ-nowkɨ. The major development is clearly the rounding of a to ow under the influence of the following syllable. One alternative is to claim that ko became kw (this is natural if the stress was on pɨ, as it is in the modern language), with w floating into the preceding syllable and rounding the a: *pɨ-nakoyɨ > *pɨ-nakw(y)ɨ > *pɨ-nawk(y)ɨ > *pɨ-nawkɨ > *pɨ-nowkɨ. I will assume that something along these lines is correct. We will come back to this matter in section 3.3.

We turn now to Cupan. Proto Takic *pɨ becomes pe in Cahuilla, pə in Cupeno, and po in Luiseno by regular sound changes (UA-L-VP). In all

---

[6]The first person singular clitic =n appears to be in the process of being reanalyzed as part of the reflexive pronoun in sentences like (4). Note the following, where the presence of =n on the subject pronoun precludes its occurrence later in the sentence: nɨ²=n nokun čaahču (I-I REFL sing) 'I'm the only one who sings' (SR-C-PC).

three of the Cupan languages, the *pɨ-nakoyɨ construction allows a pronoun
of any person with the reflexive pronoun base. It is not obvious whether
the construction should be viewed as involving a postposition, as in Serrano,
or a possessor prefix, since the pronominal forms are virtually the same
for the two. However, Luiseno plural forms such as čaama-ha 'we ourselves' (L-KG-SG-102) may provide some evidence for the postpositional
analysis, since čaam 'we' expands to čaamo- before postpositions but not in
possessive use; similarly for the other plural pronouns. In Cupeno, the
vowel of the pronominal element has harmonized to that of the reflexive
pronoun base -qi, e.g. pi-qi 'by himself' (CUP-H-SCD-50).

The reflexive pronoun base is our primary concern here. P-TAK
*-nakoyɨ is reflected in Cahuilla as -qiʔ(i), in Cupeno as -qi, and in Luiseno
as -xay. The ʔ(i) of the Cahuilla form is secondary and will not be considered further. Our first step, then, is to reconstruct the Proto Cupan form,
which evolves to -qi and -xay in Cahuilla-Cupeno and Luiseno respectively.
The obvious reconstruction for P-CUP is *-qay. Luiseno -xay then results
from spirantization of q to x, while the natural vocalic evolution ay > ey >
iy > i yields -qi. The problem now is to relate P-TAK *-nakoyɨ to P-CUP
*-qay.

Various alternatives are possible, but the pivotal development is clearly
the loss of the initial syllable. A similar loss occurred in the first person
singular Serrano form, where it could be explained as an instance of haplology to avoid two successive syllables of the form nV. I suggest that this
haplology took place at the Proto Takic stage, before Serrano and Proto
Cupan had definitively split off. The anomaly of a shortened form in the
first person singular was retained in Serrano, but in Proto Cupan the reflexive pronoun system was regularized, resulting in the truncated *-qay
for all persons.

The details of this evolution are rather tricky, enough so that the claim
just made (namely that the haplology affecting Serrano can be identified with
the one affecting Proto Cupan) must remain somewhat tentative. The problem, essentially, is that the most natural subsequent development requires
that the pronoun *nɨ- be dropped in Serrano, while the *-na of *-nakoyɨ be
lost in Proto Cupan. Though bothersome, this is hardly a crucial difficulty.
Given the Proto Takic first person singular *nɨ-nakoyɨ, the awkward nVnV

sequence could be avoided by dropping either syllable. It is not unreasonable to suppose that the alternative forms *nɨkoyɨ and *nakoyɨ coexisted
for a time; the former eventually won out in Proto Cupan, the latter in
Serrano. In Serrano, then, *nakoyɨ evolves to nowk(ɨ) along the lines suggested above: *nakoyɨ > *nakw(y)ɨ > *nawk(y)ɨ > *nawkɨ > nowk(ɨ).

The only special development required for Proto Cupan is the change of
*-koyɨ to *-kayɨ; granted this, the backing of k to q before a low vowel is
not unexpected,[7] and the fading away of final ɨ is quite regular. The natural claim to make is that the o of *-koyɨ harmonized to the preceding a of
*na before the latter was lost, but here we run into an ordering problem: I
claim that the haplology was common to Serrano and Proto Cupan, but the
harmonization must be restricted to Proto Cupan (it could not occur in
Serrano, since it would prevent the devocalization of *ko to *kw) and yet
precede haplology. We need not take this ordering conflict too seriously,
since it is inspired by the oversimplified family tree model of genetic relationships, but still one would like to avoid it. This we will do when the
analysis is refined in section 3.3.

3.2.6. Papago

The Papago reflexive pronoun is hɨǰɨl, and the reciprocal pronoun is
ʔaʔay. Neither of these fits our P-UA reconstruction as perfectly as one
would like, so the postulated connection must be somewhat tentative.
Nevertheless, both forms bear a clear partial resemblance to the P-UA
form said to underlie it, and the contrast between the reciprocal pronoun
with initial ʔa and the non-reciprocal pronoun without it correlates directly
with the proposed reconstruction.

In the case of hɨǰɨl, we must posit an evolution in function from locative
to emphatic to reflexive, which is quite in line with our previous observations. The evolution in form from *pɨ-nakoyɨ to hɨǰɨl is of course considerably more problematic. I will claim that hɨǰɨ reflects *koyɨ of the proto

---

[7] *k supposedly becomes q in Cupan after a nasalizing vowel (UA-VVH-TCG-73).
This might suggest the more detailed development *nɨ-nakoyɨ > *nɨ-nakayɨ >
*nɨ-nkay(ɨ) > *nɨ-ŋkay > *nɨ-qay > *nə-qay.

form, and its derivation from the latter is quite plausible.[8]   The derivation
of hi̇ji̇l from *pi̇-nakoyi̇ requires numerous steps, a couple of which may
seem ad hoc, but enough of the steps are regular or easily explicable that
the relationship of these forms does not seem overly speculative.

The change of k to h is not a regular sound change in Papago, but it has
parallels in the derivation of reflexive pronouns in other languages (e. g.
Hopi); most likely it occurred while k was still intervocalic, before the initial part of the word had disappeared: *pi̇-nakoyi̇ > *pi̇nahoyi̇. The loss
of na has no obvious motivation, so I must posit it without explanation:
*pi̇nahoyi̇ > *pi̇hoyi̇. In view of its environment, the harmonization of o to
i̇ in *pi̇hoyi̇ is hardly surprising. The addition of final l is less expected,
to say the least. A phonological explanation is out of the question, but we
may speculate about a grammatical one. I will argue in section 3.2.9 that
*-nakoyi̇ can be analyzed into smaller elements in a semantically coherent
and appropriate way, and that the final syllable yi̇ originally meant 'be'.
There is another morpheme 'be' reconstructable (in several variant shapes)
for P-UA; its Papago reflex might be expected to be li (cf. section 5.2.2).
Conceivably, then, l(i) was added to the reflexive pronoun form to reinforce
the meaning of yi̇ as this sense faded from yi̇ itself. These two changes,
together with the regular sound changes *y > ǰ and *p > w, give us the following development: *pi̇hoyi̇ > *pi̇hi̇yi̇ > *pi̇hi̇yi̇l > *wi̇hi̇yi̇l > *wi̇hi̇ǰi̇l.
All that remains is the loss of initial wi̇, not improbable given the phonologically weak character of this syllable. Perhaps its loss was related to

---

[8]The prior existence of the full sequence *pi̇-nakoyi̇ in the history of Papago receives some support (speculative to be sure) from the postposition wi̇i̇nadk 'with' (P-
SS-D-130). This derives by reanalysis of the pronoun-postposition sequence *wi̇i̇-nadk.
Since initial *p becomes w in Papago, we may hypothesize the following evolution:
*pi̇-nakoyi̇ > *pi̇i̇naky > *pi̇i̇nayk > *wi̇i̇nayk > wi̇i̇nadk. The reanalysis of *-nakoyi̇ as a
postposition meaning 'with' has parallels in other subfamilies (cf. sections 3.2.5 and
3.4.1.2), so only the metathesis of ky to yk can be regarded as possibly problematic.
If this analysis is correct, the verb wi̇i̇nad 'put with' (P-SS-D-47; P-M-LPA-37) represents a back formation.

Wick Miller has suggested that hi̇ji̇l derives from the P-UA form for 'one' rather
than from *pi̇-nakoyi̇. He reconstructs *se(me) for 'one' (UA-M-CS-68); my own reconstruction is *si̇mayi̇, which is in basic agreement with his. Since P-UA *s > P h,
this derivation is quite plausible. However, I tend to reject it for two reasons. First,
the Papago form for 'one' is hi̇ma(ko), and there is no current evidence from Papago
or the other Pimic languages for the loss of *ma from *si̇mayi̇ (cf. NT ʔumo, TO
hi̇mad). Second, this derivation loses the parallelism (sketched below) between the evolution of reflexive and reciprocal pronouns in Papago. The matter nevertheless deserves further attention.

Some suggestions by Eric Hamp have considerably improved my analysis of the derivation of the Papago reflexive pronouns.

the change of the third person singular postpositional object pronoun from wi to zero; see UA-L-SP.[9]

If this view of the derivation of hijil is accepted in its essentials, that of ?a?ay from P-UA *?a-nakoyi becomes reasonably straightforward. The change of k̲ to h̲ and the loss of na̲ are exactly the first two steps in the derivation of hijil, and it is naturally to be expected that the two forms based on *-nakoyi would evolve in parallel fashion, at least in the initial stages: *?a-nakoyi > *?anahoyi > *?ahoyi. Vowel harmonization of o̲ to a̲ also parallels the previous derivation, the quality difference reflecting the different initial syllable, and beyond that only two phonetically natural changes are required: *?ahoyi > *?ahayi > *?a?ay(i) > ?a?ay. The only potential problem is the failure of final y̲ to become d̲ or ̆j̲ as expected on the basis of normal sound change. Perhaps this relates to syllable structure or word-final position, but this is only speculation.

3.2.7. Tarahumara

The reconstruction of reciprocal *?a-nakoyi and locative/emphatic *pi-nakoyi is corroborated most directly by reciprocal ?anagu and reflexive/emphatic/possessor binoy of Tarahumara. The latter has evidently generalized in function to the point where it can play almost any reflexive pronoun role; its plural, ?aboy, can even be reciprocal. ?anagu, however, has apparently remained narrowly reciprocal.

The Papago and Tarahumara forms are somewhat complementary. While in Papago the reflexive pronoun attests only the syllables koyi of *-nakoyi and the reciprocal pronoun attests every syllable except na̲, the converse largely obtains in Tarahumara: the reflexive pronoun binoy shows remnants of each proto syllable (but ko̲ only indirectly), and the reciprocal retains na̲ but loses yi. Taken together, then, these two languages strongly support our reconstruction of the full sequence *-nakoyi for both the reciprocal and the non-reciprocal form, even though both have been simplified

---

[9] If hijil was reanalyzed as a postposition, then, the loss of wi was completely regular. We have just seen that the Takic reflexive pronoun was reanalyzed as a postposition, and the loss of na̲ parallels the loss of na̲ (attributed to haplology) in the Proto Cupan form. Mutual influence between Papago and Cupan in the evolution of the reflexive pronouns is therefore a real possibility that deserves to be studied further. It may explain certain Papago changes that appear ad hoc in terms of Papago alone.

in each language.

The loss of y̶ɨ is the only major event in the evolution of ʔanagu from *ʔa-nakoy̶ɨ; the change of ko to gu is a matter of minor phonetic detail, and given the considerable allophonic variation attributed to Tarahumara, it may not even represent a change. Initial *p becomes b in Tarahumara, and *ɨ becomes i, so the derivation of binoy from *pɨ-nakoy̶ɨ is reasonably straightforward. I will assume the following evolution (variations can of course be devised): *pɨ-nakoy̶ɨ > *bɨnakoy̶ɨ > *binakoyi > *binahoyi > *binahoy > *binohoy > *binooy > binoy. Note that while the syllable ko is lost per se, it is responsible for the quality of the final vowel.

Two more things need to be examined, the plural reflexive pronoun ʔaboy and the ending -po optionally found on all three reflexive pronouns in Tarahumara. ʔaboy is apparently innovative. Perhaps this is due to the fact that binoy came to be used independently as a (possibly somewhat emphatic) subject pronoun, e.g. binoy koʔ-mea (he eat-FUT) 'He will eat' (TA-H-TE-ix). Third person subject pronouns almost invariably distinguish singular and plural, so it is quite conceivable that ʔaboy was innovated to serve as a plural counterpart for binoy. The nature of the innovation is not difficult to see; given the pressure to form a plural counterpart to the reflexive pronoun binoy, and given the existence of the (inherently plural) reciprocal pronoun ʔanagu, ʔa was interpreted as an indication of plurality and added to binoy. *ʔa-binoy then evolved to ʔaboy, perhaps in this manner: *ʔa-binoy > *ʔabonoy > *ʔabooy > ʔaboy. (The loss of n could be concomitant with vowel nasalization.) This analysis is supported to some degree by the existence of the variant ʔaboni, in which the n of binoy is retained. Both ʔaboy and ʔaboni can derive from the postulated intermediate stage *ʔabonoy, the former through loss of n and the latter through loss of o.

Previous discussion should make it evident that reflexive pronouns are closely connected with postpositions. In some instances a reflexive pronoun becomes a postposition diachronically (cf. Serrano); in other cases postpositions are added to a pronominal entity of some kind, one which may itself be a reflexive pronoun, to form a derived reflexive pronoun, typically with locative value, but not necessarily restricted to this function (cf. Tubatulabal). Thus it should come as no surprise that the ending -po which

attaches optionally to reflexive pronouns in Tarahumara derives from a
postposition. This postposition translates as 'in' or 'place of' and is usually written -bo: sate-bo 'in the sand' (TA-B-G-19); sewa-bo (flower-
place of) 'garden' (TA-T-TED-30); ?a?we-bo 'place where eagles are found'
(TA-H-TE-x).

While the source of -po seems fairly clear, the evolution of its semantic
value is less so. One would suppose that it was originally added to the reflexive pronouns, which had varied functions as noted earlier, to make
them explicitly locative. They apparently serve this function no longer,
however. In fact, Brambila states explicitly that the presence of -po
makes the pronoun explicitly reflexive, and that if -po is omitted it is ambiguous between reflexive and merely emphatic sense:

    (1) binoypo me?a-re
        REFL kill-PAST
        PRON
        'He killed himself.'   (TA-B-G-410)

    (2) binoy me?a-re
        REFL kill-PAST
        PRON
        'He himself killed him.' / 'He killed himself.'   (TA-B-G-410)

This specialization of -po to specifically reflexive value may have been
facilitated by the loss of the reflexive verb prefixes in Tarahumara.

3.2.8.   Locative versus Reciprocal

The preceding sections establish, quite firmly in my opinion, the reconstruction of the reflexive pronouns *?a-nakoyɨ and *pɨ-nakoyɨ for
Proto Uto-Aztecan. The claim that *?a-nakoyɨ was reciprocal in function
while *pɨ-nakoyɨ was locative and emphatic also seems reasonably well supported, but it deserves systematic discussion.

I observed in section 3.0 that locative reflexive pronouns tend to take on
emphatic function by extension, as indicated by the ambiguity of English
expressions such as by himself. It is not implausible to suppose that a
locative/emphatic pronoun could generalize still further in function and
come to play reflexive and possessor roles as well. It is somewhat less
plausible to claim that a reflexive pronoun with a multiplicity of functions
would narrow in function (with no change in form) until it played only a

locative or locative/emphatic role; instead, generalized reflexive pronouns
appear (in Uto-Aztecan at least) to be specialized in meaning and function
through the addition of postpositions (cf. Tubatulabal and Tarahumara).

   With this in mind, let us examine Table VI, in which the reflexive pronouns of Table V are grouped in accordance with whether they descend from
*ʔa-nakoyɨ or *pɨ-nakoyɨ.

*ʔa-nakoyɨ			*pɨ-nakoyɨ		
NP	nahoy	RCPR	SR	PRON-nuk	LOC/EMPH/POSSR
TU	ʔomoix	REFL/EMPH	CA	PRON-qiʔ(i)	LOC/EMPH
	ʔomohic	RCPR	CU	PRON-qi	LOC/POSSR
	ʔomoixp	LOC	L	PRON-xay	LOC/EMPH/POSSR
H	nahoy	RCPR	P	hɨjɨl	REFL
P	ʔaʔay	RCPR	TA	binoy	REFL/EMPH/POSSR
TA	ʔanagu	RCPR			

Table VI

With the exception of the innovative hybrid ʔaboy of Tarahumara, none
of the forms reflecting *pɨ-nakoyɨ is reciprocal. Locative and emphatic
sense predominate, and while numbers alone are misleading here (because
of the disproportionately large number of Takic examples), our prior observations on the evolution of reflexive pronouns make it highly probable
that we were correct in assigning a locative or locative/emphatic role to
P-UA *pɨ-nakoyɨ.

   The situation in the first column is even clearer. All of the forms are
reciprocal, and so far as is known only reciprocal, with the exception of
the Tubatulabal forms, which cannot be taken as counter-evidence to the reconstruction of *ʔa-nakoyɨ as reciprocal. *pɨ-nakoyɨ was lost entirely in
Tubatulabal, as were the reflexive and reciprocal verb prefixes, so the remaining form was naturally generalized in function, with postpositions being incorporated later for greater precision. The conclusion that
*ʔa-nakoyɨ was reciprocal in function and contrasted with the non-
reciprocal *pɨ-nakoyɨ therefore seems inescapable.

3.2.9.   The Origin of *-nakoyɨ

   Proto Uto-Aztecan *ʔa-nakoyɨ was a reflexive pronoun with reciprocal

value, while *pɨ-nakoyɨ was basically locative and tended to assume emphatic value by extension. These are clearly morphemically complex
forms, and by probing further we can hope to learn something about pre-
Proto-Uto-Aztecan as well as the synchronic and diachronic derivation of
reflexive pronouns.

We can begin by identifying the different pieces. As noted previously,
*ʔa and *pɨ are both well-attested as third person singular pronouns in
Uto-Aztecan (cf. Chapter 1, footnote 7, and also UA-L-SP); clarification of
their roles must await further study, however. If we assume that each syllable represents a separate morpheme, at least diachronically, *-nakoyɨ
decomposes into *na, *ko, and *yɨ. *na is almost certainly related to the
reciprocal verb prefix *na- reconstructed for P-UA, whatever the nature of
the relationship may be. What can we now suggest for the origin of *ko and
*yɨ?

*ko can be related to a locative postposition meaning something like 'at',
'with', or 'near'. Postpositions possibly supporting this reconstruction
present a very complex picture, however, and we cannot explore the details
here. It is difficult to know how many of the postpositions resembling *ko
actually derive from it; some of these are parts of complex postpositions
which themselves require further analysis; more than one cognate set may
be involved; there is some possibility of confusion with (or derivation from)
a noun meaning 'edge', 'top', or 'forehead' (e.g. P ko(k)a 'forehead' (P-
SS-D-25)); and so on.

Despite these many uncertainties, one does find in Uto-Aztecan a substantial number of postpositional elements roughly of the form -ko, -ho, or
-ku (or reconstructable to such a form) whose meanings cluster around
'at/with/near'. (If these are all related, we can consider *-ko to be basic,
with development to either -ho or -ku constituting an assimilation in height.)
Here is a sample of these elements; no attempt at exhaustiveness is made:
NP -ku-pa 'on/above'; M -ho-'tu 'with'; SH -'ku 'at', -hoi 'around'; P -ko
'at/in'; NT -ko 'next to'; TA -ho-nesa 'from', -ku-wana 'after/behind'; Y
-ku-ni 'toward'; CR -kɨ-me 'with'; HU -kɨ 'with/through/by means of'; A
-ko 'in/on'. (Note that ɨ in Cora and Huichol descends from P-UA *u.) As
indicated, the analysis of this and similar data is anything but straightforward. However, it does establish the existence of one or more P-UA

locative postpositions of roughly the shape *-ko, and this is all the present
discussion requires. (The analysis will be refined in section 3.3.)

*yɨ means 'be'. Once again the existence of this entity in P-UA is rea-
sonably certain, although a detailed reconstruction will demand extensive
and careful research. The most direct evidence for P-UA *yɨ 'be' is provided by the southernmost languages, where its expected reflex is ye. ye
is in fact the Aztec root for 'be' in all unrealized forms (e.g. future, con-
ditional, subjunctive). Cora yei 'live/dwell' and Huichol yeikaa 'be' are
both used in expressions of location. In the northern languages, the Cupan
stem yax 'be' could easily derive from *yəx, with *yə the expected reflex
of *yɨ. The Shoshoni non-singular form for 'sit', yɨk^{w}i, may be related,
and so may the Southern Paiute present tense suffix -yɨ.[10] A number of
other forms might be cited as supporting P-UA *yɨ 'be', but these should
be sufficient to establish the probability of the reconstruction.

Now that we have identified the pieces of *ʔa-nakoyɨ and *pɨ-nakoyɨ, let
us see how they fit together. *-nakoyɨ can be regarded as a unit of some
kind, since it remains unchanged while occurring with either of two pronominal elements. There are grounds for believing that the division between the pronoun and *-nakoyɨ goes back to an older subject-predicate

---

[10]Sapir tentatively relates this suffix to the past durative -ya of Aztec rather than to
ye 'be' (UA-S-SPN2-321), incorrectly I believe. The vowel correspondences point to a
-yɨ/ye relation rather than to -yɨ/-ya; the common suffixal status of -yɨ and -ya clearly influenced Sapir, but there is nothing implausible about 'be' becoming incorporated
as a tense-marking suffix (for a discussion of an analogous development in Cupan, see
CUP-J-SC). Sapir himself gives further evidence for relating the present tense suffix
-yɨ of Southern Paiute to a stem meaning 'be'. He observes that the SP verbs meaning
'be', e.g. ʔatoʔa, generally do not take the suffix -yɨ when present tense is intended
(SP-S-G-235). This failure of 'be' and -yɨ to co-occur probably reflects a slightly
earlier stage when both meant 'be' so that combining the two was redundant and point-
less.
    The history of Uto-Aztecan 'be' is interesting and highly complex. On the basis of
partial and very unsystematic examination, I believe at least three verbs meaning 'be'
can be reconstructed for the proto language, *yɨ, *ka, and *tɨ, with *yɨ being the new-
est of these forms and *tɨ the oldest. The relative age of these forms correlates with
their tendency toward suffixal status. Thus *tɨ, the oldest, functions as a suffix on the
less ancient *ka in the well-established *ka-tɨ 'sit' (UA-VVH-TCG-139; UA-M-CS-55);
cf. *wɨ-lɨ 'stand' (UA-M-CS-58) (see section 5.2.3 for the alternation between *t and
*l). In similar fashion, *ka is found as a suffix on the still newer *yɨ, as attested by
Huichol yeikaa and Cupan yax (< *yəx < *yɨ-ka). This multiplicity of simple and derived forms lends itself to the development of suppletion. In Aztec, for example, *yɨ
(> ye) specialized as the unrealized stem for 'be', and *katɨ (> kate > kaʔ) became the
realized stem. In Shoshoni, katɨ and yɨ-k^{w}i have specialized as singular and non-
singular.
    For additional tantalizing data pertaining to yɨ/ya in Uto-Aztecan, see UA-VVH-
TCG-140 and UA-M-CS-55.

division, and also for believing that *ʔa-nakoyɨ was historically prior to
*pɨ-nakoyɨ. Therefore we will consider *ʔa-nakoyɨ first.

Evidence has been presented for reconstructing expressions of the form
*na-P for P-UA. Since *ko is a locative postposition, *na-ko represents a
special case of the *na-P construction and further corroborates the reconstruction of this pattern. *na-ko meant something like 'with one another',
so combining this with *yɨ 'be' (whose use with locatives is well-attested)
results in a locative predicate *na-ko-yɨ 'is with one another'. *ʔa is a
third person singular pronoun, which I will analyze as the subject of
*na-ko-yɨ in *ʔa-na-ko-yɨ and translate as 'it'. *ʔa-nakoyɨ therefore
originally meant approximately 'It is with one another'.

Next we must determine the referent of *ʔa 'it'. The referent of 'it', I
will claim, is the clause designating the reciprocal activity. I am claiming, in other words, that P-UA sentences such as 'They fight with one another' derive historically from expressions such as 'They fight, (and) it
(= their fighting) is with one another'. Granted this claim, which is semantically motivated and diachronically plausible, we may posit, for pre-
P-UA, synchronic underlying structures like Figure VI.

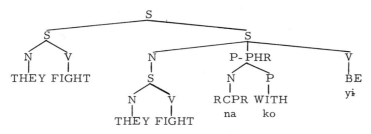

Figure VI

Sentence pronominalization reduces the second occurrence of 'they fight' to
the pronoun *ʔa, so that the surface form of the second conjunct is nothing
other than *ʔanakoyɨ. I would claim that Figure VI derives synchronically
from a still more abstract structure in which *ko is a predicate and the
clause which *ko defines is embedded to the higher predicate *yɨ, but this
analysis has no special implications for the matter at hand and will not be
pursued any further.[11]

[11]One advantage of analyzing postpositions as predicates is that this greatly mini-
mizes the difference between the use of *na in the na-P construction and its use as a
verb prefix.

Two aspects of this derivation require elaboration. First, not every reciprocal sentence lends itself to a locative interpretation; for example,
while it is reasonable to say that 'They fight with one another' is equivalent
to 'They fight, and their fighting is with one another', it is much less reasonable to equate 'They bite one another' with 'They bite, and their biting
is with one another'. However, the proposed derivation does not require
that the 'with' interpretation be appropriate in all instances, only that it be
appropriate in some. At some stage of pre-Proto-Uto-Aztecan, structures
like Figure VI presumably represented a productive pattern, of which
*ʔanakoyɨ was only one exponent. Eventually this one expression became a
fixed unit and generalized in both meaning and function, allowing little or no
variation in form and serving for reciprocal sentences of all kinds. By the
time we reach P-UA, this grammaticization had already been accomplished.
There is no evidence for positing a series of alternative reciprocal pronouns at the P-UA level, and no reason to believe that Figure VI was necessarily still valid as a synchronic underlying representation at this level.

Next, the coalescence of *ʔa-na-ko-yɨ into a fixed lexical unit was accompanied by loss of its clausal status, certainly in terms of surface
structure, and possibly (depending on how one analyzes reciprocal pronouns) in terms of underlying structure as well. Purely for illustrative
purposes, we may think in terms of a development like 'They fight, and it is
with each other' > 'They fight, with each other' > 'They fight with each
other' > 'They fight each other', in which what is originally an independent
clause gradually reduces to a non-clausal reflexive pronoun.

Let us now turn to *pɨ-nakoyɨ. The evidence clearly indicates that
*pɨ-nakoyɨ was locative rather than reciprocal, meaning something like
'by himself'; by extension this takes on emphatic and then possibly other
senses. The only problem that arises in explaining the origin of *pɨ-nakoyɨ
is the occurrence of *na in this form, since everything else leads us to believe that *na was specifically reciprocal, not reflexive as required by the
meaning of *pɨ-nakoyɨ.[12] This is certainly not a major problem, especially

---

[12] The Hopi emphatic pronoun naa-p does not establish a non-reciprocal use of P-UA
*na, since it could well be a later coinage following the na-P pattern. The verb prefix
naa- in Hopi became reflexive as well as reciprocal when the reflexive prefixes were
lost, so there is nothing surprising about naa- being reflexive with postpositions as
well.

when we bear in mind the grammaticization of *$^?$a-na-ko-yɨ sketched
above. Once *$^?$a-na-ko-yɨ began to coalesce as a fixed unit, with the identity of the component morphemes perhaps starting to become less certain
in the minds of speakers, the necessary conditions were present for the innovation of *pɨ-nakoyɨ. *PRON-nakoyɨ already existed as a model to follow, with *$^?$a serving as the pronoun, and the close similarity between reflexive and reciprocal sense made it easy to ignore the difference between
reflexive and reciprocal value for *-nakoyɨ.

Specifically, I propose synchronic underlying structures analogous to
Figure VII for pre-P-UA sentences like 'He works by himself'.

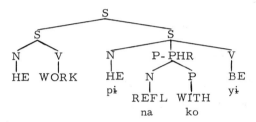

Figure VII

Note that in 'He works by himself' we are expressing the togetherness of
'he' and 'himself' (he is with himself but with nobody else), not the reciprocal character of a verbal relation as in Figure VI. Thus the subject of the
second conjunct is a clause in Figure VI, but in Figure VII it is a pronoun
designating an individual. I am therefore proposing a diachronic derivation something like the following: 'He works, and he is by himself' > 'He
works, by himself' > 'He works by himself'. By the P-UA stage,
*pɨ-nakoyɨ had reduced to a locative pronoun and started to take on em-
phatic sense, and Figure VII may no longer have been valid as a synchronic
underlying representation.

If this analysis of *$^?$a-nakoyɨ and *pɨ-nakoyɨ is roughly correct, it has
several implications. First, it strongly supports the reconstruction of
*na-P for P-UA, and even for pre-P-UA. Second, it provides a potentially
valuable clue for the reconstruction of the Uto-Aztecan pronouns, for it
suggests that the difference between *pɨ and *$^?$a in the third person singular was basically the difference between human and non-human referents,
or possibly between personal and sentential pronouns. Third, this almost

transparent analysis of the origin and development of reciprocal and locative reflexive pronouns in Uto-Aztecan may prove typical of the evolution
of reflexive pronouns in general; at the very least it shows one possible
path along which they may evolve. Finally, the analysis has implications
for the synchronic analysis of reflexive pronouns and other constructions.
In particular, it tends to support the claim that non-clausal surface elements may derive from full underlying clauses, including conjuncts of the
surface main clause. This analysis was proposed for passive by-phrases
in English (and other languages) in the Introduction, and we will return to
it in Chapter 5.

3.3.   The Kawaiisu Evidence

3.3.1.   Reformulation

In section 3.2 we reconstructed the reflexive pronoun base *-nakoyɨ,
which could be used in either the locative/emphatic form *pɨ-nakoyɨ or the
reciprocal form *ʔa-nakoyɨ. The *na of *-nakoyɨ was identified as the reciprocal *na- reconstructed in Chapter 2, while *yɨ was equated with a reconstructed predicate meaning 'be'. *ko was tentatively identified as a
postposition meaning something like 'at', 'with', or 'near'. However, the
precise semantic value of this postposition is not of central importance,
for a wide range of postpositional meanings would be compatible with reciprocal meaning for a subclass of predicates (under the analysis offered
in section 3.2.9), providing a reciprocal pronoun form that could be generalized to all semantic classes of predicates and later to reflexive use as
well.

No Numic reflexes of *-nakoyɨ were known when I first reconstructed
this element. Since that time two Numic forms have come to light. The
Northern Paiute form, nahoy, is from an unpublished work by Liljeblad
(NP-L-M). It matches the Hopi reflex and fits in well with the analysis
presented so far. In addition, field work on Kawaiisu by Pamela Munro
and others has uncovered what is almost certainly a cognate form, one
that strongly confirms the reconstruction in its essentials and at the same
time allows us to refine it. The usual form in Kawaiisu is nɨwayɨ, but
nawayɨ also occurs. This form has both reflexive and reciprocal use. As

we might expect in view of the general innovation of enclitics for possessor
use in Southern Numic, it is followed by the appropriate possessor enclitic
rather than being preceded by a pronominal prefix. The enclitic =pɨme,
which one would expect to be third person plural, is apparently not restricted to this person, since it is also attested with the third person singular
and with first person plural (K-M-SPO-17). I posit realignment of recent
origin in the Kawaiisu reflexive possessor enclitic system and will not consider such forms any further, except to note that =pɨme corresponds to the
reflexive possessor enclitic =pɨ of Southern Paiute. The reflexive and reciprocal uses of nɨwayɨ are illustrated in (1) and (2) respectively.

K (1) nɨwayɨ=ni pɨ 'kee-tɨ po²o-'paana
    self-my   see-TNS water-in
    'I saw myself in the water.'   (K-M-SPO-16)

K (2) nɨm nɨway=nɨm pɨni-'kar-tɨ-mɨ
    we   self-our   look-sit-TNS-PL
    'We sat and looked at each other.'   (K-M-SPO-17)

The first and last syllable of nɨwayɨ can be equated with those of
*-nakoyɨ in a non-problematic way. The final yɨ in the two forms needs
no comment. For the first syllable, recall that both nɨwayɨ and nawayɨ
are attested, though the former is evidently the most common form at present. This alternation is related to the fact that Kawaiisu has two reflexive
prefixes, na- and nɨ-, as does Shoshoni. na- of course reflects the reconstructed reciprocal prefix *na- treated in Chapter 2; the source of nɨ- is
considered in Chapter 4. The functions of na- and nɨ- were originally distinct, as the discussion of these reconstructions shows, but in Kawaiisu
they have merged at least in part. With two reflexive prefixes so similar
in form, this is hardly surprising. Nor is it surprising that the reflexive
pronoun nawayɨ would give rise to the variant nɨwayɨ once the effective
equivalence of na- and nɨ- had been established.

Only the middle syllable appears problematic; the wa of nawayɨ is not
terribly similar to the *ko of *-nakoyɨ. One possible explanation for this
discrepancy is that another postposition displaced the reflex of *ko in the
Kawaiisu form. I doubt very strongly that this is the proper explanation.
Instead I will claim that the reconstruction of *ko as the postpositional
element in the P-UA reflexive pronoun base is correct only as a first approximation. The best reconstruction is rather *k^{w}a, which is reflected

as either *$\underline{ko}$ or $\underline{wa}$. The P-UA reflexive pronoun base is therefore
*-$\underline{nak^{w}ay\dot{i}}$ rather than *-$\underline{nakoy\dot{i}}$.

3.3.2.   *$\underline{k^{w}a}$

There is ample justification both for positing a postposition *-$\underline{k^{w}a}$ for
P-UA and for claiming that Kawaiisu $\underline{w}$ sometimes reflects proto *$\underline{k^{w}}$. P-
UA *-$\underline{k^{w}a}$ meant approximately 'to/at/against' and took on other senses
when used in combination with other elements. *-$\underline{nak^{w}ay\dot{i}}$ therefore originally meant something like '(it) was to each other', but by P-UA times this
sequence had achieved general reciprocal use and been extended to reflexive (specifically, locative/emphatic) use, so that *-$\underline{k^{w}a}$ had no doubt been
reduced to very general locative sense in this form.

Further investigation of Uto-Aztecan postpositions will be necessary before the evidence for P-UA *-$\underline{k^{w}a}$ can be presented in definitive form.
Here I must be content to sketch the reconstruction only in its broad outlines, bringing in enough data to show that it is highly probable if not certain. I will omit many possible reflexes and concentrate on those that
seem reasonably secure.

*-$\underline{k^{w}a}$ occurred by itself as a postposition and figured as one member of
at least three complex forms (in addition to *-$\underline{nak^{w}ay\dot{i}}$). None of these
uses is attested in a terribly large number of subfamilies, but each is attested in both northern and southern languages. Moreover, when all four
uses are taken into account, the attestation is respectably wide.

By itself, *-$\underline{k^{w}a}$ is straightforwardly attested at least in Hopi and
Pimic: H $\underline{?ak^{w}}$ 'into'; P $\underline{?ab}$ 'there/on near side of'; NT -$\underline{aba}$ 'on/against';
TO -$\underline{a?ba}$ 'in/at'. (Also note Aztec -$\underline{ko}$ 'in/on' and various other postpositions cited in section 3.2.9.) All of these forms are decomposable into
*$\underline{?a-}$, originally a third person singular pronoun that takes postpositions,
and *-$\underline{k^{w}a}$. The reanalysis of a pronoun plus postposition sequence into a
complex postposition is a widespread phenomenon in Uto-Aztecan (UA-L-
SP), so the segmentation of these forms is fully justified. Note as well
that $\underline{b}$ is the expected Pimic reflex of *$\underline{k^{w}}$.

Probably also reconstructable is the sequence *-$\underline{k^{w}a-ni}$, where *-$\underline{ni}$
can be attributed the meaning 'be/do' (e.g. P-NUM *$\underline{ha(')ni}$ 'do/make/fix'

(NP-N-HG-321, 322); L <u>nive$^?$</u> 'be in'; P <u>ǰuñi</u> 'do'; TA <u>ni</u> 'be'; Y <u>ʔaane</u> 'be'; HU <u>ʔaane</u> 'be'). The sequence is clearly represented in Cupeno -k^waani and Luiseno -q^waan(i), both benefactive postpositions. The Yaqui postposition -<u>kun(i)</u> 'toward' is a likely cognate, though not a certain one. The semantic value of *-k^wa-ni must have approximated '(it) is to X', where X represents the postpositional object. This meaning could easily underlie both the Cupan benefactive sense and the 'toward' sense of Yaqui -<u>kun(i)</u>. It also suggests the incorporation of these locutions from a juxtaposed clause, as outlined for *-nak^{w}ayɨ in section 3.2.9.

If Yaqui -<u>kun(i)</u> derives from *-k^wa-ni, we must posit the development *k^wa > Y ku in at least some forms. This development is corroborated by the third pattern, which is represented by Southern Paiute and Kawaiisu -tu'k^{w}a 'under' and Yaqui <u>betuk(u)</u> 'under/below'. The <u>be-</u> which initiates so many potentially free-standing postpositions in Yaqui is clearly segmentable and derives historically from *pɨ-, a third person singular pronoun (UA-L-SP). The relation between Southern Numic -tu'k^{w}a and Yaqui -<u>tuku</u>, both with the basic meaning 'under', is therefore beyond serious doubt.

The final reconstructable sequence is something approximating *-na-k^{w}a (perhaps *-na-^{n}k^{w}a), with a meaning of 'toward' (or possibly 'direction'). It is most clearly attested in the three branches of Numic, e.g. Northern Paiute -<u>na'k^{w}a</u> 'toward/beyond/behind/to', Shoshoni -<u>na^{n}k^{w}a</u> 'from direction of', and Southern Paiute -<u>na^{n}k^{w}a</u> 'direction' (note that prenasalization and gemination merge in Western Numic). In Yaqui we find a likely cognate sequence <u>nuku</u> in the two complex forms <u>benukut</u> 'until (direction)' and <u>nukusia</u> 'to beneath'. The <u>be-</u> of <u>benukut</u> derives from the pronominal *pɨ-, as noted above, and there are likely possibilities in the Yaqui postpositional system for corroborating the segmentation of -<u>sia</u> and -<u>t</u>.

We see, then, that it is quite reasonable to reconstruct for P-UA the postposition *-k^wa meaning roughly 'to/at/against'. Next we must turn our attention to the possibility of an alternation between *k^w and *w in medial position, since such an alternation at some stage is needed to relate Kawaiisu <u>nawayɨ</u> to P-UA *-nak^{w}ayɨ. It is well known that certain Uto-Aztecan languages display a regular process of medial consonant lenition, resulting in strong/weak alternations such as <u>p/v</u>, <u>t/r</u>, etc. depending on a morphological trait of the preceding element. (This consonant gradation is discussed much more carefully in section 5.2.3.) These alternations are largely retained as a productive synchronic process in the Numic languages, but outside this subfamily the allophonic variation has become phonemic in character. This process of medial consonant lenition is a natural place to look for the change of $*k^w$ to w in Kawaiisu.

I will claim that there was a regular $*k^w$/$*w$ alternation in P-UA parallel to the others mentioned. There was also a regular alternation between $*m$ and $*w$, though I will not try to substantiate the latter claim here in any detail. w in a daughter language can therefore reflect any of three proto phonemes: $*w$, $*k^w$, or $*m$. While the fortis/lenis alternation has long been recognized for other consonants, to my knowledge no one has previously pointed out that $*w$ can be reconstructed as the lenis or "spirantized" version of $*k^w$ or $*m$. The reason for this is easy to perceive. The lenited forms of $*p$, $*t$, etc. did not coincide in phonetic shape with any other phonemes and hence were easily recognized as allophonic variants of their fortis counterparts (though the difference later became phonemic in most daughters). In the case of $*k^w$ and $*m$, on the other hand, the lenis allophone $*w$ was bound to be confused with the phoneme $*w$ and eventually to merge with this phoneme. Comparative Uto-Aztecan scholars have been primarily concerned with roots, and since a root-medial consonant typically displays only a single allophone, medial $*w$ has simply been taken as representing the P-UA phoneme $*w$ in all instances. The situation is quite different when suffixes are reconstructed, however. Here the $*k^w$/$*w$ and $*m$/$*w$ alternations remain overt, since different roots and stems select different allophones; when the allophonic variation became phonemic, it gave rise to alternate versions of the same suffix, with some daughters retaining one version and other daughters the second. Morphological reconstruction can therefore provide evidence to substantiate the claim that w can reflect $*k^w$ and $*m$ as well as $*w$.

To illustrate the $*m$/$*w$ alternation I offer only a single brief example. We can clearly reconstruct for P-UA a non-proximal demonstrative $*ma$; in some daughters it is retained as ma or something similar, in others it approximates wa, and these sets of daughters are roughly complementary. Various daughter forms (especially in Hopi, Serrano, Gabrielino, Pimic, and Mayo) show that $*ma$/$*wa$ was or could be preceded by another syllable

in the demonstrative form, so that *ma itself can be considered a medial
syllable. Recall that g is the expected reflex of *w in Pimic: NP ma-; M
ma-; SH ma-; SP ma- (accusative wa-ya); K ma-; TU wa?; H pam (plural
pɨma); SR ?ama?; GA maraama?, piema; L wunal (< *wanal, but cf. NP-N-
HG-194-196); P hɨga(i); NT ?ɨgai; TO hɨgga; TA (w)era; Y wa; MA ?ama;
CR mɨɨ(mɨ); HU mɨɨ; PO ma. This cognate set leaves little doubt about
the validity of the *m/*w alternation, and other sets could easily be added
to corroborate the hypothesis.

Our primary concern is however with the *k^w/*w alternation, and while
the evidence presently available is not as extensive as it is for *m/*w, it
is certainly sufficient. What follows is a brief and non-exhaustive survey.

One bit of evidence for this alternation is a direct trace it left in the
Western Numic languages as a phonological rule. Specifically, w surfaces
as 'k^w in fortis environments in both Northern Paiute and Mono (UA-XXX-
WC1; NP-N-HG-56; M-L-G-96). In Mono, for example, we find
?i-waqa-'na (my-say-NR) 'what I said' with the non-geminating possessor
prefix ?i-, but ?ɨ-'k^{w}aqa-'na (your-say-NR) 'what you said' with the geminating prefix ?ɨ-. While I have not investigated the historical phonology of
Western Numic, this alternation clearly supports the *k^w/*w hypothesis.

Next, considerable lexical evidence is provided by initial consonants in
reconstructed roots. In a number of instances Wick Miller (UA-M-CS)
found reason to reconstruct alternate forms for the same meaning, one be-
ginning in *k^w and the other in *w. He could not collapse the variants because it was not recognized that *k^w and *w bore any systematic relation
to one another, but by treating *w as the spirantized form of *k^w, and by
noting that consonant gradation sometimes occurs across word boundaries,
the pairs can be related in a natural way. These pairs include at least the
following (identified by the number of the cognate set in UA-M-CS): *k^{w}i
(1), *wi (2) 'acorn'; *wɨ (39a), *k^{w}ɨ (39d) 'big'; *k^{w}ɨ (76), *wɨ (77) 'carry';
*k^{w}a (110a), *wa (110b) 'coyote'; *k^{w}a (191), *waka (192) 'frog'; note also
*k^{w}a (152a), *suwa (153) 'eat'. Closer examination will doubtless reveal
further lexical evidence for the alternation.

Definitive evidence from suffixes and other grammatically significant
elements cannot be presented here, both because reconstructions are still
quite tentative and because adequate discussion of each of them would

require a lengthy presentation. Preliminary indications can however be offered. For example, Kawaiisu ʔiwʔana, Serrano ʔahk^w, Gabrielino ʔik^{w}a, and Opata ʔig^{w}ati (Opata g^w derives from earlier *w) suggest the reconstruction *ʔi-k^{w}a 'here'. This form clearly incorporates the proximal demonstrative base *ʔi, and the second element can no doubt be equated with the postposition *-k^{w}a 'to/at/against' under discussion, which provides direct evidence for the *k^w/*w alternation being able to affect this postposition. I will present just one other example here. There is a fair amount of evidence for reconstructing the subordinator *-k^w(a), with the approximate meaning 'when/while', possibly restricted to instances where the main and subordinate clause subjects are non-identical. Reflexes that point to the fortis variant *-k^w(a), with possible vocalization of (or assimilation to) the labial component to yield a rounded vowel, include Southern Paiute -ku 'while/as/when', Chemehuevi -kwa? 'when', Yaqui -tek(o) 'if/when', Mayo -k(o) 'when', and others. Reflexes that point to the lenis variant *-w(a), also with vocalization or assimilation to yield a rounded vowel, include Serrano -u/-w 'while/as', Yaqui -o 'when/while', and Tarahumara -o (non-adverbial subordinator). Other sets could be added, but they would not be convincing except in the context of a broader study.

3.3.3.   Development

Granted that the P-UA reflexive pronoun base was *-nak^{w}ayɨ rather than *-nakoyɨ, we must now refine our conception of the evolution of this form in the daughter languages, since the previous description of this evolution was based on *-nakoyɨ. Certain details are uncertain or potentially problematic, but they can be treated at least in a tentative manner.

It is reasonable to suppose that *-nak^{w}ayɨ and *-nakoyɨ both occurred in the proto language, the latter representing a phonetic simplification of the former. For most of the daughters in which this reflexive pronoun base is retained, *-nakoyɨ is the more convenient starting point for characterizing the evolution of the reflex, so the previous description of this evolution need not be altered. Thus we can confine our attention here to Takic and Numic.

Certain minor difficulties arose in our discussion of the development of the reflexive pronouns in Takic, difficulties that can be eliminated if *-nak^{w}ayɨ rather than *-nakoyɨ is taken as the point of departure. Recall that *nɨ-nakoyɨ was reconstructed as the first person singular form. From this developed the alternative haplological forms *nɨkoyɨ and *nakoyɨ, the former eventually prevailing in Cupan and the latter in Serrano. The problems arise in relation to the precise sequence of changes to be posited for Serrano and also in relation to the ordering of haplology and the vowel harmonization needed for Cupan.

First consider the Serrano development posited earlier: *nakoyɨ > *nakw(y)ɨ > *nawk(y)ɨ > *nawkɨ > nowk(ɨ). The most problematic step is the first one, the devocalization of o to yield w, which subsequently filtered into the preceding syllable and precipitated the natural change *aw > ow. While the devocalization is certainly not inherently implausible, it can be eliminated in favor of a more commonly attested process if *nak^{w}ayɨ is reconstructed instead, namely syncope of the medial vowel: *nak^{w}ayɨ > *nak^{w}yɨ > *nawk(y)ɨ > *nawkɨ > nowk(ɨ).

Now consider the ordering difficulty. Haplology took place in both Serrano and Cupan, so it was reconstructed for the Proto Takic stage. The variant *nɨkoyɨ won out over *nakoyɨ in Proto Cupan, since the Cupan languages uniformly display reflexive pronouns that begin with a pronominal element descended from *nɨ- (or the corresponding form for other persons), lack na, and end in a reflex of *-koyɨ. However, P-CUP *-koyɨ became *-kayɨ (> *-qay); this change in vowel quality is most naturally regarded as harmonization of *o to the *a of *na, but presumably this *na had already been lost in Proto Takic times in the alternant that Proto Cupan retains.

The need for this problematic vowel harmonization is avoided if *-nak^{w}ayɨ is posited rather than *-nakoyɨ. The first person singular *nɨ-nak^{w}ayɨ then simplifies to either *nak^{w}ayɨ, which accounts for the Serrano reflex as illustrated above, or *nɨk^{w}ayɨ, which was chosen in Proto Cupan. Precisely how the labial component of *-k^{w}ayɨ was lost is an open question for which I have no definite answer. One possibility is that the labialization filtered through to the preceding syllable, as suggested for Serrano, where it caused the backing of *k to *q: *nɨk^{w}ayɨ > *nɨwkayɨ > *nɨqay(ɨ) > *nɨqay. Other possibilities could also be entertained.

Overall, then, reconstructing *-nak^{w}ayɨ renders the subsequent Takic evolution somewhat more natural and less problematic, though the difference is less than dramatic. Now we must return to Numic, where reflexes are known only for Northern Paiute and Kawaiisu. *-nakoyɨ is the obvious starting point for Northern Paiute nahoy, leaving Kawaiisu nawayɨ as the only obvious reflex of *-nak^{w}ayɨ. I have related the shift *-nak^{w}ayɨ > nawayɨ to the *k^w/*w medial consonant alternation established in section 3.3.2 (recall that the preceding *pɨ- of *pɨ-nak^{w}ayɨ is replaced by a series of pronominal enclitics as part of the more general innovation of such enclitics in Southern Numic). However, it would not do simply to posit free variation between *-nak^{w}ayɨ and *-nawayɨ for Proto Uto-Aztecan, for two reasons. First, the variant with the lenis or spirantized w is not attested in any other subfamily. Second, consonant gradation is determined by the preceding morpheme, and since the preceding morpheme is always *na in the sequence *-nak^{w}ayɨ, we would not expect to find any alternation between fortis *k^w and lenis *w.

While the *k^w/*w alternation can be reconstructed for P-UA, I would suggest that its extension to the reflexive pronoun in Numic is much more recent, perhaps even subsequent to the split between Southern Paiute and Kawaiisu in Southern Numic (recall that Northern Paiute nahoy reflects the fortis member of the alternation). Only very limited information concerning Kawaiisu is available, but even on the basis of this it appears that Kawaiisu sometimes shows the lenis variant of a medial segment for which Southern Paiute and the other Numic languages display the fortis variant. For example, in the following four partial cognate sets for postpositions, Kawaiisu simply shows w where the other Numic languages have a variant of k^w or m--often the lenis variant, but one that is nevertheless distinguishable from w: NP -ma 'on', SH -ma^n 'on', SP -ma^n 'on', K -wa 'on'; NP -ma 'with', M -'maha 'on/with', SH -ma 'with', SP -ma 'with', K -waa'ku 'with'; SP -tuk^{w}a 'to/toward' (cf. NP -tuku 'through'), K -tuwa 'to/toward/ through'; NP -tami 'toward', SP -mi 'direction', K -tawi 'to'. Kawaiisu has apparently reanalyzed the lenis variant of k^w and m as w in these forms. The third set probably involves the postposition -k^{w}a reconstructed as the medial portion of *-nak^{w}ayɨ.

3.4. Other Reflexive Pronouns

3.4.1. Numic

3.4.1.1. The na- Forms

I have shown that the *na-P construction of P-UA is still active in at least some Numic languages and must definitely be reconstructed for Proto Numic. Thus we find examples such as the following in Mono and Southern Paiute:

M (1) na'na-pa?aha
RCPR-on
top
of
'on top of one another'   (M-L-G-182, 287)

SP (2) na-ŋ^{w}a-^{n}tuk^{w}a
REFL-on-to
onto
'onto himself'   (SP-S-G-211)

SP (3) na-ŋ^{w}a?ai
REFL-with
'with each other/both'   (SP-S-G-212)

Note that this construction can be either reflexive or reciprocal in Southern Paiute.

This construction is one source of reflexive pronouns in Numic. We have already observed this in regard to the forms na-noo and na-ma in Northern Paiute, both of which translate as 'together' and can be regarded as a special kind of reciprocal pronoun. na-'noo is also found in Southern Paiute, but here it has been reanalyzed from a basically locative reciprocal meaning 'with one another' or 'together' to become an emphatic reflexive (cf. section 1.4):

SP (4) na'noo='su
self-NOM
'he himself'   (SP-S-G-212)

SP (5) na'noo-p
self-at
'for himself'   (SP-S-G-212)

The incorporation of the additional postposition -p(a) in (5) is good (though not conclusive) indication that na'noo has been reanalyzed in Southern Paiute as an emphatic reflexive pronoun base and that -'noo is no longer recognized as a postposition in this base.

Directly parallel to Southern Paiute na'noo='su is Kawaiisu nano'so,
which has locative and emphatic value:

> K (6) nano'so katɨ - t   nɨ ʔ
>   self   live- TNS I
>   'I live by myself. '   (K- M-SPO- 17)

Both SP na'noo='su and K nano'so incorporate the clitic ='su, whose original meaning in Numic was apparently 'just/precisely' or something similar.
The nominative label for this element in the Southern Paiute form should
not be taken too seriously; it drops in the oblique form na'noo-p, but the accusative na'noo-tɨa='su retains it. In any event, ='su is evidently segmentable synchronically in Southern Paiute, but there is no clear evidence that
the same holds for the 'so of Kawaiisu nano'so. We saw in section 1.4 that
='su has itself taken on reflexive value of some kind in Southern Paiute
(nɨnia='su 'myself ACC', nɨ'nia 'me ACC'). The same is true in Kawaiisu,
but the form is ='su rather than 'so when it occurs alone:

> K (7) nɨ ʔɨ='su saʔa'kata=a'ka
>   I- self   cook- it
>   'I cooked it myself. '   (K- M-SPO- 18)

We can reconstruct this transfer of reflexive sense to *='su for Proto
Southern Numic and attribute it to its occurrence in the complex reflexive
pronoun *na- 'noo='su.

The evolution of the Southern Paiute emphatic and reflexive pronoun expressions in (4) and (5) merits recapitulation, both because it is complex
and because of what it shows about the factors influencing syntactic change.
One hypothesis concerning the origin of P- NUM *- 'noo was presented in
section 2.2. There I claimed that *- 'noo reflects an earlier *na-w(i)
(RCPR- to), an exponent of the P- UA *na- P construction also attested as
Cahuilla- Cupeno *- nəw. For pre- Proto- Numic, we can posit a reciprocal
particle *na-w 'together'. (If this had a clausal source, as posited for
*- nak^Wayɨ in section 3.2.9, only the central portion of the clause, i. e.
*na- P, was lexically expressed or retained; there is no trace of the subject
pronoun and 'be' of Figure VI.)

In the first round of reanalysis, the RCPR- P sequence *na-w was reanalyzed as a postposition, *- 'noo. The instigating factor was probably

phonetic, the merger of <u>aw</u> to <u>oo</u>.[13] Once this merger had taken place,
speakers lost sight of the relation of this form to *<u>na-</u>, causing the following reanalysis:

(8) na-w   >   noo   >   N-'noo
    RCPR-with   RCPR-with   N-with
    'together/with   'together/with   'with N'
    one another'   one another'

The formerly bimorphemic sequence became monomorphemic and retained
the locative meaning of the postposition, while the reciprocal element disappeared as an independent element and its meaning was lost. The syntactic details of this reanalysis were sketched in section 2.2.

Because the *<u>na-P</u> construction was retained in Numic, this reanalysis
affecting only one combination, the newly derived postposition *-'noo could
itself combine with *<u>na-</u>. This gave rise to P-NUM *<u>na-'noo</u> 'with one an-
other/together', which is retained as such in Northern Paiute. We have
just seen that the Southern Paiute <u>na-P</u> construction may be reflexive as
well as reciprocal, and apparently the reflexive sense took over in Proto
Southern Numic *<u>na-'noo</u>, leading eventually to a second round of reanalysis.

P-SNM *<u>na-'noo</u> meant 'with oneself/by oneself', i.e. it was a locative
reflexive pronoun construction. We have already noted a tendency for locative reflexives to become emphatic reflexives, and this semantic extension, together with the incorporation of the clitic =<u>'su</u> (which is characteristic of reflexive pronouns throughout Numic), yields the P-SNM emphatic
reflexive *<u>na-'noo='su</u> reflected in the Southern Paiute example (4) and the
Kawaiisu example (6) (example (6) happens to be locative).

The semantic difference between locative and emphatic reflexive pronouns is subtle, but it is real; the locative sense of 'with/by' is literal in
locative reflexives, but only figurative in emphatic reflexives (I can do
something <u>by myself</u>, i.e. personally, when I am not <u>by myself</u>, i.e. alone).
The shift of <u>na-'noo</u> from locative to emphatic value in Southern Numic
therefore involves a change in the status of the postposition -<u>'noo</u>. This
postposition is meaningful only figuratively, and the expression containing
it is vulnerable to the reanalysis shown in (9).

[13]For P-CAC *-<u>nəw</u>, the factor triggering the corresponding reanalysis was the
loss from the language of *<u>na-</u> and the *<u>na-P</u> construction.

(9) na-'noo   na-'noo   na'noo
     REFL-with   REFL-with   REFL
     'by oneself'   >   'oneself'   >   'oneself'
     (LOCATIVE)   (EMPHATIC)   (EMPHATIC)

This second reanalysis apparently took place in Proto Southern Numic, and in
Southern Paiute another postposition was added to the new reflexive pronoun
na'noo to make it oblique, as shown in example (5). Viewed historically,
then, (5) contains three postpositions (*-w(i), *-'noo, -p) and three reflexive or reciprocal pronoun bases (two instances of *na- and na'noo).

While this chain of development is rather intricate, it seems well-
motivated and reasonably straightforward. All of the elements involved
have been identified, their combination is semantically and syntactically
regular, and the cause and details of each change are readily apparent.
The remaining reflexive pronouns in Numic are formed on the base pɨ, as
shown in Table VII.

NP	pɨɨ='su	EMPH
	pɨɨ-'sɨ?mɨ	'alone'
	pɨɨ-'noo	'with/also'
M	pɨɨ='su	EMPH/REFL
	pɨɨ-'sɨ?ɨ	'alone'
SH	pɨ'nɨ^{n}sɨ	REFL
	pɨ('nɨ)	POSSR
SP	=pɨ	POSSR
K	nɨwayɨ=pɨme	REFL/RCPR

Table VII

(Once again, the Shoshoni forms are only representatives of a larger set.)
The development of these forms is somewhat less straightforward than that
of the na- forms, chiefly because pɨ does not reconstruct as a reflexive pronoun. The reflexive use of pɨ is confined largely if not entirely to Numic.

3.4.1.2.   pɨ as a Reflexive Pronoun

With the exception of Kawaiisu nawayɨ/nɨwayɨ, Numic shows no direct
reflexes of *pɨ-nak^{W}ayɨ. I believe, however, that the reflexive use of pɨ
in Numic is an indirect reflex of this sequence. The development of
*pɨ-nak^{W}ayɨ in Takic affords some clues as to what may have happened on
the way to Proto Numic. Let us examine this development in Serrano,

where the situation is clearest.

Like P-UA *pɨ-nak^Wayɨ, Serrano pɨ-nuk is basically a locative reflexive pronoun, roughly 'by oneself'. We have seen that in pre-P-UA
*pɨ-nak^Wayɨ constituted a clause, and that *pɨ was a non-reflexive subject
pronoun (cf. Figure VII). The surface clausal status of *pɨ-nak^Wayɨ was
most likely lost by the P-UA stage, and certainly by the P-TAK stage.
Serrano pɨ-nuk is synchronically a postpositional phrase, and pɨ is a postpositional object rather than a subject pronoun. The grammaticization of
*-nak^Wayɨ and the reduction of *pɨ-nak^Wayɨ from clausal to phrasal status
entail reanalysis of the elements involved, and this reanalysis may explain
how pɨ became reflexive in Numic.

(a)

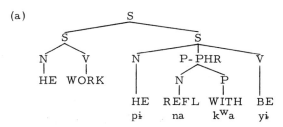

'He works, (and) he is by himself.'

(b)

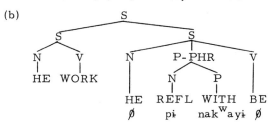

'He works, by himself.'

(c)

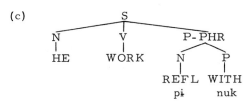

'He works by himself.'

Figure VIII

An independent locative clause has several elements: a subject nominal, the verb 'be', and a postpositional phrase consisting of the postposition and its object. A postpositional phrase has only the last two elements mentioned, namely the postposition and its object. Obviously, if a postpositional phrase derives directly from a locative clause, the elements involved must coalesce and be realigned in some fashion. Let me suggest for Serrano pɨ-nuk the development outlined in Figure VIII.

The first structure in Figure VIII, (a), is essentially the same as Figure VII. The crucial semantic information conveyed by the second conjunct in this structure is that contained in the postpositional phrase; the subject 'he' is coreferential to the subject of the first conjunct and is therefore in a sense semantically redundant, and the meaningfulness of 'be' is subject to dispute.[14] Furthermore, both third person singular pronouns and 'be' are often realized as zero, in Uto-Aztecan and in languages generally. It is not unexpected, then, that when *-nak^{w}ayɨ coalesces into a fixed expression, and speakers no longer recognize within it the separate components from which it derives, the resulting realignment will favor the postpositional phrase, as shown in (b). *-nak^{w}ayɨ is reinterpreted as 'with', and *pɨ as the reflexive object of 'with', while 'he' and 'be' remain unlexicalized. The lack of an explicit subject and verb in (b) make this structure susceptible to further reanalysis, in which the postpositional phrase is interpreted as being part of the preceding clause. The result is structure (c). (c) represents the surface situation in modern Serrano. I would suggest (b) both as a likely surface structure for an earlier stage of development and as a possible synchronic underlying structure for (c) in the contemporary language.

Whether or not one regards Serrano pɨ- as a reflexive pronoun is largely just a matter of definition. pɨ- happens to be the regular third person singular postpositional object, and the reflexive value of the construction illustrated in (c) might be attributed to -nuk instead of to pɨ-. pɨ- has evidently not been extended with reflexive sense to other constructions,[15] so the reflexive status of this element is somewhat conjectural.

---

[14] I believe that 'be' is in fact meaningful, having (stative) existential sense; cf. section 5.4. The important point, of course, is that 'be' has more restricted semantic content than most other elements and is often lexicalized as zero.

[15] There is a possessor use, but pɨ-nuk as a unit plays this role, in contrast to the situation in Numic.

It is not conjectural in Numic, however. The forms in Table VII point clearly to pɨ as a reflexive pronoun which may be elaborated by the addition of other elements. pɨ has non-reflexive uses in Numic, but this is perfectly compatible with the present analysis, which seeks only to explain how it could have taken on reflexive value in certain constructions. Specifically, I postulate a Numic analog of the evolution sketched in Figure VIII, at least for Western and Central Numic. A similar development can be posited for Southern Numic, but one that differs in detail.

3.4.1.3.   The pɨ- Forms

My data on Numic reflexive pronouns based on pɨ- is somewhat haphazard and probably incomplete. A full description of their origin and syntactic development is therefore not at the moment possible, but a number of observations can nevertheless be made.

For Proto Numic, we can reconstruct at least the following: the reflexive pronouns *-nakoyɨ (from *ʔa-nakoyɨ and needed for Northern Paiute nahoy) and *pɨ-nak^{w}ayɨ; the clitic *='su 'just/precisely'; and the *na-P construction. The meaning of *='su is quite compatible with that of reflexive pronouns, and it combines with reflexive pronouns in all three branches of the family, but beyond that I have little to say about it at this time. The *na-P construction has already been discussed; this construction is still productive in Mono and Southern Paiute, and it is reflected in the Northern Paiute reciprocal pronouns na-noo 'together' and na-ma 'together' and the Southern Numic emphatic pronouns based on na-'noo, but I have found no reference to the construction in Shoshoni.

An examination of the Numic reflexive pronouns based on pɨ in Table VII shows two basic differences between Western and Central Numic on the one hand and Southern Numic on the other hand. First, Western and Central Numic have reflexes of *pɨ-'noo, a postpositional expression, but no such reflexes are found in Southern Numic. Second, Southern Numic has a reflexive possessor enclitic =pɨ (elaborated to =pɨme in Kawaiisu for reasons beyond the scope of this discussion); thus the reflexive pɨ is possessive rather than postpositional. It is no accident that the postpositional and possessive reflexive locutions based on pɨ are in complementary distribution within Numic. This is a direct consequence of a difference in the way in which speakers reanalyzed *pɨ-nak^{w}ayɨ once the literal interpretation of this form was lost sight of.

In Southern Numic, speakers reanalyzed *pɨ-nak^{w}ayɨ as a POSSR-N construction analogous to English <u>myself</u>. Since *-nak^{w}ayɨ was treated as a noun rather than as a postposition, *pɨ- never became a reflexive postpositional base, hence the non-occurrence of postpositional expressions like *pɨ-'noo in Southern Numic. Moreover, since *pɨ- was a (reflexive) possessor pronominal, it was subject to the subsequent change in Southern Numic whereby possession came to be expressed by enclitics to the possessed noun. The noun *nak^{w}ayɨ was eventually lost in Southern Paiute, but the reflexive possessor enclitic =pɨ, illustrated in (1), reflects the prior existence of *nak^{w}ayɨ=pɨ.

SP (1) pu^{n}ku-^{n}k^{w}ɨ-a=pɨ   ko-ko?i-yɨ
          horse-PL-ACC-REFL RDP-kill-PRES
                              DISTR
          'kills his own horses'   (SP-S-G-188)

This N=POSSR reflexive pronoun is directly attested in Kawaiisu, of course.

In Western and Central Numic, *pɨ-nak^{w}ayɨ was reanalyzed as a PRON-P sequence, as outlined earlier for Serrano. That is, *-nak^{w}ayɨ was treated as a postposition, and *pɨ- as the reflexive object of that postposition. Once established as a reflexive pronoun, *pɨ- was extended to the various other syntactic roles it has in these languages. The postposition *-nak^{w}ayɨ does not itself survive, but the *pɨ-P construction is attested through reflexes of *pɨ-'noo in Northern Paiute and Shoshoni. We may speculate that *pɨ-nak^{w}ayɨ was replaced by the simpler *pɨ-'noo by analogy to *na-'noo, which can clearly be reconstructed for Proto Numic.[16]

---

[16] I have considered the possibility that *-'noo might itself be the descendant of *-nak^{w}ayɨ but tend to disfavor it. We saw earlier (section 3.3.3) that the k^w of *-nak^{w}ayɨ must be presumed to have been fortis rather than lenis, with its weakening to w most likely being a fairly recent development in Kawaiisu. Thus it is doubtful that we could validly posit for Proto Numic a variant of *-nak^{w}ayɨ with lenis k^w, and even if we could, it is hard to see how this form could give rise to both the highly conservative reflex nawayɨ and the drastically modified -noo, even within the same daughter (Kawaiisu). Deriving *-'noo from *-nak^{w}ayɨ rather than from *-na-w(i) would also make it difficult or impossible to relate Numic *-'noo to Proto Cahuilla-Cupeno *-nəw(i), which is reflected in Cupeno by -nəw and in Cahuilla by the doublets -new and -niw. I am suggesting, then, that the contrast in Takic between the Serrano postposition -nuk (< *-nak^{w}ayɨ) and P-CAC *-nə-w(i) (< *na-w(i)) is matched in Numic by the contrast between a postpositional reflex of *-nak^{w}ayɨ, which was lost, and *-'noo

Apart from NP p<u>i</u>i-'noo 'with/also', two kinds of reflexive pronouns based on p<u>i</u>i are found in Western Numic. p<u>i</u>i combines with ='su to form an emphatic pronoun that, in Mono at least, has taken on reflexive use as well in conjunction with the verb prefix <u>na</u>-:

> M (2) p<u>i</u>i='su na-yawi-'ti
>   REFL REFL-laugh-TNS
>   'He's laughing at himself.'   (M-L-G-180)

> M (3) p<u>i</u>i='su ?a-hipi
>   REFL   it-drink
>   'Drink it yourself!'   (M-L-G-388)

> NP (4) p<u>i</u>i='su mia-u   ?isa?a
>   REFL go-PNCT coyote
>   'Coyote went.'   (NP-AF-N-335)

In both languages, p<u>i</u>i combines with the word for 'one' (NP s<u>i</u>?m<u>i</u>, M s<u>i</u>?<u>i</u>) to yield a form meaning 'alone'. The fact that 'one' can also be used in this fashion without p<u>i</u>i in Northern Paiute may indicate that p<u>i</u>i was a secondary incorporation in this construction:

> M (5) p<u>i</u>i-'s<u>i</u>?<u>i</u>-'ki'ma-'ti
>   <u>REFL-one-</u>come-TNS
>   alone
>   'came alone'   (M-L-G-69)

> NP (6) n<u>i</u> s<u>i</u>?m<u>i</u> ki'ma
>   I   one   come
>   'I came alone.'   (NP-AF-N-333)

If P-WNM *s<u>i</u>?m<u>i</u> 'one' could mean 'alone', and if the emphatic reflexive pronoun *p<u>i</u>i still retained some vestige of the original 'by oneself' meaning of the locative reflexive pronoun from which it is claimed to derive, there is nothing surprising about the combination of the two as *p<u>i</u>i-s<u>i</u>?m<u>i</u> 'alone', which amounts to a kind of reduplication to intensify the meaning, literally something like 'by himself alone'.

In Shoshoni, both *p<u>i</u>- and *p<u>i</u>-'noo have taken on reflexive possessor use. The former is proclitic to the possessed noun, like other possessor

---

(< *<u>na-w(i)</u>), which displaced it.

    The daughter forms I have related to *<u>na-w(i)</u> deserve more careful scrutiny than I am able to give them here. For one thing, the postposition *-<u>w(i)</u> (based on CA -<u>niw</u>, Y -<u>w(i)</u>, A -<u>wi-k</u> among others) is probably to be regarded as the lenited variant of *-<u>mi</u> 'to/toward' (cf. NP -<u>tami</u> 'toward', SP -<u>mi</u> 'direction', TU -<u>mii-k</u> 'toward', H -<u>mi</u> 'to') on the basis of the *<u>m</u>/*<u>w</u> alternation established in section 3.3.2. It is also possible that *-<u>w(a)</u> figures in some of these forms instead of *-<u>w(i)</u>, where *-<u>w(a)</u> could reflect *-<u>ma</u> or *-k^wa as well as *-<u>wa</u>. Further discussion must await detailed reconstruction of the P-UA postpositional system.

elements of the language. Sometimes the possessor reflexive co-occurs with the reflexive verb prefix na-.

SH (7) cuku'pɨ'ci pɨ'nɨ k^{w}ɨh-i   waci^{n}kɨ-'nu
          old   REFL wife-ACC lose-PERF
          man
          'The old man lost his (own) wife.'   (SH-M-IN-3)

SH (8) su-'tɨ   te'na-pɨʔɨ pɨɨ=^{n}tɨhɨɨyaa na-ʔu'tu-^{n}tɨ
          that-NOM man-ABS REFL-deer   REFL-give-PROG

          su-'ka   wai-'pɨʔ-a
          that-ACC woman-ABS-ACC
          'That man is giving his own deer to that woman.'
          (SH-D-PMS-61)

pɨɨ can be used regardless of the number of the possessor. pɨ'nɨ (< *pɨ-'noo) on the other hand, is restricted to singular possessors; pɨhɨ is used in the dual, and pɨ'mɨ in the plural. These expanded forms have clearly developed by analogy to the non-reflexive possessor pronouns. In the second person, for example, the singular, dual, and plural possessor pronouns are ʔɨ'nɨ, mɨhɨ, and mɨ'mɨ respectively (SH-M-NN-20).

Shoshoni displays an elaborate set of non-possessive reflexive pronouns. These are given in Table VIII (SH-D-PMS-82, 83).[17] (Note that the third person possessor forms are essentially the same as the non-possessor forms except that they lack the final syllable.) This paradigm is basically regular. Moreover, it accords quite well with those of the non-reflexive subject and object pronouns. In particular, nɨ is the regular first person non-inclusive form; ta the regular inclusive base; ^{h}wɨ (or some close

		DL		PL	
	SG	INCL	EXCL	INCL	EXCL
1P	nɨ-sɨ-sɨ	ta-^{h}wɨ-sɨ	nɨ-sɨ-sɨ	ta-'mɨ-^{n}sɨ	nɨ-'mɨ-^{n}sɨ
2P	ʔɨ-'nɨ-^{n}sɨ	mɨ-^{h}wɨ-sɨ		mɨ-'mɨ-^{n}sɨ	
3P	pɨ-'nɨ-^{n}sɨ	pɨ-^{h}wɨ-sɨ		pɨ-'mɨ-^{n}sɨ	

Table VIII

[17] The set is still more elaborate than shown in the table. For the third person, an alternate system lacking the final syllable -sɨ has evolved; it is inflected for singular/dual/plural and also for nominative/accusative/genitive (SH-M-NN-20). These inflections also follow those of the non-reflexive pronominal paradigms quite closely, so it is reasonable to assume that the forms all developed from the original base pɨɨ. I have no detailed information concerning their syntactic and semantic properties.

variant thereof) the dual marker; 'mɨ the plural marker; and ʔɨ and mɨ the second person singular and non-singular forms. The only real irregularity in the set is the occurrence of nɨ-sɨ-sɨ in two of the first person slots instead of the expected nɨ-'nɨ-^{n}sɨ and nɨ-^{h}wɨ-sɨ. This we may attribute to assimilatory influence of the third syllable on the second.

I will claim that this entire paradigm grew out of the single early Shoshoni form *pɨ-'noo='su. It was modeled on the non-reflexive pronominal paradigms, which explains why it incorporates the same elements as these. By claiming that the paradigm represents an innovation, we account both for its regularity (there has not been sufficient time for elaborate restructuring to take place) and for the lack of such a paradigm for the reflexive pronouns of other languages. This analysis also explains the origin of the elements 'nɨ and (^{n})sɨ in various forms of the paradigm--they derive from *-'noo and *='su respectively. The development of *pɨ-'noo='su to pɨ-'nɨ-^{n}sɨ involves little more than vowel harmonization, and one or both of these elements was retained in each form of the set as the paradigm was elaborated, in order to preserve the trisyllabic model of the original.

3.4.2. Takic

We have already dealt with the Takic descendants of *-nak^{w}ayɨ, which are basically locative and emphatic. The Takic languages use another reflexive pronoun, based on the form for 'person', for the reflexive and reciprocal functions. This pronoun has taken over the role formerly played by the reflexive and reciprocal verb prefixes, which were lost in Takic.

Specifically, we can reconstruct for Proto Takic a reflexive pronoun consisting of a possessor prefix plus *-taqa (< *-taka). The q of *-taqa spirantizes to x in the Cupan languages, and the Serrano form -taqa is sometimes recorded as -taxa. I will mention only in passing a possessive construction in Cora that uses a similar form, -itax. This form combines with the reflexive possessor prefix ru- as follows:

CR (1) k^{w}atas   ru-itax
      sp. flower own-?
      'their own kwatas flowers'   (CR-P-G-27)

The similarity is suggestive but most likely fortuitous. I have nothing of substance to say about the syntax or the origin of this Cora construction.

It will be recalled from Chapter 1 that the Takic reflexive pronouns
sometimes involve more than POSSR-tax. Oblique expressions incorporating a postposition are attested in Serrano and Cahuilla and should perhaps
be reconstructed for Proto Takic.

      SR (2) pɨɨ-taxa-ika
                   their-self-to
                   'to one another'   (SR-H-G-120)

      CA (3) tax-ŋa
                   self-on
                   'on themselves'   (CA-H-BSK-46)

Cahuilla tax- has been incorporated as a verb prefix, and even when it is
not a verb prefix it lacks the possessor prefix characteristic of the other
languages, as shown by (3).[18] Possible instances of a plural and an absolutive form of tax have also been noted in Cahuilla.

One problem which came up in conjunction with the oblique reflexive
pronoun construction in Cahuilla is resolved when we look at further Cupan
data, only to give way to a broader problem. The problem concerned sentences like (4), in which the postposition appears to be -wika instead of the
expected -ika (cf. (2)).

      CA (4) ne-qiʔ tax-wika ne-kuktaš-qa
                 my-self self-to   I-talk-DUR
                 'I'm talking to myself.'   (CA-B-IN)

The status of the extra w is solved when we note that the reflexive pronoun
always takes the suffix -wi in Cupeno, and that the ending -w is also attested in Luiseno:

      CU (5) čəm-tax-wi
                   our-self-POSSD
                   'ourselves/one another'   (CUP-H-SCD-50)

      L (6) supul=up čam-taxa-w loʔxa-lut
               one-he   our-self-? do-gonna
               'One of ourselves is gonna do it.'   (L-KG-SG-101)

These examples make it evident that taxwika should be segmented as tax-
w-ika rather than tax-wika, and that the sequence *POSSR-taxa(-wi) can be
reconstructed for Proto Cupan. But now we are faced with the problem of

---

    [18]The lack of a possessor prefix in (3) and similar examples may be some indication
that the tax-P construction of Cahuilla does not in fact derive from an oblique reflexive
pronoun construction of P-TAK but is rather innovative. The loss of the possessor prefix is a natural consequence of incorporating the reflexive pronoun in the verb, and if
the oblique construction represents a subsequent innovation, it could be expected to con-
tinue the non-possessed pattern.

identifying *-wi.

Hill identifies Cupeno -wi as a rare suffix attached to possessed nouns
(CU-HN-M-124). Several things make this analysis plausible. First,
Cupeno does have a series of suffixes, including -ki, -ʔa, and -kiʔa, that
accompany possessed nouns (CU-H-G-63), so all the analysis requires is
the addition of -wi to this set. Next, (7) seems to corroborate the existence of a possessed suffix -wi in Cupeno.

      CU (7) pə-xutax-wi
              his-back-POSSD
              'his back'   (CU-HN-M-124)

Finally, a possessed suffix involving -w recurs in various Uto-Aztecan
languages, Luiseno for example:

      L (8) no-paa-w
             my-water-POSSD
             'my water'   (L-H-I-138)

Nevertheless, I believe there are grounds for doubting the validity of
this analysis. It should be made clear that these doubts pertain only to the
analysis of *-wi as a possessed suffix at the level of Proto Cupan; they do
not necessarily reflect on the adequacy of the analysis in modern Cupeno,
which is all that Hill was concerned with. If Cupeno -wi does in fact function as a possessed suffix, this use probably represents a Cupeno innovation to bring -wi into line with the other possessed suffixes of the language.

The first point to be made is that the possessed suffixes in other Uto-
Aztecan languages point to *-wa rather than *-wi. This appears to be the
case in Cahuilla:[19]

      CA (9) ne-paʔ-wa
              my-water-POSSD
              'my water'   (CA-B-IN)

*-wa is definitely indicated by Northern Tepehuan -ga (g < *w) and Yaqui
-wa:

      NT (10) bavi-ga-dɨ
               bean-POSSD-his
               'his own beans'   (PMC-B-PT-61)

---

[19]The ʔ in (9) is probably intrusive. In the absence of more extensive data and a
careful analysis, not too much weight should be put on this Cahuilla example, which
may be susceptible to alternative treatments.

Y (11) ʔa-tami-wa-m
        his-tooth-POSSD-PL
        'his teeth'   (Y-F-YP-13)

The possessed suffix is -wi in the Matlapa dialect of Nahuatl, but it is -wa
in the Tetelcingo dialect, -w in Classical Nahuatl, and in general it is correct to say that there is little or no evidence for reconstructing *-wi in this
capacity.

Rare affixes tend to be archaic, so we become suspicious when they do
not readily articulate with similar affixes in related languages, which is
the case with the putative possessed suffix -wi in Cupeno. Cupeno -wi is
even more suspicious in view of the fact that I have seen it cited only with
the reflexive -tax and the noun xutax 'back', which bears a striking resemblance to -tax. Furthermore, lexical evidence from other languages indicates strongly that xutax can be decomposed into xu and tax, with xu itself
meaning 'back'; Miller justifies P-UA *ho 'back' and establishes hu as a
form for 'back' in Cahuilla (UA-M-CS-18). There seems little doubt, then,
that xutax 'back' derives from a compound of some kind involving xu 'back'
and tax 'person/body', the latter being the same noun on which reflexive
pronouns are formed. The fact that xutax takes the suffix -wi when possessed is then a direct consequence of the fact that tax takes -wi and cannot be
regarded as independent evidence for a possessed suffix of this shape in
terms of which we can explain the -wi found in reflexive pronouns. Synchronically -wi may be a possessed suffix in (7), but diachronically (7) only
shows that the reflexive noun tax takes -wi, which is the very observation
we are trying to account for.

What, then, is the source of *-wi in the P-CUP *POSSR-taxa(-wi) construction? Several possibilities suggest themselves, and I must be content
to outline them without attempting to arrive at a final decision. One possibility is that *-wi is none other than the postposition *-w(i) previously discussed. *-nəw(i) was reconstructed for Proto Cahuilla-Cupeno, and it can
be projected back to Proto Cupan and beyond, ultimately deriving from
*na-wi. Since the reciprocal *na was lost in Takic, and was in effect re-
placed by *taxa, the innovation of *taxa-wi parallel to *na-wi is certainly
not out of the question. -w(i) has of course lost its postpositional status if
this derivation is correct.

Hill herself provides a clue to a second possibility in another context. She notes the existence of a suffix -wi used to form derived nouns, as in (12) and (13). She glosses this suffix 'person' (CU-H-G-221).

CU (12) kəwi-kə-wi-š
west-from-person-ABS
'Luiseno/person from the west'   (CU-H-G-221)

CU (13) məm-ŋəx-wi-š
ocean-from-person-ABS
'white man/person from the ocean'   (CU-H-G-221)

Similar derived forms are found in Luiseno:[20]

L (14) paala-ŋa-wi-š
PN-from-person-ABS
'person from Pala'   (L-L-FN)

If -wi does in fact mean 'person', it is not at all implausible to claim that this is the element optionally added to *POSSR- taxa in Proto Cupan. *-taxa itself means 'person/body', and the addition of another morpheme with the same sense could serve a reinforcing function, just as in the derivation of P-WNM *pɨɨ-sɨʔmɨ 'by himself alone'.

Relating *-wi to forms for 'person' in other Uto-Aztecan languages is possible but problematic. Miller does in fact reconstruct *tewi 'person/ people' (UA-M-CS-45), but this reconstruction is based only on Cora tebi and Huichol tewi. Other reconstructed forms for 'man/person' include *taka, *tawa, and *ta(na), which point to *ta as the basic root. Possibly *tawa and *tewi both derive from *ta-wi, the former by vowel harmonization and the latter by umlaut, but this still leaves the origin and semantic value of *-wi to be accounted for, as well as its relation to the *-wi of P-CUP *taxa-wi.

Another hypothesis is that P-CUP *-wi did mean 'person' but that this element originally meant something else and acquired the meaning 'person' by a subtle reanalysis of the forms containing it. As (12) - (14) indicate, derived nominals containing *-wi virtually always mean something like 'that which comes from N', where N is the root, and normally they designate people. Also relevant is the fact that the absolutive suffix often serves a nominalizing function in Uto-Aztecan. It is possible, then, that *-wi

---

[20]Not all of the segmentations and glosses in (12) - (14) can necessarily be justified synchronically. For example, Luiseno ŋawi is probably now a single morpheme. A good case can however be made for their diachronic validity.

originally meant 'come', with the absolute suffix contributing the sense
'person who'. This construction could then undergo the reanalysis sketched
in (15).

(15) N - ka - wi - š   N - ka - wi - š
   from come ABS > from person ABS
      ('person who')

That is, speakers reinterpreted expressions meaning literally 'person who
comes from N' as meaning 'person who is from N'; 'be' is unlexicalized in
this reinterpretation, as it often is, and <u>wi</u> shifted in sense from 'come' to
'person', picking up this sense from the absolutive suffix (or from the semantic value of the derivational pattern).

 Can we now relate *-<u>wi</u> to some broader cognate set roughly meaning
'come'? Here there are two possibilities. There is an irregular verb <u>wic</u>
'come' in Classical Nahuatl. Moreover, <u>wi</u> also functions as a recurrent
element in the paradigms of the two basic motion verbs in Classical
Nahuatl, one meaning 'come' and the other 'go'; the history of these two
verbs is obviously complex, but a good case can be made for assigning <u>wi</u>
the meaning 'come' (A-C-CG). Of the two possibilities, I definitely find
this the more plausible. The second possibility is to relate *-<u>wi</u> to the
well-established P-UA stem *<u>nɨ mi</u> 'live/wander' (UA-M-CS-44). The fact
that the medial <u>m</u> in this form has been lenited to <u>w</u> in Western Numic to
yield <u>nɨ wi</u> (UA-C-ODA-183) makes this analysis at least worth considering.
<u>nɨ</u> could easily be lost in a complex derived form, and the Luiseno could
very well be considered by the Cupeno to be 'ones who wander from the
west'.

3.4.3. Classical Nahuatl

 The Aztec reflexive pronoun construction <u>POSSR-noʔma</u> does not look
very much like any of the others we have encountered.

  A (1) to-noʔma
      our-REFL
      'we ourselves' (A-R-AM-18)

  A (2) no-noʔma ni-k-no-maka
      my-REFL I-it-myself-give
      'I give it to <u>myself</u>.' (A-S-DLN-311)

It does however bear certain resemblances to other kinds of elements in

Aztec and other languages. no- is the same as the first person singular
possessor prefix in Classical Nahuatl (also the reflexive 'myself'), and ma
is the stem for 'hand'; no-ma thus means 'my hand'. Interestingly enough,
Luiseno combines expressions like these with the postposition -ŋay 'from'
to indicate causation:[21]

L (3) xʷaan po-ma-ŋay   mariya ŋee-q
      PN   his-hand-from PN   leave-PRES
      'Juan made Maria leave.'   (L-L-FN)

L (4) yuuyi-t   po-ma-ŋay   mariya ŋee-ŋi
      snow-ABS its-hand-from PN   RDP-leave
                                     PAST
      'Maria left because of the snow.'   (L-L-FN)

A construction such as this could perfectly well give rise to an emphatic
reflexive pronoun; note the effective equivalence between 'I myself did it'
and 'I did it by/from my (own) hand'.

I will propose that this is indeed the origin of -noʔma. We can reconstruct earlier expressions of the form *POSSR-ma-P, where the postposition meant something like 'from' or 'with'. Since the first person singular
was no doubt one of the most frequently used forms in this emphatic reflexive construction, the possessor prefix no- 'my' and ma could easily have
been reanalyzed as a reflexive pronoun, as in (5).

(5) no-ma-P   >   noma-P
    my hand from   REFL from
        REFL

Once this reanalysis had occurred, the expression no longer bore any
special relation to the first person singular, and possessor prefixes were
added again to make the reference more precise. The postposition was
eventually lost.

This analysis is strongly confirmed by the variant -noʔmatka. The added -tka is transparently the same as -ti-ka; -ka is a postposition meaning
'with/from', and -ti- is a connective used to join this and other postpositions to nouns:

A (6) lienso-ti-ka
      bandage-CONN-with
      'with a bandage'   (A-DA-FC10-161)

-noʔmatka is thus the unreduced (or only partially reduced) version of the

---

[21]A similar construction is found in Cupeno: pə-ma-ŋax (his-hand-from) 'for his
sake' (CUP-H-SCD-37).

structure posited above. We have the development *-no$^?$ma-ti-ka >
-no$^?$ma-t-ka > -no$^?$ma, with the second reduction being optional.[22]

The other reflexive pronoun of Classical Nahuatl, POSSR-ne$^?$wiyaan,
has emphatic and possessor uses.

  A (7) no-ne$^?$wiyaan
          my-REFL
          'I myself'   (A-S-DLN-307)

  A (8) no-ne$^?$wiyaan no-ƛaƛakol
          my-REFL   my-fault
          'my own fault'   (A-S-DLN-307)

The components of this pronoun are most likely ne$^?$ 'I', -wi 'to/at', and
-yaan 'place of', all of which exist independently with these meanings.[23]
I will forgo a detailed derivation pending fuller investigation of these and
related forms (the similarity to nowiyaan 'everywhere' is suggestive),
noting only that a reanalysis similar to the one posited above for -no$^?$ma
is likely, with the first person singular ne$^?$ being incorporated in the reflexive base and losing its original meaning.

3.5.   Evolution

3.5.1.   Proto Uto-Aztecan

   There were two P-UA reflexive pronouns formed on the base *-nak^{w}ayɨ.
*$^?$a-nak^{w}ayɨ was reciprocal, and *pɨ-nak^{w}ayɨ was locative and possibly
also emphatic. *-nak^{w}ayɨ probably had *-nakoyɨ as a phonetic variant.

   Extensive modifications affected this system in the daughter languages.

   I3.5.1.1/CD3.5.1.1. Both pronouns were lost completely in P-CCH
and P-AZN.

---

[22] A somewhat more speculative version of this hypothesis could explain the $^?$ in
-no$^?$ma. The original form of this construction may have been *no-ma-ka 'from my
hand', directly parallel to Luiseno no-ma-ŋay. *-ka, being word-final, reduced to
*-k and then *-$^?$ (for *k > $^?$ in Aztec, cf. UA-S-SPN2-324-325), which was later dis-
placed to medial position. The variant -no$^?$matka then arose by the addition of -ti-ka
to relexicalize the meaning component 'from', which speakers no longer recognized in
the displaced $^?$.
   The basic correctness of this overall analysis is confirmed by the existence of another version of the reflexive pronoun, -matika, attested in early colonial documenta-
tion: moči $^?$oo-ki-k^{w}i-k $^?$i-ma-ti-ka (all PERF-it-take-PAST his-hand-CONN-from)
'He took it all for himself' (A-ABL-BC). These early texts, which represent dialects
other than that codified as Classical Nahuatl, also show an apparent reflexive pronoun
use of seel 'only/alone', itself based on the root for 'one': ma ki-čiiwa-kaan $^?$iin-seel-
tin (EXHRT it-do-PL their-self-PL) 'Let them do it themselves' (A-ABL-BC).

[23] I am identifying -wi with the first component of -wi-k 'toward/against'.

I3.5.1.2. Reflexive pronouns of the form *POSSR-noˀma(tka) and
*POSSR-neˀwiyaan were innovated in P-AZN. (Pertinent data from PO is
lacking, so possibly these innovations took place in A rather than at the
P-AZN stage.)

I3.5.1.3. *ˀa-nakoyɨ simplified to *ˀanako in P-TRC. Also,
*pɨ-nakoyɨ became *bɨ-nakoyɨ by regular sound change. (Attestation is
only in TA.)

I3.5.1.4. *-nakoyɨ simplified to *-hoyɨ in P-PMC, through loss of *na
and spirantization of medial k; the spirantization of k to h is an innovation
shared by NP, H, TU, and TA (CD3.5.1.2). Through vowel harmonization,
*pɨ-hoyɨ became *pɨhɨyɨ and *ˀa-hoyɨ became *ˀahayɨ. The former re-
sulted in hɨjɨl through regular sound changes, loss of the initial syllable,
and incorporation of final l (whose origin is not definitely known). The
latter simplified to ˀaˀay. The forms are attested only for P.

I3.5.1.5/CD3.5.1.3. *ˀa-nakoyɨ simplified to *nakoyɨ in P-NUM and
H. In H this became *nahoyɨ (CD3.5.1.2) and then nahoy.

I3.5.1.6/CD3.5.1.4. The clitic *='su 'just/precisely' was commonly
used with reflexive constructions in P-NUM.

I3.5.1.7/CD3.5.1.5. *pɨ-nak^{w}ayɨ was lost in TU and H.

I3.5.1.8. In TU, *ˀa-nakoyɨ became *ˀa-nahoyɨ (CD3.5.1.2) and was
further reduced by various phonetic processes to *ˀomohy, which may still
be valid as a phonological representation. The postpositions *-c and -p
were incorporated to form more specialized reciprocal and locative reflexive pronouns.

I3.5.1.9. In H, naa-p was innovated (or possibly retained) as an emphatic reflexive.

I3.5.1.10/CD3.5.1.6. *ˀa-nak^{w}ayɨ was lost in P-TAK.

I3.5.1.11/CD3.5.1.7. *POSSR-taqa was innovated as a reflexive and
reciprocal pronoun in P-TAK.

I3.5.1.12/CD3.5.1.8. In P-TAK, *-nak^{w}ayɨ could be used with pronouns for all persons. The first person singular form *nɨ-nak^{w}ayɨ simplified by haplology, yielding the variants *nɨ-k^{w}ayɨ and *nak^{w}ayɨ.

3.5.2. Proto Numic

P-NUM had the reflexive pronouns *nakoyɨ and *pɨ-nak^wayɨ. It retained the *na-P construction, and *-'noo 'with' was one postposition that could participate in this construction. The clitic *='su 'just/precisely' tended to combine with reflexive expressions. This system derives from the P-UA system by means of changes I3.5.1.5 and I3.5.1.6.

I3.5.2.1/CD3.5.2.1. In P-WNM and SH, *pɨ-nak^wayɨ was reanalyzed as a *REFL-P sequence, giving *pɨ the value of a reflexive pronoun, which came to be used independently.

I3.5.2.2/CD3.5.2.2. In P-WNM and SH, the postposition *-nak^wayɨ (cf. I3.5.2.1) was lost; *-'noo 'with' replaced it to yield the sequence *pɨ-'noo, parallel to *na-'noo.

I3.5.2.3. *na-'noo was lost in SH and also in M, a non-immediate daughter of P-NUM (CD3.5.2.3). The entire *na-P construction was evidently lost in SH.

I3.5.2.4. In SH, the new reflexive pronoun *pɨ was extended to possessor use. It and *pɨ-'noo='su were elaborated into full paradigmatic sets on the model of the non-reflexive pronouns.

I3.5.2.5/CD3.5.2.4. In P-WNM, *pɨ combined with *sɨ?mɨ 'one' to form the new reflexive pronoun *pɨɨ-'sɨ?mɨ 'alone'.

I3.5.2.6/CD3.5.2.5. In P-SNM, *pɨ-nak^wayɨ was reanalyzed as a *POSSR-REFL sequence; that is, *pɨ- was taken to be a (reflexive) possessor prefix, and *-nak^wayɨ a reflexive noun (analogous to English self). *pɨ- then became an enclitic as part of the general SNM change to the use of enclitics for possessor pronouns.

I3.5.2.7. The clitic ='su achieved reflexive value in P-SNM by virtue of its regular occurrence in the sequence *na-'noo='su (CD3.5.2.6). This sequence shifted from reciprocal to locative/emphatic value (CD3.5.2.7).

I3.5.2.8/CD3.5.2.8. The reciprocal pronoun *nakoyɨ was lost in M (a non-immediate daughter of P-NUM), SH, and P-SNM.

3.5.3. Proto Western Numic

P-WNM had the reflexive pronouns *pɨɨ-'noo and *pɨɨ='su; the reciprocal pronouns *na-noo and *nakoyɨ; and the form *pɨɨ-'sɨ?mɨ 'alone'. This system descends from that of P-NUM by changes 1, 2, and 5 of set I3.5.2.

I3.5.3.1. *pɨɨ-'noo was evidently lost in M, as were *na-noo (CD3.5.2.3) and *nakoyɨ (CD3.5.2.8).

I3.5.3.2. *nakoyɨ in NP became *nahoyɨ (CD3.5.1.2) and then nahoy.

3.5.4. Proto Southern Numic

P-SNM had a locative/emphatic reflexive pronoun *na-'noo='su, an emphatic reflexive clitic *='su, and the reflexive/reciprocal construction *nak^{w}ayɨ=POSSR. This resulted from the P-NUM system through changes 6-8 of set I3.5.2.

I3.5.4.1. *nak^{w}ayɨ=POSSR was lost in SP, though =pɨ was retained as a reflexive possessor clitic.

I3.5.4.2. SP *na-'noo='su narrowed to emphatic value. The postposition *-p(a) was incorporated for oblique forms, and an accusative form was also innovated.

I3.5.4.3. In K, the lenis variant of k^w, namely w, was adopted in *nak^{w}ayɨ, yielding nawayɨ. By influence of the reflexive prefixes, the variant nɨwayɨ was innovated and eventually became the preferred variant.

3.5.5. Proto Takic

P-TAK had a reflexive/reciprocal pronoun construction *POSSR-taqa. In addition there was a reflexive pronoun series based on *pɨ-nak^{w}ayɨ, which had locative, emphatic, and possibly possessor value. In the first person singular of this series, the reduced forms *nɨ-k^{w}ayɨ and *nak^{w}ayɨ coexisted. Changes 10-12 of set I3.5.1 are responsible for deriving the P-TAK system from that of P-UA.

I3.5.5.1. In SR, the variant *nak^{w}ayɨ won out in the first person singular and evolved phonetically to nowk(ɨ). *pɨ-nak^{w}ayɨ evolved to pɨ-nuk, and in other persons, where the pronoun base ended in m, -nuk simplified to -uk.

I3.5.5.2. In P-CUP, the *nɨ-k^{w}ayɨ variant won out in the first person singular, and the reflexive pronoun paradigm was then regularized, yielding *PRON-k^{w}ayɨ in all persons (CD3.5.5.1). *-k^{w}ayɨ evolved phonetically to *-qay (CD3.5.5.2).

I3.5.5.3/CD3.5.5.3.   *POSSR-taqa became P-CUP *POSSR-taxa(-wi) through spirantization of q and the optional incorporation of *-wi (of uncertain origin).

3.5.6.   Proto Cupan

The reflexive pronouns of P-CUP included *POSSR-taxa(-wi), with reflexive and reciprocal use, and *PRON-qay, with locative, emphatic, and probably possessor use. This system derives from the P-TAK system by changes 2 and 3 of set I3.5.5.

I3.5.6.1/CD3.5.6.1.   *-qay changed to *-qi in P-CAC.

I3.5.6.2.   *-qay became -xay in L.

3.5.7.   Proto Cahuilla-Cupeno

P-CAC had the reflexive/reciprocal pronoun *POSSR-tax(-wi) and the locative/emphatic pronoun *PRON-qi. I3.5.6.1 is the only substantial change in the evolution of this system from that of P-CUP.

I3.5.7.1.   In CA, tax- was incorporated as a verb prefix; the POSSR -tax construction was lost.

I3.5.7.2.   The inclusion of -wi in the reflexive pronoun became obligatory in CU.

3.5.8.   Proto Pimic

The P-PMC system consisted of the reflexive pronoun *hɨ̆jɨl and the reciprocal pronoun *ʔaʔay and derives from the P-UA system through I3.5.1.4. Since hɨ̆jɨl and ʔaʔay are attested only in P, we cannot be sure how much of the evolution described in I3.5.1.4 had taken place by P-PMC times.

3.5.9.   Proto Taracahitic

The P-TRC system is attested only through TA. It consisted of the reflexive pronoun *bɨnakoyɨ and the reciprocal pronoun *ʔanako. Change I3.5.1.3 derives this system from that of P-UA.

I3.5.9.1.   *bɨnakoyɨ became *binakoyi by regular sound change and

then *binahoyi by spirantization of k̲ (CD3.5.1.2). Other phonetic processes yield binoy.

I3.5.9.2.   *ʔanako evolved phonetically to ʔanagu.

I3.5.9.3.   ʔaboy was innovated as the plural counterpart of binoy.

I3.5.9.4.   The postposition -po̲ was optionally added to the reflexive
and reciprocal pronouns.

These forms were presumably lost in Y.

3.5.10.   Proto Aztecan

P-AZN had no reflexive pronouns directly descended from P-UA (cf.
I3.5.1.1). The reflexive pronouns *POSSR-noʔma(tka) and
*POSSR-neʔwiyaan are found in A (I3.5.1.2), but it is not clear whether
they were innovated at the P-AZN stage or only in A.

IV. UNSPECIFIED ARGUMENT PREFIXES

4.0.   Introduction

Non-distinct argument affixes combine and generalize two functions, that of marking coreferential arguments and that of marking unspecified arguments. Specifically reflexive prefixes serve the former function and were dealt with in Chapter 2. In this chapter we will examine those prefixes which serve the latter function.

We saw earlier that reflexive prefixes are often extended to passive use. This constitutes a generalization in function of the prefix, as shown in Figure IX (N_1 and N_2 are the subject and direct object respectively).

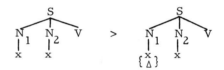

Figure IX

Instead of marking only clauses in which the subject and object are coreferential, the prefix comes to mark clauses in which the subject and object are non-distinct, coreference being a special case of non-distinctness. When N_2 substitutes for an unspecified N_1 and functions as the surface subject, the resulting sentence meets our definition of a passive.

The notion of non-distinct arguments does not in itself require that it be the subject rather than the object that is unspecified. Our formulation of this notion therefore implicitly predicts the possibility of a reflexive prefix undergoing the generalization shown in Figure X as an alternative to the one in Figure IX.

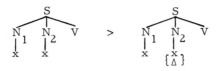

Figure X

Precisely this development seems to have taken place in Huichol, where reflexive prefixes indicate an unspecified object, at least with certain stems:

HU (1) we- p- te- yu- ka- naaki?eeri
         they- ASSR- DISTR- REFL- down- love
                          PL
         'They love.'   (HU- G- S- 96)

The correctness of this prediction has a number of implications. First, it further supports the notion of non- distinct arguments as a significant one meriting inclusion in linguistic theory. Second, it indicates that the usefulness of the notion is not inherently tied to passive constructions. The common denominator in Figures IX and X is the equivalence between a coreferential argument and an unspecified argument, and this equivalence can hold with respect to either subject or object. Passivization is not involved in (1) or in Figure X, and in Figure IX it is only secondarily involved, resulting from a cross- linguistic tendency for specified nominals to replace unspecified subjects in surface structure.[1]

The third implication is that it is not sufficient, in describing the use of a morpheme, to state that it indicates non- distinctness of the subject and object. For example, the reflexive prefixes in Aztec can mark the situation in Figure IX but not that in Figure X, while the converse is true of the reflexive prefixes in Huichol. Therefore we must specify whether a morpheme marking non- distinct arguments has "subject focus" or "object focus". The Aztec reflexive prefixes have subject focus, since they require that the subject be either unspecified or coreferential to the object. The Huichol reflexive prefixes have object focus, since they require that the object be either unspecified or coreferential to the subject.

The final implication pertains to syntactic change. A specifically reflexive prefix (one that requires coreference rather than non- distinctness) is ambivalent in regard to subject and object focus. We normally conceive of

---

[1]Cf. Ronald W. Langacker, 'Movement Rules in Functional Perspective', *Language* 50. 630-664, 1974.

such a prefix as requiring that the object be coreferential to the subject,
but we could also view it as requiring that the subject be coreferential to
the object; that we typically do not is probably due to the fact that it is virtually always the subject which is lexicalized in reflexive clauses, but this
may only reflect the tendency for lexical content to surface in prominent
positions (see the reference in footnote 1). Because of this ambivalence,
reflexive prefixes could perfectly well evolve quite differently in two closely related languages, taking on unspecified subject function in one and unspecified object function in another. A prefix could also shift from marking
non-distinct arguments with subject focus to marking non-distinct arguments with object focus, perhaps passing through an intermediate stage
with narrowly reflexive function.

Just as the notion of non-distinct arguments predicts the possibility of
the developments shown in Figures IX and X, so it predicts the possible
changes shown in Figures XI and XII. That is, alongside the generalization
in function from marking coreferentiality to marking non-distinctness, we
would expect to encounter generalization in function from marking unspecificity to marking non-distinctness.

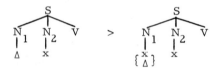

Figure XI

Figure XII

By and large this prediction is borne out. When we extend the notion of
non-distinct arguments so that it can hold, not only with respect to subject
and object of the same predicate, but also with respect to nominals in a
main and subordinate clause, a number of examples of generalization from
unspecificity to non-distinctness in Uto-Aztecan can be found. (One example is given in section 5.2.4; others are discussed in UA-LM-PM.) Moreover, the Tarahumara passive suffix -tu has been extended to reflexive use;

this is essentially the change depicted in Figure XI.[2] Uto-Aztecan provides
no examples of the change in Figure XII, however, where an unspecified
object prefix takes on reflexive use as well. Restricting our attention to
subject and object within the same clause, then, we find only one instance
of generalization from unspecificity to non-distinctness.

That this type of change did not occur more often in Uto-Aztecan is
probably due to the fact that these languages have always had other devices
available to mark reflexives, hence the generalization would be superfluous
in terms of marking reflexivization and would result in loss of precision in
terms of indicating unspecified arguments. In Tubatulabal and Takic, the
only well-documented languages where both the reciprocal *na- and the reflexive prefixes of P-UA disappeared, the unspecified argument prefixes of
P-UA were also lost. Thus there was probably never an instance in the
history of Uto-Aztecan where a reflexive or reciprocal prefix was lacking
with an unspecified argument prefix in existence which could fill the gap.
By contrast, we have seen that the extension of reflexive prefixes to passive use, as in Figure IX, correlates quite well in Uto-Aztecan with the
loss of the original passive suffix. Similarly, Huichol has lost the P-UA
unspecified argument prefixes, so the extension of the reflexive prefixes to
unspecified object use, as in Figure X, did not entail competition with an
existing unspecified object morpheme.

Of course, it is not quite fair to appeal to the competition or lack of
competition of other morphemes, for some morphemes probably disappear
because others invade their domain and eventually render them superfluous.
It may be merely a matter of chance that the developments in Figures XI
and XII are not more commonly attested in Uto-Aztecan (within the boundaries of a single clause). If it is not a matter of chance--that is, if such developments occur only with extraordinary infrequency in languages of the
world--we must explain this in some manner. One possibility is to posit a
hierarchy of "strength" among grammatical markers, claiming that reflexive markers are inherently stronger than unspecified argument markers
and can invade their domain, but not conversely; this would correlate with
the fact that reflexive markers are much more common cross-linguistically

---

[2] The extension of -tu to reflexive use was no doubt prompted by the loss of reflexive
prefixes in Tarahumara.

than unspecified argument markers. Another possibility would be to modi-
fy the notion of non-distinct arguments in some appropriate way to bring it
in line with the facts of language change.

In any event, I think it would be a mistake to reject out of hand the possible relevance of the presence or absence of competition from other morphemes, given how frequently this notion appears to be useful and how
little we really know about the dynamics of language change. The important
thing is that we not abuse the notion and that we bear in mind that competition with other morphemes is at best only one factor out of many that come
into play in determining the direction of change.

4.1.   Data

Of the twenty languages under primary consideration, ten have verb prefixes that clearly descend from P-UA prefixes whose primary function was
to indicate unspecified arguments. One such prefix is also attested in
Southern Tepehuan (PMC-B-PT-26). These prefixes and their functions
are listed in Table IX.[3]

Assuming that all of these prefixes belong in the set and that their function has been correctly labeled (the problematic cases will be discussed
subsequently), we can clearly reconstruct for P-UA the prefixes *ta-, *ti-,
and *ni-. With one exception, the daughter forms derive by means of regular sound changes. *i becomes e in Yaqui and Aztec, which accounts for
the vowel of ne- and te-. *t becomes λ before a in Classical Nahuatl, and
Papago t becomes č before high vowels, accounting for the only consonantal
changes. The only irregular development is the change of *i to u in the
Pimic languages. This may of course be posited for P-PMC.

I will mention only in passing the possibility of reconstructing a partitive
use for *ti-. A partitive use for this prefix is attested in Mono and
Tepecano, and it might be found in other languages given fuller information.
The partitive use of Luiseno -taxaw is also suggestive given the close relation established here between reflexive and unspecified argument constructions.

---

[3]The Southern Paiute prefix tii- 'well/thoroughly' possibly should be added to this
set: ti-ⁿti'ka-yi (well-eat-PRES) 'eats well/has a feast' (SP-S-G-101). A semantic
shift from marking unspecified objects to 'well/thoroughly' is not out of the question,
and none of the four examples Sapir cites has an explicit object.

M (1) ʔi-ʔa'po-na   nɨɨ tɨ-weni-tɨhɨ
       my-basket-ACC I   UNSPEC-sell-PRES
                       OBJ
       'I'm selling some of my baskets.'   (M-L-G-189)

TO (2) yam-haštu   n-iš-tu-kaʔ   ga-hoovit
       <u>NEG-something</u> I-AFF-UNSPEC-eat ART-zapote
          nothing   OBJ
       'I have never eaten zapotes.'   (TO-M-PL-379)

L (3) supul=up čam-taxaw loʔxa-lut
      one-he   our-self   do-gonna
      'One of ourselves is gonna do it.'   (L-KG-SG-101)

I am inclined to believe that P-UA *tɨ- did in fact have a partitive function, but this can hardly be verified with so little data.

NP	tɨ-	UNSPEC OBJ
M	tɨ-	UNSPEC OBJ
SH	ta-	UNSPEC SUBJ
	tɨ-	UNSPEC OBJ
	nɨɨ'-	PASS/REFL
K	nɨ-	REFL
H	tɨɨ-	UNSPEC OBJ
P	ta-	UNSPEC SUBJ
	ču-	UNSPEC OBJ
TO	tu-	UNSPEC OBJ
ST	tu-	UNSPEC OBJ
Y	ne-	UNSPEC H OBJ
PO	ta-	UNSPEC NH OBJ
A	ƛa-	UNSPEC NH OBJ
	te-	UNSPEC H OBJ
	ne-	UNSPEC H COREF SUBJ

Table IX

4.2.   *ta- and *tɨ-

There seems little doubt that *ta- marked unspecified subjects in Proto Uto-Aztecan while *tɨ- marked unspecified objects. This is the nature of the *ta-/*tɨ- contrast in both Numic and Pimic, two widely divergent sub-families. The distinction between human and non-human objects in Aztec is almost certainly secondary, since there is no indication of such a contrast in any other subfamily.

Granted the likelihood of this reconstruction, only two things remain: substantiating the functions of the reflexes of *ta- and *tɨ- as represented in Table IX, and determining the nature of the realignment of these prefixes in Aztecan. As it turns out, the function of the daughter prefixes is problematic only in Papago; for the other languages the data presented in Chapter 1 should be sufficient.

Papago ta- and ču- are highly restricted in their distribution, occurring primarily in a class of derived adjectives or adverbs. I have nothing of substance to say about the means by which this restricted distribution came about and will concentrate instead on the validity of Hale's claim (P-H-G-75) that ta- and ču- indicate unspecified subject and unspecified object respectively. (His terms are "indefinite agent" and "indefinite object".) His claim is almost certainly correct diachronically, and I believe it can probably be justified synchronically for Papago as well, but the semantic value of ta- and ču- is not at all straightforward in terms of surface structure, as it is in other languages. To determine their semantic value, we must try to sketch reasonable semantic representations for the derived forms in which they appear.

(1) and (2) exemplify the type of expressions in which ta- and ču- occur.

```
P  (1)  s-ta-ʔɨɨbida-m
         AFF-UNSPEC-fear-ADJR
              SUBJ
         'frightening'    (P-H-G-75)

P  (2)  s-ču-ʔɨɨbida-m
         AFF-UNSPEC-fear-ADJR
              OBJ
         'fearful'    (P-H-G-75)
```

Other forms with ta- are glossed as 'funny/laughter-inducing', 'worth seeing', and 'urine-inducing'. The corresponding forms with ču- are glossed as 'full of laughter', 'interested/always wanting to see things', and 'full of urine' (P-H-G-75, 132).

The designations unspecified subject and unspecified object are not appropriate for these expressions as a whole. For example, (1) may take a specified subject--it is not the subject of 'frightening' as a whole that is unspecified--and in (2) the unspecified object cannot be the object of 'fearful' as a whole, since (I presume) this adjective does not allow a direct object. It is much more reasonable to suppose that the unspecified subject and

object are the subject and object of the verb from which the adjective derives, not of the adjective per se. All of these expressions are semantically complex, and when we decompose them, the unspecified character of
the subject or object of the verb root becomes apparent. This approach
runs into difficulty with 'urine-inducing' and 'full of urine', since a verb
meaning 'have urine' or 'urinate' is most probably intransitive, but the
other three sets are straightforward.

The forms with <u>ta</u>- mean 'frightening', 'funny/laughter-inducing', and
'worth seeing'. The first two are causative in character; something
'frightening' has the property of 'causing one to fear it', and something
'funny' has the property of 'causing one to laugh (at it)'. If we let <u>x</u> stand
for the individual with the property in question, and Δ for an unspecified
argument, we can represent these properties as follows:

(3) x CAUSE [Δ FEAR x]

(4) x CAUSE [Δ LAUGH AT x]

The third example, 'worth seeing', is not causative, but it lends itself to a
similar interpretation:

(5) x WORTH [Δ SEE x]

In all three cases the unspecified argument is the subject of the root verb,
supporting the claim that <u>ta</u>- marks unspecified subjects.

The forms with <u>čŭ</u>- mean 'fearful', 'full of laughter', and 'interested/
always wanting to see things'. Here aspectual notions seem more important than any notion of causation, but the latter cannot definitely be excluded; for example, a 'fearful' person may be one who 'tends to fear things',
one who 'fears things habitually', or one who, at the present time, has the
property that 'something causes him to fear it'. The proper semantic representation might be ascertained by a careful examination of the usage of
these forms, or by better knowledge of the derivational process involved,
but for present purposes the choice is not terribly important, since any
obvious analysis leads to the same conclusion.

For sake of discussion, let us follow the hint contained in the gloss for
the third form and regard all three as habitual and non-causative in character.[4] Thus a person who is 'fearful' has the property that 'his fearing

[4]I do not wish to exclude the possibility that the semantic representations in (3) - (5)
might also require some aspectual specification.

something is habitual'; a person who is 'full of laughter' has the property
that 'his laughing at something is habitual'; and a person who is 'always
wanting to see things' has the property that 'his wanting to see something is
habitual'. These properties are sketched in (6)-(8).

(6) [x FEAR Δ] HAB

(7) [x LAUGH AT Δ] HAB

(8) [x WANT [x SEE Δ]] HAB

In all three cases the unspecified argument is the object of the root verb,
which supports the claim that čü- marks unspecified objects.

Naturally these representations cannot be taken too seriously without
fuller information. I assume that the examples which Hale cites fairly
portray the tendencies of derived adjectives with ta- and čü-, but I am in
no position to assess how consistently the contrast is maintained or to explain the genesis of problematic forms. Nevertheless I hope this discussion
does at least establish the plausibility, for purposes of grammatical reconstruction, of regarding ta- and čü- as marking unspecified subjects and objects respectively.

Let us turn now to Aztecan. Only ta- is attested for Pochutla, but since
this prefix stands for an unspecified object rather than an unspecified subject, it is fair to assume that the realignment of te- (< *tï-) and ta-/λa-
took place at the Proto Aztecan stage and was not confined to Classical
Nahuatl. Our question, then, is this: How did P-AZN *te- and *ta-, which
originally indicated unspecified object and subject respectively, come to
designate instead unspecified human and non-human objects?

The most obvious proposal is perhaps the following. Subjects tend to be
human in transitive clauses, while objects are more likely to be non-human
than subjects are, so on the basis of frequency, what originated as a sub-
ject/object contrast could easily be reinterpreted as a human/non-human
contrast. Unfortunately this proposal leads to the wrong results. It predicts that *ta- should be human and *te- non-human, but the reverse is
what we actually find. Thus we must look for some less obvious solution.
There are limits on our ability to explain language change; perhaps we
should aim only for description and not explanation, and in any event our
attempts at "explanation" must be viewed with some skepticism. In the
case at hand, however, we can at least hope to delimit the factors that

made change possible and helped to determine its direction.

I will hypothesize that the third unspecified argument prefix of Proto Aztecan, *ne-, was the instigating factor. This prefix is problematic in a number of ways, but two things seem fairly clear: it has subject focus, in the sense of section 4.0, and it indicates that the unspecified argument is human. Because *ne- and *te- have the same vowel and belong to the same highly limited population of unspecified argument prefixes in P-AZN, it is not unreasonable to suppose that one could influence the other.

Specifically, let me propose the two-step reanalysis indicated in (9); the prefixes are characterized in terms of what kind of unspecified argument they designate.

(9) ne- H SUBJ   ne- H SUBJ   ne- H SUBJ
     te- OBJ   >   te- H OBJ   >   te- H OBJ
     ta- SUBJ   ta- SUBJ   ta- NH OBJ

In the first step, *te- changes in value from marking any unspecified object to marking only unspecified human objects. This restriction to human objects is by analogy to the phonetically similar *ne-. The system which results is unstable for various reasons. *te- and *ta- were formerly in direct contrast along one parameter, subject versus object, but now the contrast mixes two parameters, holding between subject and human object. With *te- now restricted to human objects, there is no way to indicate an unspecified non-human object. These factors together with the similarity in form between *te- and *ta- triggered a second realignment, in which *ta- switched from subject to non-human object function. This restored the simple contrast between *te- and *ta- and provided a way to indicate unspecified non-human objects. *ta- could be spared from its unspecified subject function, since two other devices were available in the language to mark unspecified subjects, namely reflexive prefixes and passive/impersonal suffixes.

4.3.   *nɨ-

Only four reflexes of P-UA *nɨ- are known, and they differ considerably in their semantic value: SH nɨɨ'- PASS/REFL; K nɨ- REFL; Y ne- UNSPEC H OBJ; and A ne- UNSPEC H COREF SUBJ. One would naturally like a larger and more uniform set, but for several reasons this cognate set is reasonably secure. First, these reflexes are well-distributed, including the northernmost subfamily (Numic), the southernmost (Aztecan), and one intermediate. Second, there are no problems in the sound correspondences. Third, two of the four languages involved are Shoshoni and Aztec, and these two, of all the Uto-Aztecan languages, are precisely the two that best preserve the other unspecified argument prefixes. Finally, the semantic value of *ni̵- was both complex and highly unusual, as we will see, so its loss or simplification in a large number of daughters is not terribly surprising.

Determining the meaning of *ni̵- is no simple matter, not only because of the variation in its function, but also because its role in the individual daughters is not totally clear. Shoshoni ni̵i̵'- is basically a reflexive prefix which can also be used with passive sense. Thus it is not an unspecified argument prefix in the direct sense that ta- and ti̵- are, but by now the connection should be quite apparent. In the few examples available to me, the interpretation is reflexive when the (surface) subject is human, but passive when it is non-human (as is generally the case with Spanish se). I do not know whether this is a consistent pattern.

SH (1) te^{n}k^{w}a'pi̵ huuwi̵ha'ni-ma ni̵i̵-'ka?a-^{h}k^{w}a
      man   axe-with   REFL-cut-PERF
      'The man cut himself with an axe.'   (SH-M-IN-15)

SH (2) ti̵-^{n}pi   ni̵i̵-'nua
      rock-ABS REFL-push
      'The rock got pushed.'   (SH-M-IN-15)

Kawaiisu ni̵- is evidently reflexive but not passive; I have examples with human subjects only:

K (3) ni̵-pi̵'kee-ti̵   ni̵?i̵
      REFL-look-TNS I
      'I looked at myself.'   (K-M-SPO-16)

Buelna, and following him Mason, have called Yaqui ne- an "indefinite personal object" marker, and supposedly it occurs only with the verb sawe 'command' (CAH-B-A-34; Y-M-PS-206). I take the phrase "indefinite personal object" to mean unspecified human object, especially in view of the semantic requirements of the verb 'command'. Johnson's brief lexicon appears to corroborate the relic status of ne- and also its function as an unspecified object marker:[5]

Y (4) sawe-me
        command-PRTC
        'one who governs'   (Y-J-I-283)

Y (5) ne-sawe-n
        UNSPEC-command-PAST
        H OBJ   DUR
        'was ordering'   (Y-J-I-279)

The disappearance of ne- has almost certainly been facilitated by the innovation of the prefix yo(r)e- (< 'person') having precisely the same function
(cf. example (14) of section 1.16).

Despite voluminous data, the function of Aztec ne- is the most problematic. We saw in Chapter 1 that it is basically reflexive and almost always requires a human subject. More precisely, we can characterize
Aztec ne- as indicating an unspecified human coreferential subject. That
is, a clause containing ne- must have an unspecified subject, this subject
must be human, and it must be coreferential to the object (also unspecified),
either as a reflexive or as a reciprocal.[6] All of these requirements are
met in example (6).

A (6) ne-XaʔsoʔXa-lo
        UNSPEC-love-IMPRS
        H SUBJ
        'There is loving of one another.'   (A-R-AM-30)

While the unspecified coreferential human subject function of Aztec ne-
appears to be the most basic one (and presumably the original one historically), examples such as the following show that the conditions on the use of
this prefix are not always so strict:

A (7) ne-mač-ti-lo
        UNSPEC-know-CAUS-IMPRS
        H SUBJ
        'One is taught.'   (A-S-DLN-272)

---

[5]The verb suffix -neka '(do) with one another' (Y-M-PS-204) may also incorporate
this element. It is equally likely, however, that it is a remnant of the *na-P construction discussed in Chapter 2.

[6]One might think it meaningless to talk about two unspecified arguments being coreferential, since an unspecified argument is by definition one that is identified by neither
reference nor lexical content. The key word here is "identified". When two unspecified arguments are said to be coreferential, they are equated only to one another, and
neither is thereby identified. To be identified, they would have to be provided with additional lexical content, or else they would have to be stipulated as coreferential to
some other nominal identified by deixis or lexical content.

A (8) ne-mak^{w}eš-ti-lo
        UNSPEC-bracelet-make-IMPRS
        H SUBJ
        'They (pearls) are made into bracelets.'   (A-A-PC)

A (9) ne-k^{w}a-lo
        UNSPEC-eat-IMPRS
        H SUBJ
        'One eats.'   (A-G-L-35, 46)

These examples represent a gradual weakening in the conditions on the use
of ne-, from the original requirement of unspecified coreferential human
subject (illustrated by (6)) to the ultimate requirement of unspecified human
subject only (illustrated by (9)).

To see the nature of this weakening in more detail, we must analyze
more carefully the unspecified coreferential human subject condition. For
sake of discussion, we may decompose this condition into five parts, listed
below as (A)-(E).

(A) unspecified subject

(B) human subject

(C) unspecified object

(D) human object

(E) subject and object coreferential

Example (6) meets all five requirements. (7) obeys (A)-(D) but not (E). (8)
represents still a further relaxation of the conditions; (D) is not obeyed, and
(C) is obeyed only in a weakened form, since the object is not (at least in
context) truly unspecified, but rather pronominal. Finally, (9) obeys only
(A) and (B), if we assume that 'eat' is the functional equivalent of an intransitive verb. (An alternative view is that ne- in (9) indicates both unspecified human subject and unspecified object, in which case it obeys (A)-
(C).)

I will claim that Aztec ne- directly reflects the semantic value of P-UA
*nɨ-; that is, *nɨ- marked an unspecified human subject coreferential to
the object. (There is no particular reason to believe that *nɨ- could be reciprocal as well as reflexive; reciprocal use quite possibly represents an
Aztec generalization.) Several considerations point to this as the proper reconstruction. It is clear that an unspecified argument is involved. The requirement that this argument be human is directly supported in Classical
Nahuatl and Yaqui, and indirectly in Shoshoni if the reflexive use of nɨɨ'- is

considered basic and the passive use an extension. The requirement of coreference between the subject and object is found in Aztec, Kawaiisu, and
Shoshoni (again considering the reflexive function basic), though not in
Yaqui. Thus all of the properties attributed to P-UA *ni̱- are found in at
least three of the four languages, and all are found together in Aztec ne-.
Furthermore, reconstructing *ni̱- as an unspecified human coreferential
subject marker offers the most plausible account of the evolution of the
daughter forms; all of the changes involved are simplifications of this complex semantic characterization.

We will consider these changes one by one. In Aztec itself, ne- has
come to be used in intransitive sentences with unspecified human subjects,
as exemplified in (9). The change involved is from marking an unspecified
human coreferential subject to marking an unspecified human subject, i.e.
the requirement of coreference with the object is lost.[7] Note that this extension supports the claim, implicit up to now, that P-UA *ni̱- had subject
focus. As long as coreference between subject and object is required, it
makes little difference whether we say that the prefix marks unspecified
human subjects or unspecified human objects. However, the extension of ne-
in Aztec to sentences like (9) indicates that the subject was the pivotal element (if subject or object focus can be posited at all in cases of coreference).

The ambivalence of reflexive/reciprocal constructions in regard to subject and object focus comes out clearly when we turn from Aztec to Yaqui.
In Yaqui the prefix ne- was taken as marking unspecified coreferential human objects rather than unspecified coreferential human subjects. This distinction has no consequences as long as the requirement of coreference is
maintained, but once it is lost the distinction becomes overt. The requirement of coreference was lost in Yaqui, much like it was in Aztec, but because of the shift from subject focus to object focus the result was different; Yaqui ne- marks unspecified human objects rather than unspecified
human subjects.

My interpretation of the Shoshoni development is as follows. First, the

---

[7]This is not quite the same as a generalization from coreferential arguments to non-
distinct arguments. It is not a matter of the subject becoming non-distinct from the
object, but rather of allowing the prefix to be used in cases where there is no object.
This distinction is subtle, but its importance has been demonstrated in terms of the extension of reflexive prefixes to passive but not to impersonal sentences.

unspecified feature was lost from the semantic representation of nɨɨ'-.
This had the effect of making the prefix reflexive, since it then marked
human coreferential subjects, i. e. human subjects coreferential to the object; this apparently remains the situation in Kawaiisu. Second, the human feature was lost, and the requirement of a coreferential subject generalized to the requirement of a non-distinct subject. The prefix thus
came to be used with either passive or reflexive force. The passive use
confirms the status of nɨɨ'- as a subject focus prefix.

These various developments of P-UA *nɨ- are summarized in Figure
XIII.

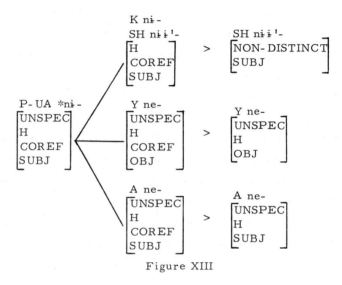

Figure XIII

Notice the great semantic complexity of P-UA *nɨ- in terms of the concepts we have been discussing. Unlike a prefix which marks non-distinct
subjects, and hence allows the subject to be either unspecified or coreferential to the object, *nɨ- requires that it be both simultaneously and requires further that this unspecified argument be human. The possibility of
such a prefix existing is not open to doubt--Aztec shows it can exist--but a
form so highly marked is quite susceptible to simplification or to loss.
This is especially so in languages with a variety of other devices to indicate coreference or unspecified arguments, and the Uto-Aztecan languages
are relatively rich in such devices.

I might comment in particular on Kawaiisu nɨ- and Shoshoni nɨɨ'-. If they do go back to P-UA *nɨ-, *nɨ- must be reconstructed for Proto Numic, yet only two among the several Numic languages retain this prefix. This tendency for P-NUM *nɨ- to be lost is quite understandable when we note the direction in which the P-UA form was simplified, namely to marking coreferential subjects and then non-distinct subjects. Numic na- plays essentially the same role, as we saw in Chapter 2, with both reflexive/reciprocal and (except in SNM where there was a special passive suffix) passive use. This duplication of effort with two prefixes so similar in form made loss of one of the prefixes highly probable, so it is hardly surprising that they both survived only in two languages. Within Shoshoni, moreover, nɨɨ'- may have generalized to marking non-distinct subjects by analogy to na-.[8]

4.4.   Evolution

4.4.1.   Proto Uto-Aztecan

P-UA had three unspecified argument verb prefixes: *ta-, which marked unspecified subjects; *tɨ-, which marked unspecified objects; and *nɨ-, which marked unspecified human coreferential subjects.

I4.4.1.1. All three prefixes were lost in TU, P-TAK, and P-CCH. Their loss in P-CCH was probably unrelated to their loss in the other languages. Therefore we may posit two common developments, the loss of these prefixes in TU and P-TAK (CD4.4.1.1) and their loss in P-CCH (CD4.4.1.2).

I4.4.1.2. *nɨ- simplified in P-NUM to marking human coreferential subjects. (Since there is attestation only in Shoshoni and Kawaiisu, we cannot safely take this change as a common development for all the Numic languages.)

I4.4.1.3. *ta- and *nɨ- were lost in H. *tɨ- was retained as tɨɨ-, which ultimately specialized to marking unspecified human objects.

---

[8]Sapir indirectly bears witness to the similarity between *nɨ- and Numic na- and their probable interaction. He offers Aztec ne- and Southern Paiute na- as cognates, despite the non-corresponding vowels (UA-S-SPN1-407; UA-S-SPN2-313). His hypothesis was not at all unreasonable in view of the limited data available to him, which apparently did not include Shoshoni or Kawaiisu. Since nɨɨ'- and na- co-occur in Shoshoni and Kawaiisu, and since both reconstruct in a straightforward way, it is evident that they are in fact historically distinct.

I4.4.1.4/CD4.4.1.3.   *nɨ- was lost in P-PMC.

I4.4.1.5/CD4.4.1.4.   *tɨ- > *tu- in P-PMC. This development is ir-regular.

I4.4.1.6.   *nɨ- > *ne in P-TRC by regular sound change. This prefix simplified in function, shifting to object focus and coming to mark unspeci-fied human objects. It is retained only in Y, so the change in function may or may not have been accomplished by the P-TRC stage.

I4.4.1.7/CD4.4.1.5.   *tɨ- and *ta- were lost in P-TRC.

I4.4.1.8.   In P-AZN, *tɨ- and *nɨ- became te- and ne- respectively by regular sound change.

I4.4.1.9/CD4.4.1.6.   In P-AZN, *te- and *ta- were realigned in func-tion to mark human and non-human unspecified objects respectively.

4.4.2.   Proto Numic

P-NUM had two unspecified argument prefixes: *ta- marked unspecified subjects, and *tɨ- marked unspecified objects. The prefix *nɨ- marked hu-man coreferential subjects. This system derives from that of P-UA by I4.4.1.2.

I4.4.2.1/CD4.4.2.1.   *tɨ- was lost in P-SNM.

I4.4.2.2/CD4.4.2.2.   *ta- was lost in P-WNM and P-SNM.

I4.4.2.3.   In SH, *nɨ- simplified to marking non-distinct subjects.

I4.4.2.4.   *nɨ- was lost in P-WNM. This change is shared with SP, a non-immediate daughter of P-NUM (CD4.4.2.3).

4.4.3.   Proto Western Numic

The verb prefix *tɨ- of P-WNM marked unspecified objects. This sys-tem derives from the P-NUM system by I4.4.2.2 and I4.4.2.4, and it is retained without modification in NP and M.

4.4.4.   Proto Southern Numic

P-SNM had the prefix *nɨ-, which marked (human) coreferential subjects. This system derives from that of P-NUM by changes I4.4.2.1 and I4.4.2.2.

I4.4.4.1.   *nɨ- was lost in SP (CD4.4.2.3).

4.4.5.   Proto Pimic

Proto Pimic had two unspecified argument prefixes, *ta- for subjects
and *tu- for objects. Innovations I4.4.1.4 and I4.4.1.5 are responsible
for the differences between this and the P-UA system.

I4.4.5.1. In P, these prefixes became highly restricted in their distribution. *tu- > ču- through regular sound change.

I4.4.5.2. In P-TEP (information is available only from TO and ST),
*ta- was evidently lost.

4.4.6.   Proto Tepehuan

The prefix *tu- marked unspecified objects in P-TEP. I4.4.5.2 derives
this system from the P-PMC system. *tu- may have been lost in NT, but
no pertinent information is available.

4.4.7.   Proto Taracahitic

The P-TRC prefix *ne- marked unspecified human objects. Changes
I4.4.1.6 and I4.4.1.7 are responsible for deriving this from the P-UA system.

I4.4.7.1. *ne- was lost in TA.

4.4.8.   Proto Aztecan

P-AZN had three unspecified argument prefixes: *te- for unspecified
human objects; *ta- for unspecified non-human objects; and *ne- for unspecified human coreferential subjects. This system derives from that of P-
UA by changes I4.4.1.8 and I4.4.1.9.

I4.4.8.1. *te- and *ne- were apparently lost in PO.

I4.4.8.2. In A, *ta- > ƛa- by regular sound change. *ne- generalized
to mark unspecified human subjects.

V. PASSIVES AND IMPERSONALS

5.0.   Introduction

The reconstructions posited for P-UA in Chapters 2-4 were unusually clear-cut. The reflexes of each proto form pointed quite unambiguously to a specific phonological shape, and it was not necessary to hypothesize any dialectal variation in the proto language. Such clarity and uniqueness cannot always be expected with such great time depth, and when we turn to passives and impersonals we begin to encounter some of the confusion and uncertainty we have a right to anticipate.

Several factors contribute to the difficulty, but they all revolve around the fact that the P-UA passive/impersonal marker was a suffix rather than a prefix or an independent particle. Suffixes are typically affected more by phonetic changes than are prefixes, since initial position tends to be phonologically more stable than medial or final position. In Uto-Aztecan the consequences of suffixal status are especially significant due to the well-known and still unresolved problem of medial consonant alternations in this family. The dental-alveolar consonants are particularly problematic in this regard, and it is these that we must deal with. Finally, the evolution of passive/ impersonal suffixes in Uto-Aztecan has been intimately tied up with the complex verb morphology and morphophonemics of these languages, areas which have barely begun to be explored in comparative terms. For all these reasons, much of what follows will be quite tentative and subject to revision and refinement as progress is made in other domains of Uto-Aztecan grammar.

5.1.   Data

The passive/impersonal markers in Uto-Aztecan are quite diverse. It is not uncommon for a single language to have a number of different passive markers. Table X summarizes the pertinent data from eighteen of the twenty languages under primary consideration here; Serrano apparently has no passive marker, and none is attested for Pochutla in the limited data available. Unless otherwise noted, a reflexive marker can only be passive, never impersonal, while other markers (so far as is known) are passive with transitive verbs and impersonal with intransitive verbs.

	PASS/IMPRS MARKER	PL SUBJ MARKING	SCOPE INVERSION	AGENTIVE PHRASE
NP	REFL			
M	REFL			+
SH	REFL			
SP	-'tɨɨ (PASS) -'tuʔa (IMPRS)	+	+	+
K	-'toʔo			
TU	-iw(a)		+	
H	-i, -(i)wa, -(i)lti			+
CA	-vel, -piš (PASS)			
CU	-vəl, -piš (PASS) -yax (PASS)	+		
L	-vol, -piš (PASS) -aat, -iš (PASS)			
P	-ǰid REFL			+
NT	-gi			
TO	REFL			
TA	-riwa, -ria, -wa -giwa, -kia, -gia -tu, -ru (REFL use)			
Y	-(i)wa			+
CR	-riwa, -(i)wa, -i -če			
HU	-ri, -rie, -rɨwa, -wa, -ya -ki			
A	-l(o), -wa, -o(a) REFL			

Table X

The markers in Table X divide into several groups. The extension of reflexive prefixes to passive use has already been dealt with in Chapter 2 and will not be considered further here. The various passive markers in Cupan constitute a second group, one that is itself heterogeneous. Southern Paiute -'tu?a and Kawaiisu -'to?o make up a third group, one that is similar to Tarahumara -tu/-ru, which will be considered a fourth. These three groups will be discussed in section 5.3. The fifth group comprises all the remaining forms and will be the subject of section 5.2.

Table X shows that reconstructing plural subject marking, scope inversion, or passive a g e n t i v e phrases for P-UA would be highly dubious. Each of these devices is attested in more than one language, but none is common. Moreover, a closer examination of the constructions in the daughter languages makes any reconstruction more dubious still. In each case, however, the question must remain open pending more complete information.

Plural subject marking is attested for passive/impersonal sentences in Southern Paiute and Cupeno:

> SP   (1)   tɨ 'ka- 'ka- 'tu?a-yɨ
>   eat-PL-IMPRS-PRES
>   'People are eating.'   (SP-S-G-148)
>
> CU   (2)   gəyiinə təm-pə-yəx-wə
>   chicken enclose-it-STAT-DUR
>   PL
>   'A chicken was cooped up.'   (CU-H-G-79)

The differences between these two constructions are immediately apparent. First, there is no similarity or relationship in form for the plural marking in the two sentences. Second, the Southern Paiute sentence is impersonal while the Cupeno sentence is passive. Third, the plural subject marker in Southern Paiute is said to be used only when the subject is understood to be "people in general" (SP-S-G-147), but it is a regular feature of the Cupeno construction. Finally, both SP -'tu?a and CU -yəx are innovative as passive/impersonal markers, and the two forms are quite unrelated.

While these observations cast considerable doubt on the reconstructability of plural subject marking, we should not foreclose this possibility, especially in view of special impersonal constructions (not otherwise discussed here) attested for Papago, Luiseno, and Hopi. The Papago construction is illustrated in (3):

P (3)   ha-haiwañ ʔa=m=t   ha-wuup
      RDP-cow AUX-IMPRS-PERF them-rope
                                 PERF
      'They roped the cows.'   (P-H-PC)

In this construction, the subject (glossed with the impersonal 'they') is left
unspecified but must be human. The underlying object remains the surface
object, as shown by object agreement on the verb, and a special impersonal =m occurs in the auxiliary sequence. Other Uto-Aztecan languages lead
one to expect a clitic with this form to mark a plural subject, but this sense
may well have been lost in Papago as part of the general loss of the plural
marker *mɨ in its various syntactic roles. Conceivably this construction
is evidence for plural subject marking on passive or impersonal sentences
in P-UA, but the evidence is at best still meager. In contrast to the situation in Southern Paiute and Cupeno, the verb is not marked in any way as
being passive or impersonal. One might try to relate =m in form to the
Cupeno durative plural suffix -wə, particularly in view of the *m/*w alternation established in section 3.3.2, but such an attempt would be misguided.
This suffix derives from P-UA *wɨlɨ 'stand', and its plural value is innovative.

An impersonal construction reported for Luiseno involves the quotative
clitic =kunu and the plural form of the present tense ending, -wun (cognate
to Cupeno -wə):

L (4)   po-y=kunu   moqna-wun
      he-ACC-QUOT kill-PRES
                      PL
      'He got killed.'   (L-M-PC)

L (5)   nawitmal-i=kunu=m čuɲi-wun
      girl-ACC-QUOT-PL kiss-PRES
                        PL
      'The girl got kissed.'   (L-M-PC)

This construction is said to require an animate logical object, which remains as the surface direct object (as shown by the accusative inflection).
The speaker must not have witnessed the event, not surprisingly in view of
the use of the quotative clitic. The agent may be understood to be singular,
despite the plural clitic and the plural tense inflection. The claim that the
Papago clitic =m cannot be related to the plural verb suffix -wə in Cupeno
is corroborated by the occurrence of cognates to both in (5). Hopi can also

convey passive or impersonal sense by means of a plural verb with unspecified subject:

H (6) taaqa-t   niina-ya
        man-ACC kill-PL
        'The man was killed. '   (H- L- EN)

These constructions do not in themselves drastically change the comparative picture with respect to reconstructing plural subject marking for P-UA,
since Cupeno and Luiseno both represent the closely related Cupan subfamily of Takic, since Hopi may be most closely related to Takic, and since
plural subject marking for impersonals may be a universal tendency. They
do however suggest that more systematic information on impersonal constructions in Uto-Aztecan, particularly the southern languages, might yield
interesting results.

Scope inversion is attested for passives in Southern Paiute and Tubatulabal:

SP (7) maai-'t$^?$ui-^{n}ki-'ti-pa=aŋa=taŋ^{w}a
         catch-CAUS-APPLIC-PASS-FUT-he-us
                                              INCL
         'He will cause us to be caught. '   (SP-S-G-147, 278)

TU (8) taŋ-iiba$^?$-iu
         kick-DESID-PASS
         'He got ready to be kicked. '   (TU-V-G-117)

In both sentences, the passive follows another suffix despite being in its
semantic scope. Thus the passive relationship is in the scope of the causative in (7), and in the scope of the desiderative (translated as 'got ready to')
in (8). Because different suffixes are involved, it is apparent that this information alone cannot establish scope inversion for passives in Proto Uto-
Aztecan. This is not to say that scope inversion may not have existed in
the proto language, only that any demonstration of its existence in regard to
passives must await fuller data and be set in the context of a broader reconstruction of P-UA verb morphology.

The case of agentive phrases, the functional equivalent of by-phrases in
English, is somewhat less clear. In some languages, e.g. Shoshoni (UA-
XXX-WC2), no such phrase is possible. Agentive phrases are definitely
attested only in Mono, Southern Paiute, Hopi, Papago, and Yaqui; the
Cupeno construction illustrated in (15) may also be pertinent.

M (9) ʔetɨ nɨ-paaʼtu na-caʼtɨ ʼkiʔi-ʼti
gun me-by REFL-fire-TNS
'The gun was fired by me.' (M-L-G-212)

SP (10) paʼka-ŋu-ʼtɨɨ=ca=aŋa kʷiyaci-ŋʷanaⁿkʷa
kill-PNCT-PASS-PAST-he bear-by
'He was killed by the bear.' (SP-S-G-221)

H (11) ʔi-mana-wya qacin-mɨ-y ʔa-ŋqʷ tihɨ-t
my-girl-DIM kachina-PL-ACC them-from doll-ACC
mak-iwa
give-PASS
'My little girl was given a doll by the kachinas.' (H-M-INO)

P (12) haiwañ ʔa=t ʔi-wuu ʔab ʔamjɨ̣d g huan
cow AUX-PERF REFL-rope there from ART PN
PERF
'The cow got roped by Juan.' (P-H-PC)

Y (13) hu maaso wepul ʔoʔoo-ta-e meʔe-wa-k
this deer one man-ACC-with kill-IMPRS-PAST
'The deer was killed by one man.' (Y-L-S-38)

Y (14) hu kučubʷaʔa-wa-k ʔim ʔusi-m-mea
that fish eat-IMPRS-PAST my child-PL-with
'The fish was eaten by my children.' (Y-L-TG-147)

CU (15) nəʔɵ=n nə-taxwi qəʔ-ni-qət kukə-t pə-či
I-I my-self bite-CAUS-gonna spider-ABS it-with
'I'm gonna get myself bitten by a spider.' (CU-H-VN-354)

Once again there are important differences among these sentences. Reflexive prefixes are involved in the Mono and Papago examples, but these
two prefixes have a different origin (cf. Chapter 2); Hopi, Yaqui, and
Southern Paiute have verbs marked by a passive/impersonal suffix, but in
Cupeno we find a special embedded sentence construction of some kind.
Moreover, there is very little resemblance among the various agentive
postpositions. At best one could attempt the reconstruction of *-ma on the
basis of the initial syllable of SP -ŋʷanaⁿkʷa, the m of P ʔamjɨ̣d (which is in
fact segmentable), Y -mea (for which the vocalism would be irregular), and
conceivably H -ŋqʷ, but while possible, this is certainly questionable, and
in any event parallel innovation could hardly be ruled out. Current evidence
therefore provides no strong reason to reconstruct agentive phrases for P-
UA passives.

Nevertheless, a certain amount of caution is warranted here. The data
clearly indicates that agentive phrases are uncommon with passives in Uto-
Aztecan, but Table X could be misleading in this regard. An agentive

locution may well be possible in more languages than Table X shows, even though its occurrence might be rather infrequent in these languages. Grammars tend to divorce morphology from syntax, treating passive suffixes under the former and postpositional phrase locutions under the latter (or under the morphology of non-verbal elements). Under these circumstances, the occurrence of agentive phrases with passive verbs is easily overlooked. Traditional accounts of syntax may also take their occurrence for granted and deem it to be too obvious for comment. In a sense this attitude is correct, for the essential aspects of passive sentences in Uto-Aztecan are clearly an unspecified underlying subject and promotion of the underlying object to surface subject position; the possibility of an agentive phrase is secondary at best. However, granted the variety and importance of postpositional expressions in Uto-Aztecan, it would not be surprising to find that speakers of the proto language had some postpositional locution available to them to specify the agent in a passive sentence when they so desired.

5.2.   The *-wa Passive

5.2.1.   Reconstruction

The passive/impersonal suffixes to be dealt with in this section are summarized in Table XI.

SP	-'tɨɨ
TU	-iw(a)
H	-i, -(i)wa, -(i)lti
P	-ǰid
NT	-gi
TA	-riwa, -ria, -wa -giwa, -kia, -gia
Y	-(i)wa
CR	-riwa, -(i)wa, -i -če
HU	-ri, -rie, -rɨwa, -wa, -ya -ki
A	-l(o), -wa, -o(a)

Table XI

The most notable feature of the forms in Table XI is the persistent recurrence of -wa, usually in association with an immediately preceding i. As a first approximation, therefore, one is justified in positing the passive/impersonal suffix *-wa for P-UA. Heath, for example, makes this reconstruction, and he associates *-wa with a class of proto suffixes reconstructable for P-UA that cause i-ablaut of the preceding vowel (UA-H-MP2-15).

Heath strongly motivates the reconstruction of i-ablaut for certain proto suffixes, and I will not recapitulate his arguments here. One consequence of this phenomenon is that i is not to be viewed as part of the *-wa morpheme itself, but rather the result of modifying the vowel of the previous syllable. For example, the final a of Yaqui toha 'carry' is ablauted to i in the passive, as shown in (1).

Y (1) tohi-wa-k
      toha
      carry-IMPRS-PAST
      'was carried' (Y-J-I-19)

In some instances, the i triggered by i-ablaut has apparently been reanalyzed as being itself a marker of passivization, with -wa then no longer required. This reanalysis is presumably responsible for the -i variant of the passive suffix in Hopi and Cora. In both cases, -i replaces the final vowel of the stem, as we saw in Chapter 1.

The forms in Table XI make it clear that more is involved with the P-UA passive/impersonal suffix than just *-wa. In most of the languages represented, at least one variant of the passive suffix contains a consonant from either the dental-alveolar region or the palatal-velar region, and in three languages both kinds are attested. It might be argued that these consonants had nothing to do with passives per se in the proto language but rather derive by reanalysis in various daughters of the final syllable of the verb stem, but I find this position implausible. The persistence of the phenomenon throughout the family makes a secondary origin through the irregular process of reanalysis quite unlikely, as does the fact that the same two general types of consonants are repeatedly involved to the exclusion of all others.

The dental-alveolar consonants are more widely distributed than the palatal-velar consonants in Table XI. The latter, in fact, are restricted to three contiguous subfamilies, Pimic, Taracahitic, and Corachol. I will

argue that the passive suffixes with palatal and velar consonants represent
an innovation and should not be reconstructed for the proto language,
though the innovation must have been an early one. Their limited distribution constitutes evidence for this position, and the possibility of identifying
the initial syllable in the forms with dental-alveolar consonants (cf. section 5.2.2) also suggests that these, rather than those with palatal-velar
consonants, are primitive.

The passive suffixes with palatal and velar consonants will be discussed
in section 5.2.5. Those which remain when these are excluded are given
in Table XII.

SP	- ꞌtɨɨ
TU	- iw(a)
H	- i, - (i)wa, - (i)lti
TA	- riwa, - ria, - wa
Y	- (i)wa
CR	- riwa, - (i)wa, - i
HU	- ri, - rie, - rɨwa, - wa, - ya
A	- l(o), - wa, - o(a)

Table XII

To account for this data we can provisionally reconstruct the passive/im-
personal suffix *-TV-wa, where T represents a dental-alveolar consonant
of some kind and V stands for a vowel. Our problem now is to identify T
and V more precisely and to sketch the derivation of the sometimes quite
varied reflexes.

T is problematic. Tarahumara, Cora, and Huichol show r for this consonant, and medial r can go back to either *t or *l in P-UA. However,
while Southern Paiute ꞌt and Hopi t (also Hopi l) reconstruct as *t, Aztec l
reconstructs as *l (UA-VVH-TCG; UA-M-CS-9). For the first time we
have a clear conflict in the testimony of the various daughters. Granted
the correctness of the correspondences, we must therefore assume one of
the following: there were two or more alternate passive suffixes in the
proto language; there was dialectal variation in the proto language in regard to the passive suffix; or an irregular sound change occurred in one or
more daughters. The first two alternatives are very similar, and I will

tentatively assume the second; the matter will be discussed more fully in
sections 5.2.2 and 5.2.3. Specifically, we may posit *ṭ for this suffix in
the northern languages, and *ḷ in the southern languages.

The quality of V is also problematic. If *-TV-wa was originally bimorphemic and *-wa triggered i-ablaut, as suggested by Heath, the high incidence of i in Table XII is not necessarily indicative of the quality of the
proto vowel. Southern Paiute suggests *ɨ with the following development:
*-tɨwa > *-tɨwɨ > -'tɨɨ. Such a development is quite plausible, since it in-
volves only the common processes of vowel harmonization and medial consonant loss (the latter also attested for the passive suffix in Tarahumara,
Huichol, and Aztec), and it explains the long vowel of -'tɨɨ. Huichol -rɨwa
does not corroborate this choice, since it reflects proto *u. *-lɨwa >
*-rɨwa > *-ruwa > *-rɨwa is conceivable, with *ɨ changing to *u by assimi-
lation and *u then becoming ɨ by regular sound change, but this is speculative, and the -rɨwa variant could be recent rather than archaic. Aztec o
does not bear on the matter, since *iwa sometimes becomes owa in this
language (UA-S-SPN1-409, 424).

The overall picture, then, is one of uncertainty. *-tɨwa, *-tiwa, *-liwa,
and possibly *-lɨwa can all be supported to some degree by certain daughter
forms, and we must posit either variation in the proto language or irregular
development in one or more daughters. Rather than choose one form arbitrarily, I will assume proto language variation. The variation between *ɨ
and *i can possibly be attributed to the incomplete consummation of i-ablaut
from *-wa on the preceding vowel ɨ. The possible origin and significance
of the *ṭ/*ḷ alternation will be dealt with shortly.

Once this proto variation is recognized, the evolution and proliferation of
the daughter forms is easy to account for in general terms, though the details are not always readily apparent. Southern Paiute -'tɨɨ and Huichol
-rɨwa have already been discussed. Tarahumara and Cora -riwa reflect
*-liwa via the regular sound change *l > r. The other forms derive through
either phonetic simplification or morphological reanalysis. Naturally the
two cannot be sharply separated.

One type of morphological reanalysis that evidently occurred was the
choice of either the first or second of the two syllables to indicate passivization by itself; this is most evident in Huichol, where some verbs take -ri

and others -wa, and it may be responsible for the -wa forms in Tubatulabal,
Hopi, Tarahumara, Yaqui, Cora, and Aztec. While the precise mechanism for this kind of split is not fully apparent, there is little doubt that it
does occur. The -(i)wa forms may also have arisen through phonologically
determined truncation of the initial consonant after certain kinds of stems
or through reanalysis of this consonant as part of the stem.[1] The -iwa
forms give rise to the -i variants in Hopi and Cora as previously described,
and Hopi -(i)lti must result from some rather different kind of morphological reanalysis that I am not presently prepared to describe.

In Tarahumara and Huichol, -riwa optionally simplified to -ria through
loss of medial w, as in Southern Paiute. Huichol -ria was no doubt rendered phonetically as -riya, which became -rie through phonetic modification
and gave rise to -ya by morphological reanalysis. *l did not become r in
Aztec, but *iwa does sometimes change to owa, as previously noted, so the
expected reflex of *-liwa is -lowa. Morphological and phonetic modifications of the kind discussed above can easily derive the variants -lo, -l, -wa,
-oa, and -o, but a more detailed account must await the careful reconstruction of diachronic Nahuatl verb morphology.

5.2.2.   The Source of *-tɨ

We have reconstructed for Proto Uto-Aztecan the passive/impersonal
suffix *-tɨ-wa, which occurred in two or more variant forms, possibly
dialectally determined. The consistency of their association in the daughter
languages indicates that *tɨ and *wa constituted a fixed unit in P-UA, and
that passive value was associated with this unit as a whole, but quite possibly the unit was of fairly recent origin. If *-tɨ and *-wa were separate
suffixes in pre-P-UA, the latter inducing i-ablaut, we can explain the alternation between *i and *ɨ in the first syllable. Presumably i-ablaut occurred
with less than full consistency in the new combination *-tɨ-wa, leading to
alternants with *ɨ and alternants with *i. The form with *i eventually won
out in most daughters, with *ɨ being preserved only in Proto Numic (as

---

[1]The widespread occurrence of -(i)wa as a variant suggests that the first syllable of
the passive/impersonal suffix may have been optional already in P-UA. The first syllable was the original passive suffix in pre-P-UA, as we will see, but the addition of
*-wa may have rendered it dispensable.

attested by Southern Paiute) and possibly Huichol.

Our task now is to identify *-tɨ and *-wa. I suggested earlier that passive/impersonal sentences consist in underlying structure of a clause with unspecified subject embedded to the verb 'be'; the motivation for this analysis will be discussed later in more detail. There is nothing in Uto-Aztecan to suggest a P-UA form anything like *tɨwa meaning 'be', so if either *-tɨ or *-wa can be shown to derive from 'be', this would support both my hypothesis concerning the underlying structure of passives and the claim that *-tɨ-wa was originally bimorphemic.

With *-wa we come close, but not really close enough. There is a derivational suffix *-wa reconstructable for P-UA; it means 'have' and sometimes takes on existential value, as in Tarahumara kona-wa (salt-have) 'have salt' (TA-H-TE-xi). But there is no indication that this morpheme *-wa causes i-ablaut, and the existential sense definitely appears to be secondary (cf. French y avoir). Another explanation for the origin of *-wa in the P-UA passive suffix will be offered in section 5.2.4.

With *-tɨ we have considerably better luck. We have already seen that P-UA *katɨ 'sit' functions as the verb for 'be' in some languages. kaa-tei, yei-kaa, and tee all function as independent verbs meaning roughly 'be' in Huichol, which suggests that *katɨ may be further segmentable into *ka plus *tɨ:

HU (1) tewi [wana m-ee-kaatei]
person there SUBR-away-live
'the person who used to live there'   (HU-G-S-38)

HU (2) kiekari-cie-niu   ni-u-yeikaa-kai-tɨni-waniu
community-in-QUOT NARR-RESTR-be-PAST-NARR-QUOT
                                      DUR
'He was in the community.'   (HU-G-S-76)

HU (3) hiipatɨ hiikɨ we-kan-a-nu-tee-ni
some   today they-NARR-toward-other-exist-NARR
                                    side
'There are some today.'   (HU-G-S-79)

The segmentability of *katɨ is further suggested by Cupan yax 'be', for which I have posited the derivation *yɨ-ka > *yəx > yax, and it is not implausible to relate to this set a Luiseno particle too used in 'if' clauses (L o < P-UA *ɨ). In addition, re (< *tɨ ?) is one form of 'be' in Tarahumara.

There is yet another source of support for positing an element *-tɨ meaning 'be' in P-UA, or at least in pre-P-UA, namely a derivational suffix added to nouns or other elements to form verbs. Usually this suffix means 'be', but it has various extensions such as 'consider to be', 'make', and 'give'. The clearest attestation of this suffix is in Taracahitic, with Yaqui -te 'make/be' and -re 'consider to be'[2] and Tarahumara (-ru)-re 'be' and -ti/-ri 'make/put on'. Here are some typical examples: Y b^{w}eka-te 'make wide' (Y-J-I-35); Y peeso-te 'be a prisoner' (Y-J-I-34); Y tu?u-re (good-consider to be) 'like' (Y-L-TG-14); TA rosa-re 'be white' (TA-B-G-208); TA reso-ru-re 'be a cave' (TA-B-G-213); TA napiso-ti 'cover with dust' (TA-B-G-625). Clearly related to this set and to each other are Cora -te/-re 'make/give' and Huichol -ri 'make/be': CR kuka-te 'provide with a necklace' (CR-P-G-47); CR sai-re (one-make) 'unify' (CR-P-G-45); CR č^{w}ika-te (song-make) 'sing' (CR-P-NE-3); HU k^{w}ika-ri (song-make) 'sing' (HU-D-I-40); HU ?inia-ri (symbol-be) 'symbolize' (HU-G-S-85).

One can also reconstruct for P-UA the active participial suffix *-ti, most familiar from Numic but in fact widely attested in Uto-Aztecan in one guise or another. The participial *-ti can be shown to be another reflex of pre-P-UA *ti 'be', but I must leave a detailed demonstration of this for another work. In sum, then, a strong case can be made for positing a pre-P-UA morpheme *ti 'be' having a variety of uses.

The existence of *ti 'be' corroborates the claim that passive/impersonal sentences derive from clauses with unspecified subjects embedded to 'be'. However, several matters require further clarification. For one thing, we must determine the source of *-wa and ask why this element was added to *-ti to form the P-UA passive suffix (section 5.2.4). Quite possibly the addition of *-wa was related to the secondary status of *ti 'be' in P-UA. Several elements or sequences of elements meaning roughly 'be' can be reconstructed for the proto language, as we have seen. *ti may very well no longer have been a surface main verb at this stage, functioning instead only

[2] Compare the use of make to mean 'estimate/consider' in English: I make her (to be) forty-seven.

Uto-Aztecan derivational verb suffixes with t/r/l present a complex picture that we cannot explore here in any detail. At least three suffixes roughly of the form *-tV can be reconstructed: *-tu 'become' (with the active variant *-tu-a 'make'); *-ti 'be'; and *-ta 'make/put on/wear'. Reflexes of all three are attested in Tarahumara and Yaqui, and most UA languages retain one or two. Considerable mutual influence and semantic shifting has occurred in the evolution of the daughter forms, as is to be expected.

as a derivational suffix, as part of *kati and other lexical items, and as an
auxiliary verb. We can confidently attribute main verb status to *ti only
for some stage of pre-P-UA, and there is no reason to assume that speakers of P-UA necessarily still identified the first syllable of *-ti-wa with
'be'.

The phonological relationship between *ti and *-ti-wa also requires
some elaboration. We have seen that there are problems with both the
vowel and the consonant. For both forms, reflexes in the daughter languages point sometimes to *i and sometimes to *i for the vowel. Here I
assume that *i is basic, with the i-ablaut of *-wa responsible for the variants *-ti-wa and *-li-wa of the passive/impersonal suffix in P-UA, and
later (post-P-UA) assimilation or other phonetic modification responsible
for the -ri reflex of the derivational suffix *-ti. The consonant poses a
greater problem. The daughter languages indicate both *t and *l for the
passive suffix (*t for the northern languages and *l for the southern ones);
the derivational suffixes reflect *t in most instances, though the situation
is slightly less clear. This situation is not unusual by comparative stan-
dards, but the analysis will be strengthened considerably if we can go beyond simply invoking proto language dialectal variation and show just how,
in view of the overall picture of consonant gradation in the family, this
state of affairs could have come about.

5.2.3.   Consonant Gradation

Consonant gradation is a classic problem in Uto-Aztecan, one that has
received a great deal of attention from both Uto-Aztecanists and linguistic
theoreticians. I have no intention here of reviewing the considerable literature on the subject[3] or treating the topic with any thoroughness. I have
not carried out the extensive lexical and phonological research needed to
provide any kind of definitive treatment. Typically, however, only limited
aspects of the problem have been dealt with, and we have little to lose (and
hopefully something to gain) by examining the problem in a broader context,
even in a somewhat speculative manner.

[3] Some pertinent references are SP-S-G, NUM-I-HP, NP-N-HG, UA-M-CS, UA-
VVH-TCG, and SP-CH-SPE. This list is far from exhaustive.

The central phenomenon is the lenition of medial consonants. Most if
not all of the consonants may be involved, but we will focus our attention on
t and other dental/alveolar consonants, since these present the most complex picture and are the ones relevant to the present discussion. Lenition
of medial t (and other consonants) is an active synchronic process in the
Numic languages, most notoriously in Southern Paiute, but in most Uto-
Aztecan languages we find only vestiges of a process that is no longer active.

In languages like Southern Paiute which preserve medial consonant gradation as an active process, the form the consonant assumes depends on
the preceding morpheme.[4]   After some morphemes (said to be "spirantizing"), t lenites, typically to r. After others (said to be "geminating" or
"unaltering"), t remains t phonetically. After others (said to be "nasalizing"), a (pre-)nasalized consonant such as nd results. A morpheme typically has the same effect (spirantizing, unaltering, or nasalizing) on the initial
consonant of any immediately following morpheme, and an initial consonant
can typically surface in spirantized, unaltered, or nasalized form depending on the character of the morpheme that it immediately follows.

In languages in which consonant gradation is no longer active, we find a
phonemic contrast in medial position between t and a voiced consonant such
as l or r. Languages may differ as to whether they have the voiced or
voiceless reflex of t for a given proto form (e.g. Y kate, L qal < *katɨ
'sit'). Moreover, a single daughter may show reflexes of both the spirantized and the unaltered version of the same proto morpheme (e.g. the absolutive suffixes -ta and -la of Luiseno both derive from *-ta: too-ta 'rock',
huu-la 'arrow'--cf. UA-S-SPN2-107). When listed in a table, therefore,
the reflexes of medial *t look very messy. These are given for representative languages in Table XIII; the correspondences for initial *t and medial
*l are included for future reference (UA-VVH-TCG; UA-M-CS-8, 9). Sec-
ondary developments such as palatalization are omitted.

In a language like Luiseno, the contrast between medial t and medial l is
synchronically distinctive; the choice must be marked for each instance of

---

[4]I will confine my attention to consonant gradation at morpheme boundaries within
single words or compounds. Preaspiration will not be discussed. Neither of these
simplifications is crucial to the possible validity of the overall picture sketched here.

	Initial *t	Medial *t	Medial *l
SP	t	$'t/t/{}^{n}t$	n
TU	t	t/l/d	n
H	t	t/l/r	n
L	t	t/l	n
P	t	t/ḍ	ḍ/l
Y	t	t/r	r
HU	t	t/r	r
A	t	t	l

Table XIII

medial t and l at the phonemic level and depends only on the segment itself, not on the character of the preceding morpheme. The nature of the under-lying phonological representation is much less clear for languages like Southern Paiute in which consonant gradation is still an active process; in fact it has been the subject of considerable controversy. It is however apparent that only one underlying segment type is involved in a set like $'t/t/{}^{n}t$, and that the choice is determined by the preceding morpheme. Note that 't is phonetically much like t and that t spirantizes to r, so that the non-phonemic 't/t distinction is quite parallel to the phonemic t/l or t/r distinction in other languages. I will take no position on the theoretical issue of how to represent spirantizing, unaltering, and nasalizing mor-phemes synchronically in Numic; rather I will discuss this type of gradation in broader historical perspective.

I will suggest that spirantizing, unaltering, and nasalizing morphemes derive historically from morphemes ending in syllables of the form CV, CVC, and CVN respectively, where C stands for a consonant, V for a vow-el, and N for a nasal consonant. This in itself is not a novel idea, but con-troversy over the adequacy of these constructs as synchronic underlying representations has obscured the question of their diachronic adequacy. Their diachronic adequacy is what I will focus on, paying particular atten-tion to the transition between a system like that of Southern Paiute and one like that of Luiseno. For ease of presentation, I will ignore the nasalizing morphemes, since nasalization is lost in most instances and the develop-ment of CVC and CVN is quite analogous.

Let us take t as a paradigmatic example, with l as its lenis counterpart.
We may posit an original suffix of the form -tV which can occur with both
CVC stems and CV stems. At the earliest stage, this suffix is realized
phonetically as -tV with both types of stems; we will call this stage A. In
(1), I sketch the probable evolution of this kind of system to the kind found
in Southern Paiute and other Numic languages, represented as stage C.

(1) CVC-tV   >   CVt-tV   >   CV-tV
     CV-tV   CV-tV   CV-lV

        (A)   (B)   (C)

The representations in (1) are phonetic rather than phonological. In the
transition from stage A to stage B, the final consonant of the stem assimi-
lates to that of the suffix, producing a surface contrast between simple and
geminated t. Lenition then accomplishes the transition between stages B
and C. The adoption of synchronic phonological rules is responsible for
both transitions. A consonant assimilation rule relates stages A and B,
and a lenition rule relates B and C. The latter has the effect of reducing
intervocalic geminate consonants to simple consonants and spirantizing (or
voicing) simple consonants.

Throughout this period, the underlying representation of the suffix remains constant, namely -tV, as in Southern Paiute. However, that of the
stem is modified, probably twice. With consonantal assimilation as an active process, there will be a tendency for the identity of final stem consonants to be lost, since these consonants typically or always derive their
phonetic shape from that of the consonant which follows. In underlying representations, therefore, final stem consonants will tend to reduce to maxi-
mally unmarked consonants or "archi-consonants"; eventually they may lose
their segmental status altogether and, at stage C, be manifest only in a
morphological distinction between unaltering stems (< *CVC) and spirantizing stems (< *CV). The phonetic representations CV-tV and CV-lV at stage
C thus derive from the respective phonological representations CV'-tV and
CV-tV, where ' may be regarded as either a morphological category feature
or an unmarked consonant, depending on one's theoretical viewpoint.

(2) shows stage C in more detail and indicates the nature of its transition
to stage D, that characteristic of languages such as Luiseno. Stage C is inherently unstable, or at least subject to modification, because a contrast

(2) $/CV'\text{-}tV/$ $/CV\text{-}tV/$ > $/CV\text{-}tV/$ $/CV\text{-}lV/$
   $[CV\text{-}tV]$ $[CV\text{-}lV]$ $[CV\text{-}tV]$ $[CV\text{-}lV]$

            (C)   (D)

manifested phonetically in one morpheme is due to an abstract property of an adjoining morpheme. The transition from C to D trades a morphological contrast for a phonemic one,[5] and it simplifies the overall phonological picture by eliminating the lenition rule and bringing the underlying representations of morphemes more in line with their phonetic manifestations.

Consider now the fate of individual morphemes in a language which undergoes the transition from C to D, suffixes in particular. What was once a single morpheme -tV will have split by stage D into two phonemically distinct morphemes, -tV and -lV, leading to several alternative paths of subsequent evolution. One possibility is for the two suffixes to be retained side by side with the same meaning or syntactic function; this is what happened with the absolutive suffixes -ta and -la in Luiseno, both from *-ta. A second possibility is for both to be retained but for them to develop different meanings or functions. A third possibility is for one of them to generalize and eventually displace the other. Naturally there is no reason to expect the fate of one pair to match that of any other.

Consider now the situation when a language at stage C is a proto language, and when the transition from C to D takes place as this proto language is undergoing dialectal differentiation or takes place independently in two or more daughters after division into daughter languages has already occurred. Under these circumstances, there is no reason to expect that the fate of a pair like -tV and -lV will be the same in all dialects, or that it will be the same in any given two daughters. -tV might be retained in one daughter and -lV in another, or both might be retained in two daughters but specialize differently, and so on. Moreover, there will be no consistent way to predict on phonological grounds whether -tV or -lV will be the reflex of proto *-tV in a given daughter, for the split of *t into two phonemes is due directly to the loss of the original environmental feature (preceding consonant versus preceding vowel) that governed the t/l alternation.

---

[5]More precisely, the morphological contrast changes from one determining whether or not the lenition rule will affect the following consonant to one determining which of two phonemically distinct suffixes will be chosen.

Proto Uto-Aztecan offers concrete illustration. There is little doubt
that P-UA represented stage C and that the transition to stage D took place
either in certain dialects of P-UA (but not all) or in most of the immediate
daughters of P-UA. Therefore we expect to find pairs like Yaqui kate and
Luiseno qal, both from *kati 'sit' (the difference depends on whether or not
the medial consonant was construed as being geminated, for one reason or
another), and we expect to find the situation shown in the second column of
Table XIII, where most daughter languages show a split of medial *t into a
fortis and lenis reflex with no apparent conditioning factor.

So far we have dealt only with P-UA *t and its reflexes. Nothing has
been said about *l, which must be recognized as a phoneme distinct from *t
in the proto language. It is the relation between P-UA *t and P-UA *l that
ultimately concerns us, because it is alternation between *t and *l that
lends an element of uncertainty to our reconstruction of the P-UA passive
suffix.

I would like to suggest that P-UA *t and *l derive from a single phoneme
*t of pre-P-UA through an earlier round of lenition and reanalysis similar
to that depicted in (1) and (2). I am suggesting, therefore, that consonant
gradation has been a continuing process in the history of Uto-Aztecan, and
that we can detect two rounds of the process for the dental consonants.[6]
The first round of lenition and reanalysis resulted in the split of pre-P-UA
*t into P-UA *t and *l, while the second round resulted in the split of P-UA
*t into Luiseno t and l, Yaqui t and r, and so on. In the first round, pre-
P-UA represented stage C and P-UA stage D, while in the second round, P-
UA represented stage C and certain of its daughters stage D.

The primary evidence for this claim is the fact that P-UA *l can be reconstructed with confidence only for medial position. This suggests quite
strongly that *l had achieved phonemic status only fairly recently, originat-
ing as the medial allophonic variant of some other phoneme, and that few if
any lexical innovations using the new phoneme in initial position had occurred by P-UA times. Miller does not reconstruct initial *l (UA-M-CS-8),
and Voegelin, Voegelin, and Hale reconstruct it on the basis of only one
cognate set, that for 'tongue' (UA-VVH-TCG-141). They reconstruct *lïŋi

---

[6]I have found some evidence to suggest that the alternation and subsequent phonemic
reanalysis of *m/*w has also recurred in the history of Uto-Aztecan.

rather than a form with initial *n because of Tubatulabal <u>lalant</u> and Hopi
<u>leŋi</u>; *n should be reflected as <u>n</u> rather than <u>l</u> in both languages. It matters
little here whether *<u>l</u> or *<u>n</u> should be reconstructed for this morpheme,
since the present discussion requires only that initial *<u>l</u> in P-UA be relatively rare (as an indication of the recent phonemic status of *<u>l</u>)--it does
not require that there be no instances of initial *<u>l</u> at all. It is interesting
to observe, however, that Sapir reconstructs initial *n for 'tongue' (UA-S-
SPN1-404). He derives Hopi <u>leŋi</u> from *<u>neŋi</u> through dissimilation. In the
case of Tubatulabal, he hypothesizes that the stem *<u>naŋu</u> dissimilated to
*<u>laŋu</u>, which then became *<u>lalu</u> and eventually <u>lala</u>- through subsequent as-
similation.

Suppose now that we reconstruct pre-P-UA *<u>t</u> to underlie both *<u>t</u> and *<u>l</u>
in P-UA, as just outlined. Suppose further that we posit the verb *<u>tɨ</u> 'be'
for pre-P-UA, as claimed in section 5.2.2. This verb had a number of
uses, as verbs meaning 'be' often do. Two of these uses concern us directly: it could suffix to a noun (or other non-verbal constituent) to form a derived verb meaning 'be N'; and it could occur in configurations like Figure
I, where it surfaced as a passive/impersonal suffix on the lower verb. If
we suppose still further that the split between *<u>t</u> and *<u>l</u> (i. e. the transition
between stages C and D) took place while dialectal differentiation was occurring, we can explain how the P-UA variation noted earlier for the passive and derivational suffixes came about. The transition from stage C to
stage D resulted in two phonemically distinct competing reflexes of *-<u>tɨ</u>,
namely *-<u>tɨ</u> and *-<u>lɨ</u>. Neither fully displaced the other in P-UA. Instead
they specialized in function, but the specialization differed somewhat dialectally, as expected. In the southern dialect(s), *-<u>lɨ</u> became a passive suffix and *-<u>tɨ</u> a derivational suffix. There is no clear evidence of a derivational suffix in the northern dialect(s), but here *-<u>tɨ</u> specialized as a passive
suffix.

5.2.4. The Source of *-<u>wa</u>

We have now identified half of the P-UA passive/impersonal suffix
*-<u>tɨ</u>-<u>wa</u>. *-<u>tɨ</u> and its variants reconstruct as 'be', partially confirming the
claim that passive and impersonal sentences derive from underlying

structures in which a clause with unspecified subject is embedded as subject complement to the verb 'be'. To complete the analysis, we must now
identify *-wa. One possible proposal, that *-wa also meant 'be', was considered briefly in section 5.2.2 and tentatively rejected. A derivational
suffix *-wa can be reconstructed for P-UA, and its reflexes sometimes
have existential import, but the basic sense of this morpheme appears to
be 'have' rather than 'be', and there is no indication that it caused i-ablaut.

I will claim that the *-wa of *-tɨ-wa derives instead from a derivational
suffix *-wa that attaches to verbs to form derived nominals. Such a derivation might at first seem strange, since passive sentences are not derived
nominals, but the connection should become apparent shortly. Strong support can be marshaled for reconstructing the nominalizing *-wa for P-UA,
and there is evidence that it caused i-ablaut. It is not inconceivable that
the nominalizing *-wa is related in some way to the *-wa which derives
verbs and means 'have', but I have no specific proposals to make along
these lines.

The derived nominals formed by the reflexes of *-wa are typically abstract, in that they designate the activity described by the verb. In at least
one daughter, however, they designate the agent of the activity rather than
the activity itself, and in another they designate the instrument of the activity. They seldom if ever designate the object, product, or location of the
activity. In discussing the reflexes of *-wa, I will confine myself to those
which seem unproblematic; several others might be added.

The most straightforward exponents of *-wa are the agentive suffix
-wa-'pi of Shoshoni (with incorporated absolutive suffix), the instrumental
-ih^{w}a-t of Serrano (also with incorporated absolutive suffix), and the abstract nominalizing suffixes -(i)w of Hopi, -(i)g of Papago (P g < *w), -wa
of Tarahumara, and -wa of Yaqui. Examples follow: SH nɨ'ka-wa-'pi
(dance-NR-ABS) 'dancer' (SH-D-PMS-89); SH tɨɨ-poo-wa-'pi (UNSPEC OBJ-
write-NR-ABS) 'writer' (SH-D-PMS-89); SR ʔöṣan-ih^{w}a-t (write-NR-ABS)
'pencil/brush' (UA-XXX-WC1); SR nɨɨp-k-ih^{w}aʔ-t (sit-PNCT-NR-ABS)
'chair' (SR-H-D2-54); H wari-k-iw (run-PNCT-NR) 'running' (H-W-L-55);
P maak-ig (give-NR) 'giving' (P-SS-D-142); P ñi-maač-ig (my-know-NR)
'my knowledge' (P-M-LPA-23); TA biči-wa (have faith-NR) 'faith' (TA-T-

TED-31); Y <u>wol-te-wa</u>[7] (?-make-NR) 'wedding' (Y-M-PS-212).

Serrano, Hopi, and Papago indicate that the nominalizing *-<u>wa</u> caused <u>i</u>-ablaut. The examples also show that the subject of the nominalized verb is normally unspecified in the daughter languages, and there is no reason to suppose that things were any different in the proto language. This is not to deny that the semantic subject may sometimes be expressed by means of a possessor prefix, as in Papago ñi-maač-ig 'my knowledge'--but this is not typical and may only show that derived nouns, like other nouns, can be possessed. Marking the subject of the underlying verb was clearly not an intrinsic property of *-<u>wa</u> nominalization in P-UA.

This observation provides the key to determining why the nominalizing *-<u>wa</u> was incorporated as part of the P-UA passive/impersonal suffix *-<u>tɨ-wa</u>: granted underlying representations of the kind proposed here for passive/impersonal sentences, we find that these representations contain as a subtree precisely that configuration required for the insertion of *-<u>wa</u>. Since it is the unspecified subject which is crucial here, not the object, let us concentrate on impersonal sentences. The underlying structure of an impersonal sentence is shown in Figure XIV. Figure XV shows the underlying structure of an abstract derived nominal such as 'running'.

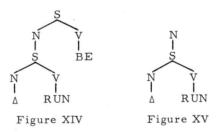

Figure XIV   Figure XV

Figure XV may not be complete as the underlying representation of an abstract derived nominal, but the essential properties shown in it do not seem terribly controversial.

From marking structures like Figure XV to marking those like Figure XIV is a small step, since XV is a proper subpart of XIV. Depending on how various minor details are to be handled, the extension may well represent a simplification of the conditions on *-<u>wa</u> insertion. The only question

---

[7] The stem of this form is uncertain; Mason speculates that it comes from Spanish <u>boda</u>.

that arises is why *-wa is positioned to the right of *-ti 'be' in derived structure instead of being suffixed directly to the verb stem, as in Figure XV. That is, why do we have *-ti-wa rather than *-wa-ti? I suggest that this merely reflects the chronology of the adoption of these elements for passive/impersonal use. At an early stage of pre-P-UA, *-ti marked passive/impersonal sentences by itself. The extension of *-wa to this construction was later, so it was natural for *-wa to be added on as an appendage to the previously existing combinations of the form *V-ti.

It should be observed that this order of suffixation does not necessarily entail any complication of the conditions for *-wa insertion. Once BE combines with the lower verb in Figure XIV to form the complex verb V-BE, perhaps by the rule of predicate raising (cf. UA-L-PR; UA-S-PTME), the derived structure is exactly analogous to Figure XV, the structure in which *-wa is normally inserted. Thus I propose the steps shown in Figure XVI both for the diachronic development of P-UA passive/impersonal sentences with *-ti-wa and, quite possibly, for their synchronic derivation.[8]

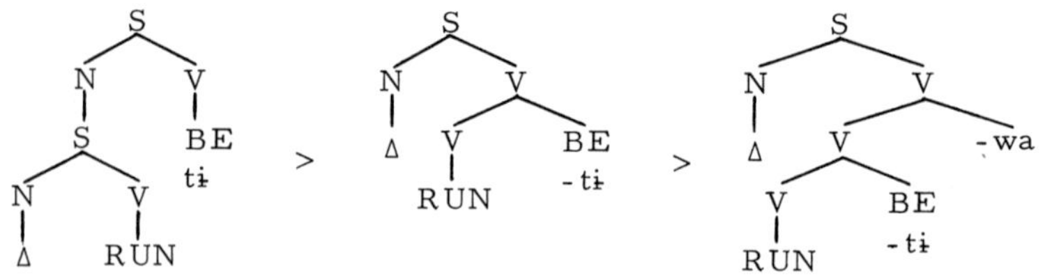

Figure XVI

If Figure XVI is valid for the synchronic derivation of passive/impersonal sentences in P-UA, we have a syntactic example of the steps in a synchronic derivation recapitulating the corresponding steps of the diachronic evolution.

The *-ti-wa passive therefore provides support for both of the major claims made in the Introduction concerning the underlying structure of passive/impersonal sentences. The origin of *-ti corroborates the claim that these sentences involve a clause embedded to 'be', while the origin of *-wa

[8]The lack of a node N dominating S in the second two structures of Figure XVI is probably not significant, since it merely reflects the fact that we are concerned with only limited aspects of the sentences involved. Discussions like this one make sense only in the context of a theory contemplating relatively abstract underlying syntactic representations, and in such representations the entire structure of Figure XVI would function as an argument of a higher clause (e.g. a clause expressing tense or modality) and hence would still be dominated by the node N.

corroborates the claim that the subject of the embedded clause is unspecified. To conclude this discussion, a few words are now in order about the evolution of derived nominals in *-wa in the various daughter languages. Their evolution strengthens the present analysis and has possible theoretical interest.

I indicated previously that derived nominals with reflexes of *-wa are normally abstract, i.e. they designate the activity described by the underlying verb. I have implicitly assumed that P-UA derived nominals with *-wa were also abstract, and this assumption hardly seems controversial. Figure XV is intended to depict the essential characteristics of the underlying representation of abstract derived nominals.

Derived nominals in *-wa are abstract in most of the daughter languages in which they are retained, but agentive and instrumental uses are also found, most notably in Shoshoni and Serrano respectively. Seldom if ever do derived nominals designate the object, product, or location of the verbal activity, despite the fact that derived nominals marked in other ways often have these values in Uto-Aztecan. This dichotomy between agent and instrument on the one hand and object, product, and location on the other hand is quite significant, because agentive and instrumental nouns are precisely those which commonly become surface subjects. This supports the claim that the subject of the embedded verb is a pivotal element in *-wa nominalization.

Figure XV depicts the underlying structure of abstract derived nominals. This is the structure triggering *-wa insertion in P-UA and in those daughters where *-wa derived nominals are still abstract. The underlying structure for agentive and instrumental derived nominals must be somewhat different; it is depicted roughly in Figure XVII (the distinction between agentive and instrumental subjects is ignored).

Figure XVII

The important feature of agentive and instrumental nominals is that the nominal as a whole is coreferential to the subject of the nominalized verbal activity. Thus a 'runner' is 'one who runs', and a 'knife' is 'something that cuts'.

Naturally this is an oversimplification, especially in the case of instrumentals. Consider, for example, the Serrano derived nominals cited earlier. One means 'pencil/brush' and is based on the stem meaning 'write', while the other means 'chair' and is based on the stem meaning 'sit'. The former potentially conforms to the configuration of Figure XVII, since expressions like 'The pencil writes' are linguistically quite common; but the latter does not, since 'The chair sits' is at best linguistically uncommon where 'chair' is intended as an instrument of sitting. My claim, then, is that *-wa was first extended to instrumental sense through cases like 'knife' and 'pencil/brush', which derived from underlying structures like Figure XVII. Once the instrumental use of *-wa had been established, it generalized to all cases where the derived noun designated the instrument of the verbal activity, regardless of whether or not the instrument could function as the subject of the underlying verb.

Consider now the relation between Figures XV and XVII. In Figure XV the subject of the embedded clause is unspecified. In Figure XVII, the subject of the embedded clause is not, strictly speaking, unspecified; rather it is coreferential to the nominal containing the embedded clause and is therefore identified to a certain degree. Since *-wa has more than once changed from marking the configuration of Figure XV to marking that of Figure XVII, we must assume that the two bear some special affinity to one another, at least for purposes of language change. The basis for this special affinity should by now be readily apparent: in both structures, the subject of the subordinate clause is non-distinct from the nominal to which the clause is embedded. In Figure XV it is non-distinct by virtue of being unspecified, while in Figure XVII it is non-distinct by virtue of coreference. Presumably the evolution of *-wa to agentive or instrumental function involved an intermediate stage in which this suffix could be used whenever the two nominals were non-distinct, whether through coreference or nonspecification.

The historical evolution of P-UA *-wa therefore provides further empirical support for the notion of non-distinct arguments. It also indicates that

we must expand the domain of this notion. In all previous cases, the non-
distinct arguments were the subject and direct object of the same verb.
Now we have found an instance in which the important feature is non-
distinctness between a nominal and the subject of a clause embedded to that
nominal. In describing the properties of a morpheme sensitive to non-
distinctness, it is not sufficient to indicate whether the morpheme has subject focus or object focus. We must also designate the "controller" of the
focused nominal. In the case of subject focus, the controller may be either
the direct object or a nominal in a higher clause.[9]

5.2.5. The *-ki-wa Variants

In Pimic, Taracahitic, and Corachol, passive suffixes involving a velar
or palatal consonant were innovated and either displaced the *-ti-wa suffix
or coexist with it. These suffixes are summarized in Table XIV.

P	-ǰid
NT	-gi
TA	-giwa, -kia, -gia
CR	-če
HU	-ki

Table XIV

In Taracahitic and Corachol, the regular passive suffix reconstructs as
*-liwa. The forms in Table XIV are the only specifically passive suffixes
attested for Pimic (Papago does have a variety of passive/impersonal constructions that do not involve a special passive suffix--cf. section 5.3.4).
I propose that all the forms in Table XIV result from a single innovation,
the adoption of *-kiwa as an alternant of *-liwa. If Pimic, Taracahitic,
and Corachol constitute a subfamily, the innovation of *-kiwa presumably
took place in the proto language immediately underlying this subfamily. If
not, the innovation took place in P-PMC, P-TRC, or P-CCH and spread by

[9]The controlling nominal need not dominate the embedded clause, as it does in the
case at hand. Consider English complement subject deletion, for example. In the sentence Met dislikes scratching, the subject of scratch must be non-distinct from Met,
either by being coreferential to Met or by being unspecified. However, Met does not
dominate the clause from which scratching derives, though it does command it. The
notion of non-distinct nominals has potentially far-reaching implications for complemen-
tation, relativization, and other complex-sentence phenomena, but I cannot pursue
them here.

diffusion. *-kiwa displaced *-liwa in P-PMC but coexisted with it in P-TRC and P-CCH. The reflex of *-kiwa was eventually lost in Yaqui.

The cause for the innovation of *-kiwa is not readily apparent. Perhaps, as Brambila intimates for Tarahumara, it represents nothing more than random consonantal interchange. One highly speculative possibility is that *-liwa split to *-liwa and *-kiwa by influence of the participial suffixes. In approximately the same subfamilies where *-kiwa appears, two distinct agentive or participial suffixes are attested, one reconstructable as *-li, *-lɨ, or *-tɨ (TA -ti; Y -reo (< *re-w(a)?); CR -ri; HU -ri) and the other as *-kame (< *-kamɨ) (TO -kam; TA -(k)ame; Y -me; CR -kame). The first set, to which we can add the Numic participial suffix -tɨ, can ultimately be equated with pre-P-UA *-tɨ 'be' (though I have not demonstrated this here). Thus the innovation of *-kiwa to parallel *-liwa is not at all implausibly related to the *-li/*-kame alternation.

Another, perhaps more likely, possibility is that *-kiwa resulted from confusion with, or reanalysis involving, some other suffix. Wick Miller (UA-XXX-WC2) has plausibly suggested for this suffix the Proto Numic causative/benefactive *-^{n}kɨ, where the nasal component can be related to a P-UA causative suffix *-na. I would add to the P-NUM form a relic causative suffix -ki of Luiseno and an applicative suffix -ki/-gi of Tarahumara. Determining the role of P-UA *-kɨ/-ki will require fuller reconstruction of the verb morphology, but for the reasons cited earlier it is most reasonable to suppose that the passive use is innovative.

Whatever the cause of the innovation may have been, the derivation of the forms in Table XIV from *-kiwa is for the most part quite straightforward. In Tarahumara, nothing is involved other than the voicing of medial k and the loss of w, the latter also multiply attested in the evolution of the *-tɨ-wa passive suffix. The loss of w was evidently fully accomplished in Proto Pimic and Proto Corachol, for there is no trace of w in their daughters. For P-PMC I will reconstruct *-gia, which derives from *-kiwa by voicing of k and loss of w, and for P-CCH I will reconstruct *-kia, derived by loss of w alone.

P-PMC *-gia was evidently lost in Tepecano, and in Northern Tepehuan it simplified to -gi. The development of Papago -ǰid is somewhat problematic, but I will propose the following. *-gia was interpreted phonetically

as *-giya, which became *-gida by regular sound change. The only special change we must assume is the assimilation of g to d, yielding *-dida.
The palatalization of d to ǰ before high vowels is regular, as is the loss of
final a: *-dida > *-ǰida > -ǰid.

P-CCH *-kia becomes -ki in Huichol by loss of final a, much as in
Northern Tepehuan. There is nothing surprising in the change of *-kia to
Cora -če; in fact, the development is largely if not fully regular. P-CCH
*k regularly becomes Cora č before high front vowels, so *-kia > *-čia is
expected. The simplification of a P-CCH diphthong to Cora e is attested in
several postpositions, so *-čia > -če is not at all unprecedented, although
I do not yet know whether this simplification is sporadic or fully consistent.
Specifically: P-CCH *-cie 'in/on' > CR -ce 'in/on/for', HU -cie 'in/on/at';
P-CCH *-tɨa 'under' > CR -te 'under', HU -tɨa 'under'; P-CCH *-kɨa
'place of' > CR -ke/-če 'place of', HU -cɨa 'with/place of'.[10]

5.3. Other Passives

5.3.1. Southern Numic

The suffix -'tɨɨ of Southern Paiute is specifically passive, and -'tuʔa is
specifically impersonal (with both transitive and intransitive verbs).
Kawaiisu -'toʔo is attested as a passive and presumably also has impersonal use. Southern Paiute -'tɨɨ derives from P-UA *-tɨ-wa, as we have
seen, but -'tuʔa and -'toʔo must have some other source.

I will posit for Proto Southern Numic the innovation of *-'tuʔa as an impersonal suffix. The innovation of this suffix facilitated or was prompted
by the narrowing of *-'tɨɨ from passive/impersonal to specifically passive
use. Southern Paiute retains the P-SNM situation unchanged, but two developments occurred in Kawaiisu. Phonologically, *-'tuʔa became *-'toʔa and
then, through vowel harmonization, -'toʔo. Syntactically, this suffix displaced *-'tɨɨ and assumed both passive and impersonal functions.

The source of *-'tuʔa is the massively attested P-UA derivational suffix

---

[10]The fluctuation between -ke and -če for Cora 'place of' suggests that the monoph-
thongization of *ɨa to e in this form was fairly recent, following the change of *k to č
before i and e. Cora -ce and -te are diachronically segmentable from the postpositions
hece and hete. he (< *pɨ) derives by reanalysis of an earlier third person singular postpositional object pronoun (UA-L-SP).

*-tu(-a) used in the formation of verbs. There has been a certain amount
of semantic shifting since P-UA times, but almost certainly *-tu by itself
originally meant 'become', while the transitivizing suffix *-a combined
with this to form *-tu-a 'make'. Unproblematic reflexes of *-tu(-a) include the following: NP -tu(u) 'make into'; M -tu 'make', -tuwa 'become
like'; SH -tua 'become/turn into'; SP -tu 'make into', -tuˀa 'become/turn
into'; TU -uu(ˀ(u)) 'make/prepare'; SR -tuˀ(a) 'make/become'; CA -lu 'act/
appear/be like'; CU -lu 'act/be like '; L -u/-o 'make/become'; TA -tu 'become'; Y -tu 'be/become/exist'; HU -tɨ 'be/become'; A -ti 'be/become',
-tia 'become/make'.

From all indications, P-SNM *-'tuˀa meant 'become'. If we assume
that impersonal sentences have underlying structures of the kind shown in
Figure XIV, the innovation of *-'tuˀa as an impersonal suffix involved two
minor innovations, probably simultaneous. First, this suffix was extended
semantically from 'become' to 'be', that is, from indicating the inception of
existence of a state to indicating simply existence of the state: INCEPT
[BE] > BE. Secondly, *-'tuˀa 'be' replaced *-'tɨ as the lexicalization of
the higher predicate 'be' in impersonal sentences.

5.3.2.   Tarahumara

The next passive/impersonal suffix to be considered is Tarahumara -tu/
-ru, which has also been extended to reflexive use, as we saw in Chapter 2.
As a derivational suffix, -tu in Tarahumara means 'become'. The innovation of passives in -tu alongside those in -riwa (and -giwa) is therefore
quite similar to the adoption of *-'tuˀa as an impersonal suffix in P-SNM,
requiring only the semantic extension of -tu from 'become' to 'be'. I have
nothing to say concerning the possible cause of this innovation. Relation to
Huichol -rɨwa (< *-ruwa ?) is not impossible but is at best highly speculative.

5.3.3.   Cupan

The original Uto-Aztecan *-tɨ-wa passive was completely lost in Takic.
Serrano apparently does without a replacement, but two new kinds of passives have been innovated in Cupan. One of them, found in all three Cupan

languages, involves the use of aspectual suffixes otherwise found only in
subordinate clauses. The other, restricted to Cupeno and presumably constituting an innovation in that language, involves the stative suffix -yax
'be'.[11]

As we have seen, passive sentences in Cupeno may be formed by using
the stative suffix -yax with a stem that normally requires the active suffix
-in:

> CU (1) gəyiinə təm-pə-yəx-wə
> chicken enclose-it-STAT-DUR
>   PL
> 'A chicken was cooped up.'   (CU-H-G-79)

The underlying subject is unspecified, and the underlying object functions
as surface subject. The underlying structure of this type of passive sentence in Cupeno is therefore approximately that shown in Figure XVIII.[12]

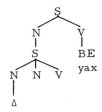

Figure XVIII

Figure XVIII is of course nothing other than the transitive version of Figure
I, which was posited for passive/impersonal sentences throughout Uto-
Aztecan and for other languages as well. There is no evidence to suggest
that this Cupeno construction directly continues the P-UA *-ti-wa passive
construction with the same underlying structure; rather it is a re-creation
of the construction at a later and quite recent stage of evolution, using the
current form of the copula to lexicalize the higher predicate 'be'. This re-
creation of structures like Figure XVIII is strong evidence that this kind of
structure has universal validity and does not simply represent retention of
an idiosyncratic P-UA construction.

[11] Kroeber and Grace report a contrast between Luiseno neč-i-ktum 'are going to
pay' and neč-ax-kotom 'are going to be paid' (L-KG-SG-31) which suggests that the innovation of -yax for passive use might go back to Proto Cupan. This possibility must
be left for more detailed investigation.

[12] For evidence that -yax derives from a higher predicate, see UA-L-PR. Detailed
discussion of Cupan -yax is provided in CUP-J-SC; cf. also Chapter 3, footnote 10
and the references cited there. For discussion of the -in/-yax alternation in Cupeno,
see CU-H-G, CU-H-VN, and CUP-J-SC-79-82.

Let us turn now to passive constructions involving aspectual suffixes
normally found in subordinate clauses. Two kinds of suffixes are involved.
In all three Cupan languages, passives can be formed by means of the descendant of P-CUP *-və-l, indicating realization of the activity designated
by the verb, and also by means of the descendant of P-CUP *-pi-š, indicating non-realization of this activity. *-l and *-š are both absolutive suffixes. *-və-l is reflected by regular sound change as -ve-l in Cahuilla, as
-və-l in Cupeno, and as -vo-l in Luiseno. *-pi-š is regularly reflected as
-pi-š in all three daughters. The second type of construction may be restricted to Luiseno. It employs the suffixes -aa-t and -i-š, which also incorporate absolutive suffixes, and which are normally associated with nominalizations. -aa-t supposedly designates ongoing activity, and -i-š the
state resulting from previous activity.

The passive use of *-və-l and *-pi-š is characteristic of all three Cupan
languages and may therefore be reconstructed for P-CUP. The forms and
pertinent constructions are so similar in all three languages that examples
may be used interchangeably for purposes of this discussion. The following
Cupeno examples illustrate the contrast between the realized forms with
*-və-l and the unrealized forms with *-pi-š:

> CU (2) hunwə-t   mamayəw-və-l
> bear-ABS help-R-ABS
> 'The bear was helped.'   (CUP-J-SR-11)

> CU (3) hunwə-t   mamayəw-pi-š
> bear-ABS help-UNR-ABS
> 'The bear will be helped.'   (CUP-J-SR-11)

Passive sentences like (2) and (3) are not terribly common and they have
received little study. For this reason I will not attempt a full description
of them; in particular, there is some uncertainty regarding their underlying structure. We can nevertheless determine how this construction arose
and acquired passive value.

We must first examine the non-passive use of these suffixes. They occur in a variety of subordinate clause types. One construction that may be
pertinent here involves subject complement clauses embedded to the verb
'be', which appears as mi-yax (reduced to miyx in Luiseno). The following

two Cahuilla examples will illustrate this construction:[13]

CA (4) [ne-taxmu-ve] miyax-we
         my-sing-R   be-DUR
                        PL
         'I have sung.'   (CUP-J-SC-165)

CA (5) [ne-taxmu-pi] miyax-we
         my-sing-UNR be-DUR
                      PL
         'I have to sing.'   (CUP-J-SC-166)

Realized complement clauses embedded to 'be' in this construction are perfective and, when 'be' is present tense, translate with the English present
perfect. Unrealized complement clauses embedded to 'be' in this construction are modal and translate with 'must' or 'have to' when 'be' is in the
present tense. The subordinate clause subject is specified, and a possessor prefix agreeing with this subject is attached to the lower verb. The
lower verb can be regarded as being nominalized, and the attachment of the
possessor prefix entails the loss of the absolute suffix, as it regularly
does in Cupan. For this reason -ve-l and -pi-š consistently appear in their
non-absolutive forms -ve and -pi in this construction.

This construction provides one possible source for the passive sentences
under consideration, since it involves a subject complement clause embedded to 'be', as in Figure XVIII. It has a specified subordinate clause subject, but were this subject to be left unspecified, the resulting configuration
would be that posited for passive sentences. Moreover, since the unspecified subject could not give rise to a possessor prefix agreeing with it, the
aspectual suffixes would be expected to surface in their absolutive form, as
they do. We need only assume deletion or non-lexicalization of 'be' to derive surface structures like (2) and (3). A sentence like (2) would thus have
the underlying structure shown in Figure XIX (leaving aside the possibility
that -ve and -pi might be underlying predicates). Deletion of BE and ad-
vancement of hunwǝ-t to subject position are the major operations required
to derive the surface structure.

[13]The occurrence of the plural form of the durative suffix in this construction, also
characteristic of Cupeno (but not Luiseno), recalls the use of the plural durative suffix
in Cupeno -yax passives. Use of the plural suffix is therefore not restricted to passives and does not necessarily indicate that the unspecified passive subject is plural,
for it is associated with non-passive constructions with 'be' as well as passive ones.
This corroborates our earlier decision not to equate plural subject marking on Cupeno
passive verbs with the plural subject marking of impersonal verbs in Southern Paiute.

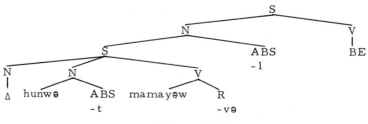

Figure XIX

While this is a possible source for the *-və-l and *-pi-š passives, I be-lieve it is not the most likely source. One problem is that (2) and (3) lack the present perfect and 'have to' sense characteristic of sentences like (4) and (5). Another problem is that miyax 'be' is not regularly deletable in sentences like (4) and (5); its deletion in the derivation of passives would have to be considered anomalous. Neither of these difficulties is over-whelming, but they prompt us to ask whether another source is available which would avoid them.

I propose that the *-və-l and *-pi-š passives derive instead from the relative clause use of these suffixes. In all three Cupan languages, they are found in relative clauses in which the subordinate clause object is co-referential to the head noun, as illustrated in (6) and (7).

> L (6) ?awaa-l [po   hunwu-t   po-mamayuw-vo]
>   dog-ABS SUBR bear-ABS his-help-R
>   'the dog that the bear helped'   (CUP-J-SR-10)

> L (7) ?awaa-l [po   hunwu-t   po-mamayuw-pi]
>   dog-ABS SUBR bear-ABS his-help-UNR
>   'the dog that the bear will help'   (CUP-J-SR-10)

The subordinator is optional. -vo and -pi occur in their non-absolutive form because of the possessor prefix on the verb. Notice that the present perfect and 'have to' meanings of (4) and (5) are not characteristic of this relative clause construction.

My specific claim is that passives like (2) and (3) derive from equative sentences in which the surface verb originates as a relative clause. (2), for example, would have the underlying structure shown in Figure XX. 'The bear was helped' is said to derive from a structure that more literally means something like 'The bear is one who was helped' or 'The bear is one

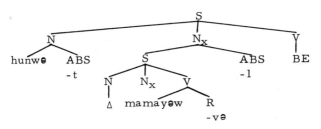

Figure XX

characterized by some unspecified person helping him'. Because the relative clause subject is unspecified, no possessor prefix is inserted and the
absolute suffix is retained. The deletion of BE is no problem, because
BE is normally deleted in present tense equative sentences:

    L (8) nawitmal no-ṣwaamay
            girl   my-daughter
            'The girl is my daughter. '   (L-H-I-13)

Both of the problems encountered with the other source are thus avoided
when structures like Figure XX are posited to underlie *-ve-l and *-pi-š
passives. The only question that arises is whether such structures are
still valid as synchronic underlying representations for sentences like (2)
or whether reanalysis has occurred making these sentences true passives
which derive from underlying structures like Figure XVIII. I have no clear
evidence which bears on the matter.[14]

The choice of the relative clause source of *-ve-l and *-pi-š passives is
confirmed to some degree by the -aa-t and -i-š passives of Luiseno, illustrated in (9) and (10).

    L (9) ʔawaa-l xeč-aa-t
            dog-ABS hit-NR-ABS
            'The dog is being beaten. '   (CUP-J-SC-178)

    L (10) ki-š   kulaw-tal loʔx-i-š
             house-ABS wood-with make-NR-ABS
                  ACC
             'The house is made with wood. '   (CUP-J-SC-178)

As nominalizing suffixes in Cupan, -aa-t and -i-š form derived nouns which
designate the object or product of the verbal activity, as in (11) and (12).

---

[14] The following Cupeno example may be relevant, but I am uncertain about its analysis: pəʔ ʔəmpə ʔə-na-y pə-tə məqni-ve-l (this there (?) your-father-ACC it-on kill-
R-ABS) 'This must be where your father was killed' (CU-HN-M-137). Note particularly the accusative inflection on the logical object of 'kill'.

CA (11) wes-a-t
         sow-NR-ABS
         'what was sown/the seed'   (CUP-J-SC-156)

CA (12) wiw-i-š
         make-NR-ABS
         acorn
         mush
         'acorn mush'   (CU-HN-M-135)

Because these nominals designate the object of the underlying verb rather than the subject or the verbal activity itself, (9) and (10) can be attributed underlying structures directly analogous to Figure XX.

For example, Figure XXI is the probable underlying structure of (9).

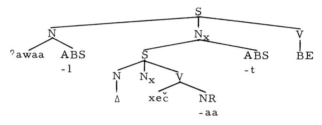

Figure XXI

Just as 'seed' means literally 'that which is sown', 'The dog is being beaten' means literally 'The dog is one who is being beaten' or 'The dog is one characterized by some unspecified person beating him'. The deletion of 'be' in equative sentences is independently attested, as we saw before, and in fact 'be' can be used in Luiseno sentences like (9) and (10) to express non-present tense (CUP-J-SC-178).

Once again the only question that arises concerns reanalysis. Is Figure XXI still valid as the synchronic underlying representation of (9), or has reanalysis converted these sentences to true passives with underlying representations like Figure XVIII? Sentence (10) suggests that reanalysis may in fact have taken place. The surface subject of (10), ki-š 'house', occurs in accusative form (the nominative form is ki-ča). If underlying structures like Figure XXI are correct, this cannot be explained, because the surface subject is also the underlying subject and remains the subject throughout the derivation. With underlying structures like Figure XVIII, on the other hand, the surface subject originates as underlying object of the subordinate clause, hence it would not be surprising for it to surface sporadically in

object form. However, further examples would be welcome to be sure that
(10) does not simply incorporate a slip of the tongue or the pen.

5.3.4. Additional Constructions

In the preceding sections I have tried to account reasonably fully for the
evolution of the central passive and impersonal constructions in the contemporary Uto-Aztecan languages. Here we will examine a number of additional constructions that possibly merit the label passive or impersonal.
Information currently available is not sufficient to allow us to reconstruct
them or trace their history in any detail. However, by assembling them
and noting certain similarities we can at least point the way for possibly
fruitful future research.

Some of these constructions were touched on in section 5.1 in conjunction with the discussion of whether or not plural subject marking could be
reconstructed for passives and impersonals. Besides the use of the plural
-'ka with Southern Paiute impersonal verbs and the plural suffix -we with
passive verbs in Cupeno, impersonal constructions possibly involving plural subject marking are attested in Luiseno and Papago. In Luiseno, the
construction involves the quotative clitic, sometimes accompanied by the
plural clitic =m, and the plural verb suffix -wun:

> L (1) nawitmal-i=kunu=m čuŋi-wun
>   girl-ACC-QUOT-PL kiss-PRES
>   PL
>   'The girl got kissed.'   (L-M-PC)

A variant of this construction has been reported in which the clitic =ṣu appears in lieu of the quotative =kunu; =ṣu normally has dubitative or inter-
rogative force:

> L (2) no-patkila-y=ṣu=m=il   ʔoyooto-wun
>   my-gun-ACC-DUB-PL-PAST steal-PRES
>   PL
>   'My gun's been stolen.'   (L-M-PC)

This variation is suggestive when compared to the situation in Papago.
As we saw, one Papago impersonal construction uses the auxiliary element
=m, not otherwise found in Papago but obviously relatable to the plural
clitic =m of Luiseno:

P (3) haiwañ ʔa=m=t   wuu
       cow   AUX-IMPRS-PERF rope
                              PERF
       'They roped the cow.'   (P-H-PC)

Papago also displays a perfective construction involving the verb suffix
-s(k) that has passive force:

P (4) ʔiida ʔoidag ʔo   hɨki hu moihuna-s
       this field   AUX already plow-STAT
       'This field has already been plowed.'   (P-H-PC)

P (5) ʔiida ʔoidag ʔa=t   o   moihuna-sk
       this field   AUX-PERF FUT plow-STAT
       'This field will be plowed.'   (P-H-PC)

It is natural to ask, then, whether the Papago stative suffix -s can be related somehow to the Luiseno dubitative clitic =ṣu. Grammatically and
semantically this is certainly possible (see UA-S-FIP for extended discussion), but phonologically there is a problem in that PUA *s normally becomes P h. The parallelism between (1) and (2) on the one hand, and on the
other hand between (3) and (4)-(5), is nevertheless striking, and the possibility of mutual influence or common inheritance should be explored further
when more complete data from other languages becomes available.

   The preceding section dealt with the development of passive constructions from nominalizations in Cupan. In particular, different kinds of relative clause inflections have apparently assumed passive force in sentences
that are not overtly complex. This relation between nominalization and
passives is not yet fully understood, but there are a number of indications
that it is not accidental and is probably quite significant. For one thing, the
prototypical passive/impersonal configuration that I have tried to justify in
a variety of ways (Figure I) involves a clause embedded to the higher predicate BE and functioning as its subject. This is precisely the kind of struc-
ture--a clause functioning as (part of) the argument of a predicate--that
underlies nominalizations and relative clauses. Second, the relation between passive/impersonal sentences and nominalization is attested by the
incorporation of the nominalizing suffix *-wa into the P-UA passive suffix
*-tɨ-wa (discussed in section 5.2.4). Finally, there are a number of fur-
ther examples, in Luiseno and various other Uto-Aztecan languages, that
show a tendency for nominalization to be associated with passive sense.

   I mention only in passing the perfective participial suffix -'pɨ found throughout Numic. It is cognate to the *-və suffix that came to mark non-subordinate verbs as passive in Proto Cupan (section 5.3.3) and can probably be reconstructed for P-UA. In Numic this suffix functions as a nominalizer (from which derives its use as an absolutive suffix in this subfamily) contributing passive sense, perfective sense, or both.[15] Of relevance here is its occurrence in the following Chemehuevi construction (I do not know how widespread this construction is in Numic):

CH (6) ʔiič kaan muwa-ya=n kani-ču-ˈp
 this house father-ACC-my house-make-PERF
 PRTC
 'This house was built by my father.' (CH-M-PC)

This sentence can be interpreted to mean literally 'This house is that which my father made' and can be attributed an underlying equative structure directly analogous to Figure XX except for the subordinate clause subject being specified. It is quite possible, then, that the use of equative sentences involving a relative clause structure and having passive value of some kind can be reconstructed for some proto stage, possibly even P-UA. The Cupan construction descended from P-CUP *-və-l and *-pi-š would then be only one reflex of this reconstructed sentence type (perhaps the only one for which we might plausibly argue that reanalysis has occurred to yield synchronic underlying structures analogous to Figure XVIII).

It would be most speculative to reconstruct complex equative sentences having passive force on the basis of Cupan and Chemehuevi alone, but the attestation is somewhat broader when we go beyond reflexes of *-pɨ and take into account examples with other nominalizers. First, this construction is also found in Chemehuevi with the nominalizer -na:

CH (7) ʔič kʷasu=n piya-ya=n maha-ˈkay-n
 this dress-my mother-ACC-my wash-PERF-NR
 'My dress was washed by my mother.' (UA-LM-PM)

Next, we find a similar construction in Luiseno where the verb lacks any subordinating suffix but is nevertheless indicated to be subordinate by the presence of a possessor prefix that agrees with its subject:

L (8) ʔiviʔ ʔaʔalvi-š naxanmal po-ʔaʔalvi
 this story-ABS old his-tell
 man story
 'This story was told by an old man.' (L-M-PC)

---

[15] The relation between passives, perfectives, and nominalizations is explored further in UA-LM-PM and CH-M-IPP.

L (9) ʔoonu=p nu-taaʔaṣ ne-yk pu-ʔoovi
       this-it   my-uncle me-to his-give
       'This was given to me by my uncle.'   (L-D-PG-212)

Finally, there is a very similar construction in Papago:

P (10) hɨgai siiki ʔo   ʔaañi wuḍ ñ-mɨʔ-a
        that   deer AUX I   be my-kill-NR
        'That deer was killed by me.'   (P-H-PC)

This Papago example is particularly interesting because the equative 'be',
which I have hypothesized on the basis of less direct evidence in the above
examples and in Figures XX and XXI, actually appears in the surface form
of the sentence.[16]

In summary, then, it is not unreasonable to suppose that equative structures analogous to Figure XXI can be reconstructed with passive value for
P-UA. At present such a reconstruction is rather uncertain, however, and
we should probably leave the matter open pending corroboration from languages farther to the south.

5.4.   Underlying Representations

Considerable evidence has been presented to justify positing underlying
representations like Figure I to underlie passive and impersonal sentences
in Uto-Aztecan. In concluding our examination of passives and impersonals,
it may prove helpful to summarize this evidence briefly and to discuss it in
a somewhat broader context. (See UA-LM-PM for more extensive discussion.)

Three aspects of Figure I distinguish it from the kinds of underlying
structures commonly postulated for passives in more familiar languages
like English. First, passive/impersonal clauses are claimed to derive
from subject complement clauses embedded to the higher predicate 'be'.
Second, the underlying subject is claimed to be unspecified. And third, it
is claimed that no analog of the English by-phrase is involved. Let us examine the evidence for each of these claims in turn. The evidence bears
directly only on the underlying structure of passives and impersonals in

---

[16]Additional, circumstantial evidence for the underlying predicate BE in this construction is provided by Luiseno perfective sentences in which the copular verb actually surfaces with the subordinate verb marked as it is in (8) and (9): ʔu-ṣṇa-ki
nu-tiiwi miiʔ-qa (your-woman-POSSD my-see be-PRES) 'I have already seen your
wife' (L-D-PG-295).

Uto-Aztecan, but it bears at least indirectly on the representation of passives in other languages if anything more than lip service is paid to the
concept of universal grammar.

All of the specifically passive/impersonal suffixes attested in Uto-
Aztecan can be equated with or directly related to 'be'. The basic passive/
impersonal suffix reconstructs roughly as P-UA *-ti-wa, and *-ti can be
identified with pre-P-UA *ti 'be'. Proto Southern Numic *-'tu?a and
Tarahumara -tu/-ru both derive from (etymologically related) derivational
suffixes meaning 'become', which clearly incorporates 'be' as a semantic
component. The innovation of Cupeno passives with -yax 'be' is especially
significant, since this represents a re-creation rather than a continuation
of the 'be' passive construction.

The descendants of P-UA *-ti-wa are virtually always used for both
passive and impersonal sentences, and the same is true of Tarahumara -tu/
-ru. Impersonal sentences are always intransitive (except in Southern
Paiute, where -'tu?a has taken over the impersonal role), and their subject
is always unspecified. Passive sentences are basically transitive versions
of impersonal sentences. The underlying object is specified, and it replaces the unspecified underlying subject in surface subject position. The overtly marked unity of passive and impersonal sentences in Uto-Aztecan is
prima facie evidence for the claim that passive sentences have unspecified
underlying subjects, since the claim is utterly uncontroversial in regard to
impersonals. Were it not for the standard analysis of English passives, in
which an underlying specified subject becomes an oblique object by transformation, the analyst of Uto-Aztecan would hardly feel any need to justify
positing unspecified underlying subjects for passive sentences in this family.

The claim that passive/impersonal sentences have unspecified underlying
subjects receives support from several other quarters. The validity of the
notion of unspecified arguments and their importance in Uto-Aztecan grammar are both strongly affirmed by the phenomenon of unspecified argument
prefixes, discussed in Chapter 4. Positing unspecified underlying subjects
for passive sentences makes it possible to account insightfully for the extension of reflexive prefixes to passive use; the extension represents a generalization in function from marking coreferential arguments to marking non-
distinct arguments. By positing unspecified underlying subjects we can also

account for the incorporation of *-<u>wa</u> in the P-UA passive/impersonal suffix *-<u>tɨ-wa</u>, as argued in section 5.2.4. Finally, the unspecified subject
claim enables us to account in a natural way for the extension of the Cupan
suffixes *-<u>və-l</u> and *-<u>pi-š</u> to passive use (cf. Figure XX). The fact that
these endings retain the absolute suffixes *-<u>l</u> and *-<u>š</u> is especially significant. Verbs marked by *-<u>və-l</u> and *-<u>pi-š</u> regularly receive a possessor
prefix to agree with their subject, which causes the absolute suffix to
drop, yielding *-<u>və</u> and *-<u>pi</u>. In their passive use, however, there is no
possessor prefix and these endings appear in their full form *-<u>və-l</u> and
*-<u>pi-š</u>, as we would expect if the subject is unspecified.

There is no evidence whatever for regarding agentive phrases as an intrinsic part of passivization in Uto-Aztecan or for deriving such phrases
from a specified underlying passive subject. Such phrases are at best uncommon in passive sentences, the ones that do occur do not obviously reconstruct, and they are not attested at all for impersonal sentences. In
view of the strong evidence for positing unspecified underlying subjects for
passive sentences,[17] it is most plausible to suppose that agentive phrases,
when they occur, are not inherent in the passive construction per se.

As a specific proposal along these lines, I suggest that they derive from
a conjunct in which the agentive postposition (or the postpositional phrase
as a whole) functions as a predicate. Schematically, a sentence like 'The
gun is fired by me' will have an underlying structure similar to Figure XXII.

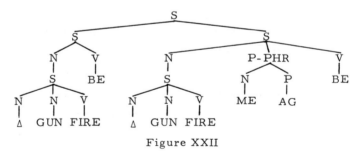

Figure XXII

'The gun is fired by me' thus derives from a fuller underlying structure

---

[17] The arguments given are generally incompatible with the alternative of creating
an unspecified subject in the course of a derivation by moving an underlying specified
subject and making it oblique. Agentive phrases identifying the semantic subject are
not to my knowledge found in impersonal sentences, reflexive passives, *-<u>wa</u> nominalizations, or Cupan *-<u>və-l</u> and *-<u>pi-š</u> passives.

meaning 'The gun is fired (and) it (= the firing of the gun) is by me'.

I will not attempt to support this analysis in any detail here, but two brief observations are perhaps in order. First, structures exactly analogous to Figure XXII were strongly motivated in Chapter 3 as (at least diachronic) underlying structures for clauses containing the reflexive pronouns *$^{?}$a-nak^{w}ayɨ and *pɨ-nak^{w}ayɨ in P-UA. The incorporation of a postpositional phrase deriving from a separate conjunct was firmly established as a historical phenomenon, and the present analysis does no more than extend this process to synchronic derivations. Second, it may be pertinent that <u>by</u>-phrases can be used overtly as predicates in English:

(1) This painting is by Seurat.

(2) The applause was by everyone in the room.

To be sure, this construction is fairly restricted; sentences like (3) and (4) are highly questionable if not ungrammatical, but they are not resoundingly ungrammatical the way many sentences are, and their meaning is readily grasped:

? (3) The killing of the duckling was by farmer MacDonald.

? (4) The student was savagely beaten, and it was by an unruly mob of policemen.

The awkwardness of these expressions may only indicate that <u>by</u>-phrase incorporation tends to be obligatory in English passives. Furthermore, something approximating Figure XXII would seem appropriate for "afterthought" <u>by</u>-phrases like that in (5):

(5) The gun was fired, by me.

I would suggest (though I cannot demonstrate here) that the presence versus the absence of the pause designated by the comma in (5) pertains, not to radical differences in underlying constituent structure, but rather to a presuppositional difference concerning how essential the speaker considers the phrase (or second conjunct) to be relative to the semantic content of the surface main clause.

The claim that Figure I approximates the underlying structure of passive/ impersonal sentences will be further supported if the semantic appropriateness of this structure can be demonstrated. I believe it can, but the problem of semantic representation in general, and the properties of 'be' in particular, are notoriously difficult, and a full discussion is well beyond the purview of this paper. I will however attempt to sketch some pertinent considerations and to suggest possible directions in which to proceed.

I trust there is nothing inherently implausible semantically about the claim that passive/impersonal sentences have unspecified underlying subjects. This follows almost as a matter of definition in the case of impersonal sentences and in passive sentences which lack an agentive phrase; it is potentially controversial only in passive sentences with a specified nominal in an agentive phrase, such as (6) or (7).

    (6) The gun was fired by me.

Y (7) hu kuču bʷaʔa-wa-k   ʔim ʔusi-m-mea
        that fish eat-IMPRS-PAST my child-PL-by
        'The fish was eaten by my children.'   (Y-L-TG-147)

Structures with unspecified underlying subjects are quite compatible with the fact that passive sentences are often used when the speaker wishes to foreground the underlying object rather than the subject. By deriving the agentive phrase from an optional following conjunct, we bring the underlying representations of passive sentences more in line with their information structure. This also accounts, without a special deletion rule, for the fact that languages typically allow the omission of the agentive phrase in passive sentences, and in some cases do not permit any such phrase at all.

The argument that the object of the agentive phrase in a passive sentence has the same selectional restrictions as the subject of the corresponding active sentence really has no force and does not necessitate a transformational derivation of the agentive phrase object from the underlying subject. Selectional restrictions amount to nothing more than semantic congruence, and if structures like Figure XXII are adopted for passive sentences with agentive phrases, the second conjunct and hence the entire sentence will be semantically anomalous if the object of the agentive postposition is not capable of instigating the activity described in the subject complement clause. This will surely follow from the meaning of the postposition by independent semantic principles, whatever their precise character may be.

The semantic significance of 'be' in passive/impersonal sentences is more elusive, and what follows will be quite tentative and will serve more to hint at what may be going on than to definitively establish and defend a position. For ease of exposition, I will limit discussion to sentences

describing states and sentences describing actions, where an action is
understood to presuppose an agent; I will not consider processes which
lack agents.[18] I will also exclude non-declarative sentences.

I will claim that every declarative sentence pertains in some way to the
existence of some process or state of affairs. The existence of this process or state of affairs may be simply asserted, or be denied, or qualified
by a modal, or located temporally or aspectually, etc. An existential notion is therefore implicit in every declarative sentence, and I will claim
that it constitutes a simple semantic predicate or a component of a complex semantic predicate. In the case of stative sentences, existence is typically expressed by means of the predicate 'be' (which may or may not have
independent lexicalization); 'be', in other words, asserts the existence of a
state. In the case of active sentences, existence is typically expressed by
means of the complex predicate 'do' or 'act'. 'Do', I suggest, combines
two strands of meaning: it asserts the causation of existence of a process,
and it implies the directness of this causation through action on the part of
the subject of 'do'.

Ross has provided very strong syntactic evidence to justify positing the
predicate 'do' in the semantic representation of all active sentences in
English;[19] in his analysis, a sentence like (8) derives from an underlying
representation like (9) through complement subject deletion and deletion or
non-lexicalization of 'do', which does however surface as do in many constructions. Just as 'do' embeds an object complement in the underlying
structure of active sentences, I will claim that 'be' embeds a subject complement in the underlying structure of stative sentences. A sentence like
(10) will therefore have the underlying structure shown in (11).

    (8) Met hissed.

    (9) PAST [DO MET [HISS MET]]

    (10) Raquel was under the table.

[18] This is not an insignificant omission. For some discussion of these notions, see
Wallace L. Chafe, Meaning and the Structure of Language, Chicago, University of
Chicago Press, 1970. The ideas developed below are explored more extensively in
Ronald W. Langacker, 'Functional Stratigraphy', to appear in Robin Grossman et al.
(eds.), Papers from the Parasession on Functionalism, Chicago, Chicago Linguistic
Society, 1975.

[19] John R. Ross, 'Act', in Donald Davidson and Gilbert Harman (eds.), Semantics
of Natural Language (second edition), Dordrecht, D. Reidel, 1972, p. 70-126.

(11) PAST [BE [UNDER RAQUEL TABLE]]

If every declarative sentence contains a predicate of existence in underlying structure, we can begin to explain why passive and impersonal sentences involve subject complement clauses embedded to 'be'. Embedding
to 'be' is a natural consequence of the unspecified character of the subject.
In an active sentence like (8), the subject of 'do' is specified and is required, by virtue of the meaning of 'do', to be coreferential to the complement
subject. It is meaningful and informative to indicate agency in a sentence
when the agent is specified. In a passive or impersonal sentence, on the
other hand, the agent--the underlying subject of the lower verb--is unspecified, and while it is semantically consistent to speak of an unspecified
agent, reference to such an agent is hardly informative. Semantically,
there is very little difference between structures like (13) and (14) for sentences such as (12); both assert the existence of the process described by
the lowest clause, but while (13) expresses agency, it does so only vacuous-
ly because the agent is unspecified.

(12) The fish was eaten.

(13) PAST [DO Δ [EAT Δ FISH]]

(14) PAST [BE [EAT Δ FISH]]

Since (13) and (14) are effectively equivalent, languages could choose either
one, and (14) is the optimal choice by virtue of its greater simplicity. In
short, 'be' is associated with passive and impersonal sentences because
these sentences assert existence but remain unspecified in regard to agency.

One matter that I have studiously avoided thus far is the underlying representations of passive sentences marked by reflexive prefixes. Presumably reflexive passive sentences originally have underlying structures analogous to (13), since they constitute extensions of reflexive active sentences
for which such structures are appropriate. When reflexive passives are
first innovated, therefore, we find sentences like the French examples (15)
and (17) paired with semantic representations like (16) and (18) respectively:

(15) Il se mord. 'He bites himself.'

(16) PRES [DO x [BITE x x]]

(17) La porte se ferme. 'The door closes.'/'The door is closed.'

(18) PRES [DO Δ [CLOSE Δ DOOR]]

Once the passive use of reflexive prefixes is established, however, it is not implausible to suppose that reanalysis might occur, leading to underlying structures like (14). I have no evidence at present to indicate whether or not this reanalysis does in fact take place.[20]

Another matter that I have largely avoided so far is the character of the mechanisms for inserting and attaching verbal affixes. I have claimed that passive suffixes in Uto-Aztecan lexicalize the higher predicate 'be', and that the attachment of this predicate to the lower verb is accomplished by the syntactic rule of predicate raising (cf. UA-L-PR). However, the precise formulation of predicate raising is problematic, as is its relationship to suffixation (UA-S-PTME), and I would not insist on any particular formulation at present. For purposes of this monograph, it is sufficient to note that passive/impersonal suffixes in Uto-Aztecan do bear a consistent relation to 'be', and that higher predicates commonly surface as verb suffixes in verb-final languages.

Although I will not explore the mechanisms for inserting and attaching verbal affixes in any detail, I would like to comment on the potential significance of the fact that passive and impersonal affixes in Uto-Aztecan are consistently suffixes, while reflexive, reciprocal, and unspecified argument affixes are consistently prefixes. In view of the fact that the Uto-Aztecan languages are basically verb-final, this distribution is probably not just accidental. I have related the passive/impersonal suffixes to a higher predicate, and with verb-final order, higher predicates occur to the right of a subordinate verb, as in the schematic passive structure (19).

(19) [Δ (N) V] BE

On the other hand, reflexive, reciprocal, and unspecified argument affixes pertain to the nature of the arguments of a verb, and with verb-final order the arguments of a verb precede it. Therefore, if passive/impersonal affixes derive from underlying predicates while reflexive, reciprocal, and unspecified argument affixes derive from underlying arguments, the fact that the former will surface as suffixes and the latter as prefixes is not unexpected. I am aware of the many theoretical and descriptive problems, both synchronic and diachronic, that arise in trying to carry these

---

[20]The fact that French reflexive sentences require être rather than avoir in the past tense is suggestive, but its significance can only be assessed in the context of a detailed examination of diachronic French syntax.

observations beyond the handwaving stage, and I cannot resolve them here.
They do however lend added plausibility to our conception of the underlying
structure of passive/impersonal sentences.

We have seen that there is evidence for deriving passive/impersonal
suffixes from the predicate 'be'. Is there any comparable evidence for deriving reflexive and unspecified argument prefixes from underlying nominal constituents? One kind of evidence is that the occurrence of a reflexive
or unspecified argument prefix on a verb precludes the co-occurrence of an
argument that the verb would otherwise require. This complementary distribution could be taken as evidence for a transformational incorporation of
underlying arguments as verbal prefixes, and while this argument strikes
me as being rather simplistic, I am not sure that any reasonable formulation of the co-occurrence restrictions would not amount to a notational variant of this analysis.

The notions of subject and object focus introduced in section 4.0 may be
relevant here. We saw that reflexive and non-distinct argument prefixes
must be specified for whether non-distinctness of the subject is required or
non-distinctness of the object. Unspecified argument prefixes such as *ta-
and *tɨ- also pertain to the character of a particular argument, not any
argument randomly chosen. The fact that these prefixes bear a special
relationship to one specific argument in a clause might be taken as further
evidence for deriving them from this argument.

A third consideration which bears on this matter is the form of reflexive
and unspecified argument prefixes. The reflexive prefixes in the southern
Uto-Aztecan languages bear a close and certainly non-accidental resemblance to the corresponding pronominal forms, as we saw in Chapter 2, and
this is of course true in many languages of the world. The P-UA unspecified argument prefixes *ta- and *tɨ- can also be related to possible pro
forms of P-UA or pre-P-UA. *ta- can be related to the various forms for
'man/person';[21] Miller reconstructs the variants *taka, *tawa, *tana, and
*ta for this form (UA-M-CS-45; cf. section 3.4.2). There are indications
that *tɨ- can be reconstructed as a pro form meaning 'thing'. Sapir, for

---

[21]The first step in this development, namely noun incorporation (leading to noun-
verb compounds), is of course quite common. Cf. Tubatulabal nɨmʔ-mɨʔɨg 'kill a
person/murder' (TU-V-WD-224), from *nɨmɨ 'person' and mɨʔɨg(a) 'kill'.

example, cites ʔi-čɨ as meaning 'this thing' in Southern Paiute (UA-S-
SPN1-393); ʔi means 'this', and t̲ can be expected to palatalize to č̲ after i.
Papago haʔiču and Tepecano has̆tu both mean 'something' and point to Proto
Pimic *tu. It will be recalled that P-UA *tɨ- irregularly became *tu- in
Proto Pimic.[22]

In view of these various considerations, it is not unreasonable to claim
that reflexive and unspecified argument prefixes derive from nominal constituents at least diachronically. Extending this analysis to synchronic derivations is another matter, one on which we might better reserve judgment.

5.5.   Evolution

5.5.1.   Proto Uto-Aztecan

The P-UA passive/impersonal suffix had several dialectal variants, including at least *-tɨ-wa, *-ti-wa, and *-li-wa. Possibly the first syllable
was optional. This suffix was passive with transitive verbs and impersonal
with intransitive verbs.

    I5.5.1.1.   *-ti-wa simplified to -iw(a) in TU.

    I5.5.1.2.   Morphological developments in H led to a number of passive
variants partially differentiated semantically, including -i, -(i)wa, and -lti.

    I5.5.1.3/CD5.5.1.1.   This suffix was lost in P-TAK.

    I5.5.1.4.   In P-TRC and P-CCH, *-li-wa became *-riwa by regular
sound change.

----

[22] The *-wa of P-UA *-tɨ-wa, which relates to the unspecified character of the subject in passive/impersonal sentences, may also be connected to a pro form. Limited
but fairly solid evidence leads to the reconstruction of *wa 'one', most unambiguously
reflected in Hopi, e.g. ʔiʔ-wa 'this one' (H-W-L-25).
Two analyses rejected earlier as untenable for the evolution of daughter languages
may prove valid, in an appropriately modified form, for the evolution of P-UA itself
from pre-P-UA. In Chapter 2 (footnote 1) we rejected the hypothesis that the reflex-
ive/reciprocal prefix na- of Numic and Hopi derives from incorporation of *taka 'man/
person' as a verbal prefix. This is indeed incorrect for na-, but a pre-P-UA root *ta
'man/person' very probably was the source of the unspecified subject prefix *ta-. (*taka
was later incorporated as the reflexive prefix tax- in Cahuilla.) The second rejected
hypothesis pertains to the cause of the change in function of te- and ta- in Aztecan. It
was suggested in section 4.2 that realignment of a subject/object contrast into a human/
non-human contrast for these prefixes might be due to the fact that transitive clause
subjects are typically human while objects may be non-human as easily as human. This
leads to the wrong results in Aztecan, but it may explain the opposite development in
P-UA. The tendency for transitive clause subjects to be human rather than non-human
makes it natural that *ta 'man/person' would develop into an unspecified subject prefix
and *tɨ 'thing' into an unspecified object prefix rather than conversely.

I5.5.1.5/CD5.5.1.2. In P-PMC, P-TRC, and P-CCH, *-<u>kiwa</u> was innovated as a variant of the passive/impersonal suffix.

I5.5.1.6/CD5.5.1.3. *-kiwa became *-kia in P-CCH.

I5.5.1.7. *-<u>li-wa</u> was lost in P-PMC (<u>CD5.5.1.4</u>). *-<u>kiwa</u> changed to
*-<u>giwa</u> and then *-<u>gia</u> (<u>CD5.5.1.5</u>).

5.5.2.   Proto Numic

P-NUM had the passive/impersonal suffix *-<u>tɨ-wa</u>, retaining the P-UA
form unchanged.

I5.5.2.1/CD5.5.2.1. *-<u>tɨ-wa</u> was lost in SH and P-WNM.

I5.5.2.2/CD5.5.2.2. The impersonal suffix *-<u>'tuʔa</u> was innovated in
P-SNM.

I5.5.2.3. *-<u>tɨ-wa</u> changed to *-<u>tɨwɨ</u> by vowel harmonization and then
simplified to *-<u>'tɨɨ</u>. It also specialized to passive function. (These changes are directly attested only in SP.)

5.5.3.   Proto Southern Numic

P-SNM was characterized by the passive suffix *-<u>'tɨɨ</u> and the impersonal suffix *-<u>'tuʔa</u>. I5.5.2.2 and I5.5.2.3 derive this system from that of
P-NUM.

I5.5.3.1. In Kawaiisu, *-<u>'tɨɨ</u> was lost. *-<u>'tuʔa</u> generalized to both
passive and impersonal use; it changed phonologically to *-<u>'toʔa</u> and then,
by vowel harmonization, to -<u>'toʔo</u>.

5.5.4.   Proto Takic

Because of I5.5.1.3, P-TAK had no passive/impersonal suffix.

I5.5.4.1/CD5.5.4.1. Passive use of the aspectual subordinate clause
suffixes *-<u>və-l</u> and *-<u>pi-š</u> was innovated in P-CUP.

5.5.5.   Proto Cupan

*-<u>və-l</u> and *-<u>pi-š</u> had passive function in P-CUP through I5.5.4.1.

I5.5.5.1. Passive use of the nominalizing suffixes -<u>aa-t</u> and -<u>i-š</u> was
innovated in L. *-<u>və-l</u> became -<u>vo-l</u> by regular sound change.

5.5.6.   Proto Cahuilla-Cupeno

As in P-CUP, the suffixes *-vǝ-l and *-pi-š had passive function in P-CAC.

I5.5.6.1.   *-vǝ-l became -ve-l in CA by regular sound change.

I5.5.6.2.   A passive construction with the stative suffix -yax was innovated in CU.

5.5.7.   Proto Pimic

P-PMC had the passive suffix *-gia.   Innovations I5.5.1.5 and I5.5.1.7 derive this system from the P-UA system.

I5.5.7.1.   *-gia was interpreted in P as *-giya, which became *-gida by regular sound change.   *-gida assimilated to *-dida, and subsequent development to *-ǰida and then -ǰid was regular.

I5.5.7.2.   *-gia simplified to *-gi in P-TEP (as attested in NT).

5.5.8.   Proto Tepehuan

*-gi was the P-TEP passive suffix.   It derives from the P-PMC suffix via I5.5.7.2.

I5.5.8.1.   *-gi was evidently lost in TO.

5.5.9.   Proto Taracahitic

P-TRC had the passive/impersonal suffixes *-riwa and *-kiwa.   I5.5.1.4 and I5.5.1.5 are responsible for deriving these from the P-UA suffix.

I5.5.9.1.   *-kiwa was lost in Y, and *-riwa simplified to -(i)wa.

I5.5.9.2.   *-riwa developed the variants -ria and -wa in TA, and *-kiwa developed to -giwa, -kia, and -gia.

I5.5.9.3.   -tu/-ru was innovated as a passive/impersonal suffix in TA. This suffix was later extended to reflexive use.

5.5.10.   Proto Corachol

P-CCH had the passive/impersonal suffixes *-riwa and *-kia.   This system derived from that of P-UA by changes 4-6 of set I5.5.1.

I5.5.10.1.   In CR, *-riwa developed the variants -iwa, -wa, and -i.   By regular changes, *-<u>kia</u> > *-<u>čia</u> > -<u>če</u>.

    I5.5.10.2. In HU, *-<u>kia</u> simplified to -<u>ki</u>. *-<u>riwa</u> evolved to -<u>ri</u>, -<u>ya</u>, -<u>wa</u>, -<u>rie</u>, and -<u>rɨwa</u>.

5.5.11.   Proto Aztecan

    P-AZN preserved the P-UA suffix *-<u>li-wa</u> unchanged. No information is available on the fate of this suffix in PO.

    I5.5.11.1. *-<u>liwa</u> became *-<u>lowa</u> in A by a change attested elsewhere. *-<u>lowa</u> simplified in various ways to -<u>lo</u>, -<u>l</u>, -<u>wa</u>, -<u>oa</u>, and -<u>o</u>.

VI. CONCLUSION

A number of reasonably well-established conclusions have emerged
from this study. Some of them pertain to languages generally and therefore to linguistic theory. Others are specific to the reconstruction of
Proto Uto-Aztecan and the evolution of its daughters.

It would be impractical to mention here all the theoretical issues which
have arisen, implicitly or explicitly, in the course of the discussion. I
have been most concerned with the concept of unspecified arguments, and I
hope to have established beyond question the linguistic significance of this
concept. Considerable evidence has also been advanced to support the importance for linguistic theory of the notion of non-distinct arguments, which
include coreferential and unspecified arguments as special cases. Non-
distinctness often holds between the subject and object of a verb, in which
case we must distinguish between instances of subject focus and instances
of object focus. Non-distinctness may also hold between a nominal in a
lower clause and a controller in a higher clause. That languages make reference to these relations is amply attested by synchronic and diachronic
evidence from Uto-Aztecan and other languages.

I have argued extensively for positing a certain type of underlying representation for passive and impersonal sentences, at least for Uto-Aztecan
and by inference for other languages as well. This underlying representation consists of a clause with unspecified subject embedded as a subject
complement to the higher predicate 'be'. When a specified object substitutes
for the unspecified subject, the result is a passive sentence. When it
does not, the result is an impersonal sentence. Agentive phrases are not
an intrinsic part of the passive construction; when they occur, they derive
from a following conjunct in which the agentive phrase functions as a predicate.

[193]

The analyses presented here provide a considerable amount of material relevant to the formulation of a theory of syntactic change. Many observations were made on the causes, mechanisms, and determining factors in syntactic change, but no attempt has been made here to formulate a theory of diachronic syntax or even to systematize the observations. Not surprisingly, the distinctive trappings of transformational grammar have not proved very useful here (e. g. the concept of transformations played virtually no role in the entire discussion). A theory of diachronic syntax must be empirically based, and while it should draw on the deepest insights of linguistic theory, it cannot profitably be tied to the idiosyncrasies of any current formulation of linguistic theory. Modern theoretical concepts have enabled us to focus on many aspects of diachronic Uto-Aztecan syntax with much greater clarity than would otherwise be possible, but for the time being diachronic syntactic studies have more to offer synchronic syntactic theory than conversely.

In regard to Uto-Aztecan specifically, we have reconstructed certain aspects of P-UA and the other, intermediate proto languages and have traced their evolution in the various daughters. The analysis naturally has implications for subclassification, and many other topics of diachronic Uto-Aztecan grammar have been touched on in the course of the discussion.

Proto Uto-Aztecan had the reciprocal verb prefix *na- and the following system of reflexive prefixes:

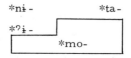

These prefixes did not have passive use. *na- occurred with postpositions and certain numerals, possibly also with nouns. There were two reflexive pronouns, *ʔa-nakᵂayɨ and *pɨ-nakᵂayɨ. The former was reciprocal, while the latter was locative and, by extension, emphatic. P-UA had three unspecified argument verb prefixes. *ta- marked unspecified subjects, *tɨ- marked unspecified objects, and *nɨ- marked unspecified human coreferential subjects. Finally, there was a passive/impersonal suffix with the dialectal variants *-tɨ-wa, *-ti-wa, and *-li-wa.

The justification of this system and its evolution were the primary subjects of this study and do not lend themselves to succinct summary. Each chapter concludes with a recapitulation of the major changes that have affected the P-UA system. The intermediate proto languages have been reconstructed and can be ascertained by assembling the summaries provided as part of these recapitulations. In tracing the evolution of the daughter languages, I have distinguished between innovations in general and what I have called common developments, which are shared innovations (or occasionally shared retentions) that are potentially significant for subclassification. Some of these corroborate the current conception of subfamilies in Uto-Aztecan, and others cross-cut these subfamilies or are shared by members of potentially larger subfamilies.

In view of the highly restricted scope of this study, nothing very certain can be deduced concerning subclassification. The number of common developments is in all cases small, and limited data has probably artificially reduced the number for subfamilies such as Tepehuan and Aztecan. Only when the figures are combined with those from many other studies of this kind will the number of common developments translate directly into solid evidence bearing on subclassification.

A tabulation of the number of common developments may prove helpful so long as these qualifications and limitations are kept firmly in mind. I will discount the numerous groupings of languages and subfamilies which display only one common development, concentrating on those with two or more. All of the major subfamilies listed in Appendix A receive some support from the phenomena studied in this work with the exception of Aztecan, and so do the Cupan and Southern Numic subfamilies. Four groupings receive support that are not generally regarded as subfamilies, namely Western Numic and Shoshoni; Numic and Hopi; Mono and Shoshoni; and Tubatulabal and Takic. The groupings are listed in Table XV according to the number of common developments.

In view of the considerations mentioned above, no importance whatever can be attached to the lack of multiple common developments for the Aztecan, Western Numic, Cahuilla-Cupeno, and Tepehuan subfamilies. On the other hand, the Southern Numic, Takic, Cupan, Pimic, and Corachol subfamilies are rather strongly corroborated, showing four or five common developments in a very limited range of data. Three of the four common

WNM-SH	5	(2.3.2.1/2.3.2.2/3.5.2.1/3.5.2.2/5.5.2.1)
SNM	5	(3.5.2.5/3.5.2.6/3.5.2.7/4.4.2.1/5.5.2.2)
NUM-H	4	(2.3.1.2/2.3.1.3/2.3.1.11/3.5.1.3)
TAK	4	(3.5.1.6/3.5.1.7/3.5.1.8/5.5.1.1)
CUP	4	(3.5.5.1/3.5.5.2/3.5.5.3/5.5.4.1)
PMC	4	(4.4.1.3/4.4.1.4/5.5.1.4/5.5.1.5)
CCH	4	(2.3.1.12/2.3.1.13/4.4.1.2/5.5.1.3)
NUM	3	(2.3.1.9/2.3.1.10/3.5.1.4)
M-SH	2	(2.3.2.3/3.5.2.3)
TU-TAK	2	(2.3.1.5/4.4.1.1)
TRC	2	(2.3.1.4/4.4.1.5)

Table XV

developments for Numic and Hopi pertain to *na-, and two of these are common retentions, so that figure may not be terribly significant. More interesting is the fact that Western Numic and Shoshoni have five common developments, while Mono and Shoshoni have two. This may be some indication that the major division within Numic is between Western and Central Numic on the one hand and Southern Numic on the other (but see NUM-FI-IC for a different proposal). This is the only non-standard subclassification that receives any substantial support.

APPENDICES

APPENDIX A
Genetic Classification

This is a highly conservative classification. None of the subfamilies indicated is considered controversial, and while more inclusive subgroupings are likely, none has been conclusively established. Only the twenty languages under primary consideration are listed.

Numic (NUM)
    Western Numic (WNM)
        Northern Paiute (NP)
        Mono (M)
    Central Numic (CNM)
        Shoshoni (SH)
    Southern Numic (SNM)
        Southern Paiute (SP)
        Kawaiisu (K)
Tubatulabal (TU)
Hopi (H)
Takic (TAK)
    Serrano (SR)
    Cupan (CUP)
        Cahuilla-Cupeno (CAC)
            Cahuilla (CA)
            Cupeno (CU)
        Luiseno (L)
Pimic (PMC)
    Papago (P)
    Tepehuan (TEP)
        Northern Tepehuan (NT)
        Tepecano (TO)
Taracahitic (TRC)
    Tarahumara (TA)
    Yaqui (Y)
Corachol (CCH)
    Cora (CR)
    Huichol (HU)
Aztecan (AZN)
    Pochutla (PO)
    Classical Nahuatl (A)

APPENDIX B
Language Abbreviations

With the exception of UA (for Uto-Aztecan), one- and two-letter abbreviations stand for individual languages and dialects, while three-letter abbreviations stand for larger genetic units. AD is used as a collective symbol for the modern Aztec dialects; this is simply a matter of practicality and is not to be taken as indicative of any claims of genetic relationship vis-à-vis Classical Nahuatl (A). The genetic significance of certain groups designated (in particular NUA, SUA, SHN, SON, TEP, TRC) is potentially subject to controversy, and by including these labels I wish to take no position on these controversies. Diacritics have been suppressed, as they are superfluous and irrelevant.

P-X = Proto X

ATN = Aztec-Tanoan

UA   = Uto-Aztecan

AZN = Aztecan
CAC = Cahuilla-Cupeno
CAH = Cahita
CCH = Corachol
CNM = Central Numic
CUP = Cupan
NUA = Northern Uto-Aztecan
NUM = Numic
PMC = Pimic
SHN = Shoshonean
SNM = Southern Numic
SON = Sonoran
SUA = Southern Uto-Aztecan
TAK = Takic
TEP = Tepehuan
TRC = Taracahitic
WNM = Western Numic

A   = Classical Nahuatl
AD   = (modern) Aztec dialects
AX   = Acaxee
B   = Bannock
CA   = Cahuilla
CH   = Chemehuevi
CM   = Comanche
CO   = Concho
CR   = Cora
CU   = Cupeno
E   = Eudeve (also Heve)
F   = Fernandeno
GA   = Gabrielino
GI   = Giamina
H   = Hopi
HU   = Huichol
J   = Juaneno
JV   = Jova
K   = Kawaiisu
KT   = Kitanemuk
L   = Luiseno
M   = Mono
MA   = Mayo
N   = Nicoleno
NP   = Northern Paiute

NT	=	Northern Tepehuan
O	=	Opata
P	=	Papago
PB	=	Pima Bajo
PI	=	Pima
PN	=	Panamint
PO	=	Pochutla Aztec
SH	=	Shoshoni
SP	=	Southern Paiute
SR	=	Serrano
ST	=	Southern Tepehuan
TA	=	Tarahumara
TO	=	Tepecano
TR	=	Tubar
TU	=	Tubatulabal
U	=	Ute
V	=	Varohio (also Guarijio)
Y	=	Yaqui

APPENDIX C
Abbreviations of Grammatical Terms

ABS	=	absolutive	CONSTR	=	construction
ABSTR	=	abstract	CONT	=	continuous
ACC	=	accusative	COORD	=	coordination
ACT	=	active	COP	=	copula
ADJ	=	adjective	COREF	=	coreference
ADJR	=	adjectivalizer	CS	=	complex sentence
ADV	=	adverb	DAT	=	dative
ADVR	=	adverbializer	DECL	=	declarative
AF	=	affix	DEF	=	definite
AFF	=	affirmative	DEM	=	demonstrative
AFFV	=	affective	DER	=	derivational
AG	=	agent	DESID	=	desiderative
AGR	=	agreement	DIM	=	diminutive
AL	=	alienable	DIR	=	direct
AN	=	animate	DIRL	=	directional
APPLIC	=	applicative	DISCONT	=	discontinuous
APPOS	=	appositive	DIST	=	distal
ART	=	article	DISTR	=	distributive
ASP	=	aspect	DL	=	dual
ASSR	=	assertive	DS	=	different subject
ATTEN	=	attenuative	DUB	=	dubitative
AUG	=	augmentative	DUR	=	durative
AUX	=	auxiliary	EMB	=	embedded
BEN	=	benefactive	EMPH	=	emphatic
CAUS	=	causative	EV	=	evidential
CESS	=	cessative	EXCL	=	exclusive
CL	=	clause	EXCLM	=	exclamation
CLSF	=	classifier	EXHRT	=	exhortative
CLT	=	clitic	EXPL	=	expletive
CMPL	=	complement	FOC	=	focus
CMPLR	=	complementizer	FREQ	=	frequentative
CMPND	=	compound	FUT	=	future
CNJ	=	conjunction	GER	=	gerund
CNJNCT	=	conjunct	H	=	human
COLL	=	collective	HAB	=	habitual
COMPAR	=	comparative	HON	=	honorific
COMPL	=	completive	HYP	=	hypothetical
COND	=	conditional	IF	=	infix
CONN	=	connective	IMP	=	imperative
CONST	=	constituent/constituency	IMPOT	=	impotentive

IMPRF	=	imperfect(ive)	POSSD	=	possessed
IMPRS	=	impersonal	POSSR	=	possessor
INAL	=	inalienable	POT	=	potentive
INAN	=	inanimate	PRED	=	predicate
INCEPT	=	inceptive	PREP	=	preposition
INCHO	=	inchoative	PRES	=	present
INCL	=	inclusive	PRIV	=	privative
IND	=	independent	PROG	=	progressive
INDF	=	indefinite	PRON	=	pronoun
INF	=	infinitive	PROX	=	proximal
INFL	=	inflectional	PRSMV	=	presumptive
INFR	=	inferential	PRSNTV	=	presentative
INSTR	=	instrumental	PRT	=	particle
INTNS	=	intensifier	PRTC	=	participle
INTR	=	introducer	PRTV	=	partitive
INTRNS	=	intransitive	Q	=	question
INVIS	=	invisible	QNT	=	quantifier
IRR	=	irrealis	QUOT	=	quotative
LOC	=	locative	R	=	realized
MAN	=	manner	RCPR	=	reciprocal
MDL	=	modal	RDP	=	reduplication
MOD	=	modifier	REC	=	recent
MOT	=	motion	REFL	=	reflexive
N	=	noun/nominal	REL	=	relative
NARR	=	narrative	REM	=	remote
NEG	=	negative	REPET	=	repetitive
NH	=	non-human	RESTR	=	restrictive
NOM	=	nominative	RSLTV	=	resultative
NR	=	nominalizer	RSMV	=	resumptive
NUM	=	number	S	=	sentence
NUMR	=	numeral	SBJNCT	=	subjunctive
NVOL	=	non-volitional	SF	=	suffix
OBJ	=	object	SG	=	singular
OBLIG	=	obligatory	SM	=	subject marker
OBLQ	=	oblique			(verbal affix)
OM	=	object marker	SS	=	same subject
		(verbal affix)	STAT	=	stative
OPT	=	optional	SUB	=	subordinate
OPTV	=	optative	SUBJ	=	subject
ORD	=	ordinal	SUBR	=	subordinator
P	=	postposition	SUPPL	=	suppletive
PASS	=	passive	TEMP	=	temporal
PEJ	=	pejorative	TNS	=	tense
PERF	=	perfect(ive)	TOP	=	topic
PERS	=	person	TRNS	=	transitive
PF	=	prefix	TRNSR	=	transitivizer
PHR	=	phrase	UNR	=	unrealized
PL	=	plural	UNSPEC	=	unspecified
PN	=	proper name	USIT	=	usitative
PNCT	=	punctual	V	=	verb
POS	=	positive	VERT	=	vertical
POSS	=	possessive	VIS	=	visible

VOC   = vocative
VOL   = volitional
VR   = verbalizer
WHQ   = WH question
WHW   = WH word
XP   = extraposition
YNQ   = yes/no question

1P   = first person
2P   = second person
3P   = third person
-         = morpheme boundary
=   = clitic boundary
= word boundary
[= clause boundary (initial)
]   = clause boundary (final)

BIBLIOGRAPHY

The principal purpose of this bibliography is to facilitate research on comparative Uto-Aztecan and the presentation of research results to others. For maximum utility in this regard, I have included virtually every source of information on Uto-Aztecan that I might ever have occasion to cite. The sources, besides published works, include dissertations, unpublished manuscripts, student term papers, lecture handouts, informal written materials of other kinds, and even personal communications. Due to their nature, some of these are unpolished and not intended for circulation; indeed, some (referred to as "informal notes" and the like) are such that the authors themselves may have difficulty identifying the work (or scrap of paper) designated. Despite this heterogeneity, it is highly useful to have all my sources of data listed in a single place.

This is not meant to be an exhaustive bibliography. I am aware of various Uto-Aztecan references that are not included here, either because they have been inaccessible to me or because I simply have not yet had time or occasion to track them down. Some of the earliest sources fall in this category. Also, no systematic effort has been made to examine works that deal with the culture of the Uto-Aztecan peoples unless they treat linguistic matters as well; the cultural studies included here are those I happen to have encountered, largely by chance, and are not necessarily to be attributed greater significance than those omitted. With a handful of exceptions, though, it is probably fair to say that this bibliography contains (along with other items) all of the major contemporary works available that deal with the Uto-Aztecan languages.

For ease of reference, each work in the bibliography is assigned a code, consisting of three parts. The first part designates the language or language family, the second stands for the last name(s) of the author(s), and the third is mnemonic for the title. For example, L-KG-SG is the code for <u>The Sparkman Grammar of Luiseño</u> by Kroeber and Grace. The works are arranged in sections according to the language or language family for which they are coded; within each section works are listed alphabetically by the author code, then by the title code. A work that deals with more than one language in a significant way is assigned to the largest appropriate category; e.g. a reference treating both Serrano and Luiseno would be listed under Takic, and only under Takic (not also Serrano or Luiseno), since there are no multiple listings. The headings Shoshonean (SHN) and Sonoran (SON) are included only for convenience and to accommodate one tradition often followed in the literature; by including them I am not taking a position on their viability as genetic units.

From time to time I hope to issue supplements to this bibliography, adding new references and bringing others up to date. To this end I would be happy to hear of omissions and new works dealing with Uto-Aztecan, and even happier to receive such works. In future references I will use the code UA-L-NA to designate the present monograph, and UA-L-PB (PB for "partial bibliography") for this constantly evolving list of references.

Abbreviations

AA = American Anthropologist

AAASP = American Academy of Arts and Sciences, Proceedings

AL = Anthropological Linguistics

CLS = Proceedings of the Regional Meeting, Chicago Linguistic Society

IJAL = International Journal of American Linguistics

JCA = Journal of California Anthropology

JSAP = Journal de la Société des Américanistes de Paris

UCPAAE = University of California Publications in American Archaeology and Ethnology

UCPL = University of California Publications in Linguistics

Aztec-Tanoan

ATN-D-TELA. Dozier, Edward P. 1956. 'Two Examples of Linguistic Acculturation, the Yaqui of Sonora and Arizona and the Tewa of New Mexico'. Language 32.146-157. [Reprinted in ATN-H-LCS, p. 509-520.]

ATN-E-AV. Epstein, Jeremiah F. 1968. 'An Archaeological View of Uto-Aztekan Time Perspective', in UA-S-UP, p. 106-130.

ATN-E-WES. Ellis, Florence Hawley. 1968. 'What Utaztecan Ethnology Suggests of Utaztecan Prehistory', in UA-S-UP, p. 53-105.

ATN-G-ZS. Gatschet, Albert S. 1876. Zwölf Sprachen aus dem Südwesten Nordamerikas. Weimar: Hermann Böhlau. [Sketches include Isleta, Jemez, Tewa, Taos, Kiowa, Ute, Comanche, Pima.] [Reprinted by Anthropological Publications, Amsterdam, and Humanities Press, New York, 1970.]

ATN-H-LCS. Hymes, Dell (ed.) 1964. Language in Culture and Society. New York: Harper and Row.

ATN-H-LSNA. Hoijer, Harry, et al. (eds.) 1946. Linguistic Structures of Native America. New York: Viking Fund Publications in Anthropology, 6.

ATN-H-SSE. Hymes, Dell (ed., with William E. Bittle). 1967. Studies in Southwestern Ethnolinguistics. The Hague: Mouton. Studies in General Anthropology III.

ATN-L-RG. Landar, Herbert. 1974. Review of Albert S. Gatschet, Zwölf Sprachen aus dem Südwesten Nordamerikas. IJAL 40.159-162.

ATN-P-CDC1. Pimentel, Francisco. 1874. Cuadro Descriptivo y Comparativo de las Lenguas Indígenas de México (Tratado de Filología

Mexicana), Volume 1. Mexico: Tipografía de Isidoro Epstein.

ATN-P-CDC2. Pimentel, Francisco. 1875. Cuadro Descriptivo y
Comparativo de las Lenguas Indígenas de México (Tratado de Filología
Mexicana), Volume 2. Mexico: Tipografía de Isidoro Epstein.

ATN-P-CDC3. Pimentel, Francisco. 1875. Cuadro Descriptivo y
Comparativo de las Lenguas Indígenas de México (Tratado de Filología
Mexicana), Volume 3. Mexico: Tipografía de Isidoro Epstein.

ATN-S-LCS. Swadesh, Morris. 1967. 'Linguistic Classification in the
Southwest', in ATN-H-SSE, p. 281-309.

ATN-S-LNA. Sebeok, Thomas A. (ed.) 1973. Current Trends in Linguistics, Volume 10, Linguistics in North America. The Hague:
Mouton.

ATN-T-SLT. Trager, George L. 1939. ' "Cottonwood" = "Tree": A
Southwestern Linguistic Trait'. IJAL 9.117-118. [Reprinted in ATN-
H-LCS, p. 467-468.]

ATN-T-TSRG. Trager, George L. 1967. 'The Tanoan Settlement of the
Rio Grande Area: A Possible Chronology', in ATN-H-SSE, p. 335-350.

ATN-VV-SGB. Voegelin, C. F. and F. M. 1973. 'Southwestern and
Great Basin Languages', in ATN-S-LNA, p. 1100-1142.

ATN-VVS-LSA. Voegelin, C. F. and F. M., and Noel W. Schutz, Jr.
1967. 'The Language Situation in Arizona as Part of the Southwest Culture Area', in ATN-H-SSE, p. 403-451.

ATN-WT-R. Whorf, B. L., and George L. Trager. 1937. 'The Relationship of Uto-Aztecan and Tanoan'. AA 39.609-624.

Uto-Aztecan

UA-A-B. Almstedt, Ruth. 1972. 'A Bibliography of Western Mexico'.
Manuscript.

UA-A-CSAR. d'Azevedo, Warren L., et al. (eds.) 1966. The Current
Status of Anthropological Research in the Great Basin: 1964. Reno,
Nevada: Desert Research Institute, Social Sciences and Humanities
Publications No. 1.

UA-B-IDM. Bright, William. 1967. 'Inventory of Descriptive Materials',
in UA-M-H, p. 9-62.

UA-B-NR. Bancroft, Hubert Howe. 1875. The Native Races of the Pacific
States of North America, Volume III, Myths and Languages. New York:
D. Appleton and Co.

UA-B-RA. Brinton, Daniel G. 1946. La Raza Americana. Buenos Aires:
Editorial Nova. [P. 116-130.]

UA-B-RM. Bright, William. 1968. Review of Wick R. Miller, Uto-
Aztecan Cognate Sets. IJAL 34.56-59.

UA-B-SCL. Bright, William (ed.) 1964. Studies in Californian

Linguistics. Berkeley and Los Angeles: University of California Press. UCPL 34.

UA-B-VD. Benson, Peter. 1971. 'Verb Derivation: Secondary Verbs'. Informal notes.

UA-C-ODA. Crapo, Richley H. 1970. 'The Origins of Directional Adverbs in Uto-Aztecan Languages'. IJAL 36.181-189.

UA-C-TS. Crook, Donald. 1971. 'Tense Suffixes in Uto-Aztecan'. Informal notes.

UA-C-YTHN. Corum, Claudia, et al. (eds.) 1973. You Take the High Node and I'll Take the Low Node. Chicago: Chicago Linguistic Society. Papers from the Comparative Syntax Festival. The Differences between Main and Subordinate Clauses.

UA-D-LASS. Dozier, Edward P. 1967. 'Linguistic Acculturation Studies in the Southwest', in ATN-H-SSE, p. 389-402.

UA-F-ICM. Fernández de Miranda, María Teresa. 1967. 'Inventory of Classificatory Materials', in UA-M-H, p. 63-78.

UA-F-IN. Flora, Jo-Ann. 1971. Informal notes on Uto-Aztecan subordinators.

UA-F-PU. Frishberg, Nancy. 1971. 'Postpositions Uto-Aztecan-in'. Informal notes.

UA-G-BU. Grimes, Larry. 1966. 'A Bibliography of the Uto-Aztecan Languages'. Educational Resources Information Center microfilm, ED 011 662, AL 000 438.

UA-G-CHI. Goss, James A. 1968. 'Culture-Historical Inference from Utaztekan Linguistic Evidence', in UA-S-UP, p. 1-42.

UA-G-PSP. Goddard, Ives. 1965. 'A Preliminary Survey of the Uto-Aztecan Pronominal System'. Manuscript.

UA-H-GBP. Hopkins, Nicholas A. 1965. 'Great Basin Prehistory and Uto-Aztecan'. American Antiquity 31.48-60.

UA-H-LD1. Hale, Kenneth. 1958. 'Internal Diversity in Uto-Aztecan: I'. IJAL 24.101-107.

UA-H-LD2. Hale, Kenneth. 1959. 'Internal Diversity in Uto-Aztecan: II'. IJAL 25.114-121.

UA-H-MP1. Heath, Jeffrey. 1973. 'Uto-Aztecan Morphophonemics I'. Manuscript.

UA-H-MP2. Heath, Jeffrey. 1973. 'Uto-Aztecan Morphophonemics II'. Manuscript.

UA-H-MP3. Heath, Jeffrey. 1973. 'Uto-Aztecan Morphophonemics III'. Manuscript.

UA-H-NCV. Heath, Jeffrey. 1974. '*-na-Class Verbs in Uto-Aztecan'. Manuscript.

UA-H-URC. Heath, Jeffrey. 1972. 'Uto-Aztecan Relative Clauses', in

UA-P-CWH, p. 230-245.

UA-HH-CT. Hill, Jane H., and Kenneth C. Hill. 1970. 'A Note on Uto-Aztecan Color Terminologies'. AL 12.231-238.

UA-J-CG. Jacobsen, William H., Jr. 1968. 'Comments on James A. Goss's "Culture-Historical Inference from Utaztekan Linguistic Evidence" ', in UA-S-UP, p. 43-52.

UA-J-CL. Jacobsen, William H., Jr. 1966. 'Comments on Linguistics', in UA-A-CSAR, p. 259-264.

UA-J-PS. Jaquith, James R. 1970. The Present Status of the Uto-Aztecan Languages of Mexico. [An index of data bearing on their survival, geographical location and internal relationships.] Greely, Colorado: Museum of Anthropology, University of Northern Colorado. Katunob--Occasional Publications in Mesoamerican Anthropology, No. 5.

UA-K-PC. Kroeber, A. L. 1911. 'Phonetic Constituents of the Native Languages of California'. UCPAAE 10.1-12.

UA-K-SFR. Key, Harold. 1965. 'Some Semantic Functions of Reduplication in Various Languages'. AL 7.88-102 [Part II].

UA-L-CUL. Lamb, Sydney M. 1964. 'The Classification of the Uto-Aztecan Languages: A Historical Survey', in UA-B-SCL, p. 106-125.

UA-L-FOLA. Langacker, Ronald W. 1972. Fundamentals of Linguistic Analysis. New York: Harcourt Brace Jovanovich.

UA-L-NCG. Langacker, Ronald W. 1975. 'A Note on Uto-Aztecan Consonant Gradation'. Manuscript.

UA-L-PR. Langacker, Ronald W. 1973. 'Predicate Raising: Some Uto-Aztecan Evidence', in Braj B. Kachru et al. (eds.), Issues in Linguistics: Papers in Honor of Henry and Renée Kahane, p. 468-491. Urbana: University of Illinois Press.

UA-L-SAIL. Langacker, Ronald W. 1974. 'Semantics and American Indian Linguistics'. Manuscript.

UA-L-SCR. Longacre, Robert. 1967. 'Systemic Comparison and Reconstruction', in UA-M-H, p. 117-159.

UA-L-SP. Langacker, Ronald W. 1974. 'The Syntax of Postpositions in Uto-Aztecan'. To appear in IJAL.

UA-L-VP. Langacker, Ronald W. 1970. 'The Vowels of Proto Uto-Aztecan'. IJAL 36.169-180.

UA-LM-PM. Langacker, Ronald W., and Pamela Munro. 1974. 'Passives and their Meaning'. To appear in Language.

UA-M-ALGB. Miller, Wick R. 1966. 'Anthropological Linguistics in the Great Basin', in UA-A-CSAR, p. 75-112.

UA-M-CS. Miller, Wick R. 1967. Uto-Aztecan Cognate Sets. Berkeley and Los Angeles: University of California Press. UCPL 48.

UA-M-H. McQuown, Norman A. (ed.) 1967. Handbook of Middle American Indians, Volume 5, Linguistics. Austin: University of Texas Press.

UA-M-HS. McQuown, Norman A. 1967. 'History of Studies in Middle American Linguistics', in UA-M-H, p. 3-7.

UA-M-IP. Munro, Pamela. 1971. 'Instrumental Prefixes'. Informal notes.

UA-M-IPC. Mason, J. Alden. 1952. 'Some Initial Phones and Combinations in Utaztecan Stems'. IJAL 18. 9-11.

UA-M-LAM. Munro, Pamela. 1971. 'Luiseño Addenda to Miller's Uto-Aztecan Cognate Sets'. Informal notes.

UA-M-M. McClaran, Marlys. 1973. 'Mexico', in ATN-S-LNA, p. 1079-1099.

UA-M-OS. Munro, Pamela. 1973. 'Proto-Uto-Aztecan *w--One Source for Luiseño ŋ'. IJAL 39. 135-136.

UA-M-QW. Munro, Pamela. 1971. 'Question Words'. Informal notes.

UA-M-SQP. Munro, Pamela. 1974. 'Chemehuevi "Say" and the Uto-Aztecan Quotative Pattern'. Manuscript.

UA-P-CWH. Peranteau, Paul M., et al. (eds.) 1972. The Chicago Which Hunt, Papers from the Relative Clause Festival. Chicago: Chicago Linguistic Society.

UA-P-ILFA. Powell, J. W. 1891. 'Indian Linguistic Families of America North of Mexico'. Seventh Annual Report of the Bureau of American Ethnology, p. 1-142. [Reprinted in Preston Holder (ed.), 'Introduction to Handbook of American Indian Languages' (Boas) and 'Indian Linguistic Families of America North of Mexico' (Powell), Lincoln, University of Nebraska Press, 1966, p. 81-218.]

UA-P-MTA. Papen, Robert. 1971. 'Some Mode/Tense/Aspect Reconstructions in *PUA'. Informal notes.

UA-R-CMR. Rigsby, Bruce. 1966. 'On Cayuse-Molala Relatability'. IJAL 32. 369-378. [P. 374.]

UA-R-PV. Roberts, John. 1971. 'Proto UA Verbs'. Informal notes.

UA-S-ALNA. Sherzer, Joel. 1973. 'Areal Linguistics in North America', in ATN-S-LNA, p. 749-795.

UA-S-BU. Shafer, Robert. 1967. 'A Bibliography of Uto-Aztecan with a Note on Biogeography'. IJAL 33. 148-159.

UA-S-FIP. Steele, Susan. 1973. 'Futurity, Intention, and Possibility: A Semantic Reconstruction in Uto-Aztecan'. Papers in Linguistics 6. 1-37.

UA-S-IIP. Steele, Susan. 1973. 'Is it Possible?'. Informal notes.

UA-S-IN. Steele, Susan. 1971. Informal notes on Uto-Aztecan clitics.

UA-S-KT. Shimkin, D. B. 1941. 'The Uto-Aztecan System of Kinship Terminology'. AA 43.223-245.

UA-S-LCP. Spier, Leslie, et al. (eds.) 1941. Language, Culture, and Personality (Essays in Memory of Edward Sapir). Menasha, Wisconsin: Sapir Memorial Publication Fund. [Reprinted: University of Utah

Press, 1960.]

UA-S-LCWN. Swanson, Earl H., Jr. (ed.) 1970. Languages and Cultures of Western North America, Essays in Honor of Sven S. Liljeblad. Pocatello: Idaho State University Press.

UA-S-PI. Steele, Susan. 1973. 'Past and Irrealis: Some Thoughts from Uto-Aztecan'. Manuscript.

UA-S-PTME. Steele, Susan. 1973. The Positional Tendencies of Modal Elements and their Theoretical Implications. San Diego: University of California doctoral dissertation.

UA-S-RA. Sherzer, Joel. 1968. Review of Warren L. d'Azevedo et al. (eds.), The Current Status of Anthropological Research in the Great Basin. IJAL 34.304-306.

UA-S-RCM. Spears, Arthur. 1971. 'Uto-Aztecan Relative Clause Markers'. Informal notes.

UA-S-RM. Steele, Susan. 1971. 'Root Modality: Some Thoughts from Uto-Aztecan'. Manuscript.

UA-S-SPN1. Sapir, Edward. 1913. 'Southern Paiute and Nahuatl, A Study in Uto-Aztekan'. [Part I.] JSAP 10.379-425.

UA-S-SPN2. Sapir, Edward. 1915. 'Southern Paiute and Nahuatl--A Study in Uto-Aztekan. Part II'. AA 17.98-120, 306-328. [Also in JSAP 11.443-488, 1919.]

UA-S-UP. Swanson, Earl H., Jr. (ed.) 1968. Utaztekan Prehistory. Pocatello, Idaho: Occasional Papers of the Idaho State University Museum, No. 22.

UA-SF-IP. Sherzer, Joel, and Lawrence Foley. 1971. 'Instrumental Prefixes in Uto-Aztecan: A Typological Approach'. Manuscript.

UA-T-AR. Tranel, Bernard. 1971. 'An Attempt at Reconstruction in Uto-Aztecan: Absolutives, Cases, and Possession'. Informal notes.

UA-T-CCN. Troike, Rudolph C. 1963. 'Uto-Aztecan Cognates in Classical Nahuatl'. IJAL 29.72-74.

UA-VVH-TCG. Voegelin, C. F. and F. M., and Kenneth Hale. 1962. Typological and Comparative Grammar of Uto-Aztecan: I (Phonology). Indiana University Publications in Anthropology and Linguistics, Memoir 17. Supplement to IJAL 28.1.

UA-W-CL. Whorf, B. L. 1935. 'The Comparative Linguistics of Uto-Aztecan'. AA 37.600-608.

UA-W-OA. Whorf, B. L. 1937. 'The Origin of Aztec TL'. AA 39.265-274.

UA-W-RK. Whorf, B. L. 1935. Review of A. L. Kroeber, Uto-Aztecan Languages of Mexico. UCPAAE 37.343-345.

UA-W-RPD. Walrad, Chuck. 1971. 'Proto Uto-Aztecan: Reconstructions of Pronouns and Demonstratives'. Informal notes.

UA-XXX-WC1. XXX. 1973. Notes from the First Uto-Aztecan Working

Conference, Reno, 22-25 August 1973.

UA-XXX-WC2. XXX. 1974. Notes from the Second Uto-Aztecan Working Conference, Long Beach, 18-19 June 1974.

UA-XXX-WC3. XXX. 1975. Notes from the Third Uto-Aztecan Working Conference, Flagstaff, 19-20 June 1975.

Aztecan

AZN-C-PA. Campbell, Lyle. 1972. 'Proto-Aztecan'. Manuscript.

Cahita

CAH-B-A. Buelna, Eustaquio. 1890. Arte de la Lengua Cahita por un Padre de la Compañía de Jesús. Mexico: Gobierno Federal. [First published in 1737 by Juan B. de Velasco.]

CAH-B-AC. Beals, Ralph L. 1943. The Aboriginal Culture of the Cáhita Indians. Berkeley and Los Angeles: University of California Press. Ibero-Americana 19.

Central Numic

CNM-M-PC. Miller, Wick R. 1974. 'Shoshoni No Baloney, or Preaspirated Consonants in Central Numic'. Manuscript.

CNM-M-PHP. Miller, Wick R. 1974. 'Some Problems in Comanche Historical Phonology'. Manuscript.

CNM-M-WWW. Miller, Wick R. 1974. 'What Went Wrong with the Growth of the Central Numic (Uto-Aztecan) Tree? Or: Leaf your Language Alone'. Manuscript.

Cupan

CUP-B-FG. Bright, William. 1965. 'A Field Guide to Southern California Indian Languages'. Archaeological Survey Annual Report, p. 393-407. Los Angeles: Department of Anthropology, UCLA.

CUP-BH-LHC. Bright, William, and Jane H. Hill. 1967. 'The Linguistic History of the Cupeño', in ATN-H-SSE, p. 351-371.

CUP-H-LD. Hill, Jane H. 1973. 'Language Death, Language Contact, and Language Evolution'. Manuscript.

CUP-H-SCD. Hill, Jane H. 1973. 'Subordinate Clause Density and Language Function', in UA-C-YTHN, p. 33-52.

CUP-HH-SC. Hill, Jane H., and Kenneth C. Hill. 1968. 'Stress in the Cupan (Uto-Aztecan) Languages'. IJAL 34.233-241.

CUP-J-IN. Jacobs, Roderick A. 1972, 1973. Informal notes on Cupan.

CUP-J-SC. Jacobs, Roderick A. 1972. Syntactic Change: A Cupan (Uto-Aztecan) Case Study. San Diego: University of California doctoral dissertation.

CUP-J-SCSC. Jacobs, Roderick A. 1973. 'Syntactic Compression and Semantic Change'. CLS 9.232-241.

CUP-J-SR. Jacobs, Roderick A. 1972. 'Syntactic Reconstruction and the Comparative Method: A Uto-Aztecan Case Study'. Manuscript.

CUP-L-MI. Langacker, Ronald W. 1969. 'Mirror Image Rules II: Lexicon and Phonology'. Language 45.844-862.

CUP-S-SR. Seiler, Hansjakob. 1967. 'Structure and Reconstruction in some Uto-Aztecan Languages'. IJAL 33.135-147.

Numic

NUM-B-HP. Booth, Curtis. 1973. 'Numic Historical Phonology'. Informal notes.

NUM-D-CC. Davis, Irvine. 1966. 'Numic Consonantal Correspondences'. IJAL 32.124-140.

NUM-F-CE. Fowler, Catherine S. 1972. Comparative Numic Ethnobiology. Pittsburgh: University of Pittsburgh doctoral dissertation.

NUM-F-GBCE. Fowler, Don D. (ed.) 1972. Great Basin Cultural Ecology: A Symposium. Reno and Las Vegas: Desert Research Institute, Publications in the Social Sciences No. 8.

NUM-FF-AN. Fowler, Don D., and Catherine S. Fowler (eds.) 1971. Anthropology of the Numa. John Wesley Powell's Manuscripts on the Numic Peoples of Western North America, 1868-1880. Washington, D.C.: Smithsonian Institution Press. Smithsonian Contributions to Anthropology, No. 14.

NUM-FI-IC. Freeze, Ray, and David Iannucci. 1974. 'Internal Classification of the Numic Languages of Uto-Aztecan'. Manuscript.

NUM-G-VV. Goss, James A. 1970. 'Voiceless Vowels (?) in Numic Languages', in UA-S-LCWN, p. 37-46.

NUM-I-HP. Iannucci, David. 1973. Numic Historical Phonology. Ithaca, New York: Cornell University doctoral dissertation.

NUM-I-MCP. Iannucci, David. 1973. 'Numic Medial Consonant Processes--An Historical View'. Informal notes.

NUM-J-IE. Jacobsen, William H., Jr. 1973. 'Development of the Inclusive/Exclusive Category in the Great Basin: Numic and Washo'. Manuscript.

NUM-J-WID. Jacobsen, William H., Jr. 1974. 'Washo Internal Diversity and External Relations'. Manuscript.

NUM-K-BS. Kroeber, A. L. 1909. 'The Bannock and Shoshoni Languages'. AA 11.266-277.

NUM-K-CMK. Klein, Sheldon. 1959. 'Comparative Mono-Kawaiisu'. IJAL 25.233-238.

NUM-L-HIT. Liljeblad, Sven. 1971. 'Notes and Excerpts of Literature Concerning the History of Indian Tribes in Idaho and Adjacent Areas of the Great Basin and the Southern Plateau'. Manuscript.

NUM-M-CCEP. Miller, Wick R. 1972. 'Comments on Cultural Ecology Papers', in NUM-F-GBCE, p. 159-160.

NUM-M-PC. Miller, Wick R. Personal communication.

NUM-N-GBLB. Nichols, Michael J. P. 1973. 'Great Basin Lexical Borrowing'. Informal notes.

NUM-N-VC. Nichols, Michael J. P. 1973. 'Numic Vowel Clusters'. Informal notes.

NUM-S-TDB. Stewart, Omer C. 1966. 'Tribal Distributions and Boundaries in the Great Basin', in UA-A-CSAR, p. 167-237.

NUM-Z-GBL. Zierhut, Norman W. 1968. 'Great Basin Linguistics: A Critical Review'. Alberta Anthropologist 2.2.63-87.

Pimic

PMC-B-PT. Bascom, Burton. 1965. Proto-Tepiman (Tepehuan-Piman). Seattle: University of Washington doctoral dissertation.

Shoshonean

SHN-DK-LFC. Dixon, Roland B., and A. L. Kroeber. 1919. 'Linguistic Families of California'. UCPAAE 16.47-118.

SHN-F-ECPH. Fowler, Catherine S. 1972. 'Some Ecological Clues to Proto Numic Homelands', in NUM-F-GBCE, p. 105-121.

SHN-G-KT. Gifford, Edward Winslow. 1917. 'Tübatulabal and Kawaiisu Kinship Terms'. UCPAAE 12.219-248.

SHN-J-SRHC. Jacobsen, William H., Jr. 1967. 'Switch-Reference in Hokan-Coahuiltecan', in ATN-H-SSE, p. 238-263. [P. 255-256.]

SHN-J-WLS. Jacobsen, William H., Jr. 1966. 'Washo Linguistic Studies', in UA-A-CSAR, p. 113-136.

SHN-K-DC. Kroeber, A. L. 1906-07. 'Shoshonean Dialects of California'. UCPAAE 4.65-165.

SHN-K-ND. Kroeber, A. L. 1909. 'Notes on Shoshonean Dialects of Southern California'. UCPAAE 8.235-269.

SHN-L-LP. Lamb, Sydney M. 1958. 'Linguistic Prehistory in the Great Basin'. IJAL 24.95-100.

SHN-M-MN. Munro, Pamela. 1974. 'On the Morphology of Shoshonean Negatives'. Manuscript.

SHN-M-NE. Munro, Pamela. 1973. 'Some Non-Explanations for Exclamations'. Manuscript.

SHN-M-SL. Miller, Wick R. 1964. 'The Shoshonean Languages of Uto-Aztecan', in UA-B-SCL, p. 145-148.

SHN-N-DCS. Nichols, Johanna. 1971. 'Diminutive Consonant Symbolism in Western North America'. Language 47. 826-848.

SHN-S-C. Shipley, William. 1973. 'California', in ATN-S-LNA, p. 1046-1078.

Southern Numic

SNM-G-ID. Goss, James A. 1966. 'Comments on Linguistics, Internal Diversity in Southern Numic', in UA-A-CSAR, p. 265-273.

SNM-G-ULAA. Goss, James A. 1965. 'Ute Linguistics and Anasazi Abandonment of the Four Corners Area', in Douglas Osborne (ed.), Contributions of the Wetherill Mesa Archaeological Project, p. 73-81. Memoirs of the Society for American Archaeology, No. 19. Supplement to American Antiquity 31.2.

Sonoran

SON-H-SG. Hale, Kenneth. 1964. 'The Sub-Grouping of Uto-Aztecan Languages: Lexical Evidence for Sonoran', in Proceedings of the XXXV International Congress of Americanists, p. 511-518. Mexico City: Instituto Nacional de Antropología e Historia. [XXXV Congreso Internacional de Americanistas, Mexico, 1962. Segunda Parte, Actas y Memorias.]

SON-K-LM. Kroeber, A. L. 1934. Uto-Aztecan Languages of Mexico. Berkeley: University of California Press. Ibero-Americana 8.

SON-K-V. Key, Harold (compiler). 1954. Vocabularies of Languages of the Uto-Aztecan Family. Chicago: Microfilm Collection of Manuscripts on Middle American Cultural Anthropology, No. 38. University of Chicago Library.

SON-M-CSL. Mason, J. Alden. 1936. 'The Classification of the Sonoran Languages', in Essays in Anthropology Presented to A. L. Kroeber in Celebration of his Sixtieth Birthday, p. 183-198. Freeport, N. Y.: Books for Libraries Press. [Reprinted: Essay Index Reprint Series, 1968.]

Southern Uto-Aztecan

SUA-M-NLMA. Mason, J. Alden. 1940. 'The Native Languages of Middle America', in Clarence L. Hay et al. (eds.), The Maya and their Neighbors, p. 52-87. New York: D. Appleton-Century. [P. 67-70. Reprinted: University of Utah Press, 1962.]

Takic

TAK-B-LSC. Bright, William. 1974. 'Uto-Aztecan Languages of Southern California'. [Report to the American Philosophical Society.]

TAK-B-TD. Bright, William. 1974. 'Tataviam Data'. Informal notes.

TAK-B-TNC. Bright, William. 1975. 'Two Notes on Takic Classification'. Manuscript.

TAK-HH-SAT. Hill, Kenneth C., and Jane H. Hill. 1973. 'Serrano and "Takic" '. Informal notes.

TAK-L-RPE. Langacker, Ronald W. 1973. 'Reconstruction of Pronominal Elements in Takic'. Manuscript.

TAK-S-AS. Strong, William Duncan. 1929. Aboriginal Society in Southern California. Berkeley: University of California Press. UCPAAE 26. [Reprinted: Banning, California, Malki Museum Press, 1972. Classics in California Anthropology II.]

Western Numic

WNM-FF-PLC. Fowler, Don D., and Catherine S. Fowler (eds.) 1970. 'Stephen Powers' "The Life and Culture of the Washo and Paiutes" '. Ethnohistory 17.117-149.

WNM-N-AR. Nichols, Michael J. P. 1971. 'Aspects of the Reconstruction of Proto Western Numic'. Manuscript.

WNM-N-LR. Nichols, Michael J. P. 1971. 'Linguistic Reconstruction of Proto Western Numic and its Ethnographic Implications', in Great Basin Anthropological Conference 1970: Selected Papers, p. 135-145. University of Oregon Anthropological Papers, 1.

Classical Nahuatl

A-A-GEER. Anderson, Arthur J. O. 1973. Grammatical Examples, Exercises, and Review. Salt Lake City: University of Utah Press. [For use with A-A-RL.]

A-A-PC. Anderson, Arthur J. O. Personal communication.

A-A-R. Almstedt, Ruth. 1973. 'Reflexives'. Informal notes on Aztec reflexives.

A-A-RL. Anderson, Arthur J. O. 1973. Rules of the Aztec Language. [Translation of Francisco Xavier Clavigero, Reglas de la Lengua Mexicana.] Salt Lake City: University of Utah Press.

A-ABL-BC. Anderson, Arthur J. O., Frances Berdan, and James Lockhart (trans. and eds.) 1974. Beyond the Codices: The Nahua View of Colonial Mexico. Manuscript.

A-B-ACA. Bright, William. 1960. ' "Accent" in Classical Aztec'. IJAL 26.66-68.

A-B-C. Booth, Curtis. 1973. 'Complements in Aztec'. Informal notes.

A-B-NA. Bright, William. 1966. 'Notes on Aztec'. Informal notes.

A-C-CA. Carochi, Horacio. 1645. Compendio del Arte de la Lengua
    Mexicana. Edited edition by Ignacio de Paredes, Mexico, Imprenta de
    la Biblioteca Mexicana, 1759. [Reprinted: Talleres El Escritorio,
    Puebla, 1910.]

A-C-CG. Crook, Donald. 1973. 'Comings and Goings in Aztec'. Infor-
    mal notes.

A-C-LWQ. Campbell, Lyle. 1970. 'Nahua Loan Words in Quichean Lan-
    guages'. CLS 6.3-13.

A-C-PI. Chung, Sandra. 1973. 'The Passive-Impersonal in Aztec'. In-
    formal notes.

A-C-SD. Croft, Kenneth. 1953. 'Six Decades of Nahuatl: A Bibliographi-
    cal Contribution'. IJAL 19.57-73.

A-CDM-P. Castillo Farreras, Víctor Manuel; Karen Dakin; and Roberto
    Moreno de los Arcos. 1966. 'Las Partículas del Náhuatl'. Estudios de
    Cultura Náhuatl 6.187-210.

A-DA-FC1. Dibble, Charles E., and Arthur J. O. Anderson. 1970.
    Florentine Codex, Book 1 -- The Gods. [Translation of Fray
    Bernardino de Sahagún, General History of the Things of New Spain.]
    Santa Fe, New Mexico: School of American Research and University of
    Utah. Monographs of the School of American Research, No. 14, Part 2.

A-DA-FC6. Dibble, Charles E., and Arthur J. O. Anderson. 1969.
    Florentine Codex, Book 6 -- Rhetoric and Moral Philosophy. [Transla-
    tion of Fray Bernardino de Sahagun, General History of the Things of
    New Spain.] Santa Fe, New Mexico: School of American Research and
    University of Utah. Monographs of the School of American Research,
    No. 14, Part 7.

A-DA-FC10. Dibble, Charles E., and Arthur J. O. Anderson. 1961.
    Florentine Codex, Book 10 -- The People. [Translation of Fray
    Bernardino de Sahagún, General History of the Things of New Spain.]
    Santa Fe, New Mexico: School of American Research and University of
    Utah. Monographs of the School of American Research and the Museum
    of New Mexico, No. 14, Part 11.

A-F-GM. Feldman, Lawrence H. 1973. 'A Guide to Nahua Morphology'.
    Manuscript.

A-G-L. Garibay K., Ángel María. 1961. Llave del Náhuatl. Mexico
    City: Editorial Porrúa.

A-G-NLA. Grasserie, Raoul de la. 1903. Le Nahuatl, Langue des
    Aztèques. Paris: Librairie Orientale et Americaine. Bibliothèque
    Linguistique Américaine, Volume 25. [Reprinted: Kraus Reprint,
    Nendeln/Liechtenstein, 1968.]

A-H-F. Hunt y Cortés, Augustín. 1895. 'Fabulas de Aesopo'. Proceed-
    ings of the XI International Congress of Americanists, p. 100-115.
    Mexico. [Text p. 100, analysis p. 100-115. Anonymous translation to

Nahuatl, translated to Spanish by Celtatecatl.]

A-H-HA. Hinton, Leanne. 1973. 'Aztec Honorific Address'. Informal notes.

A-L-LST. Langacker, Ronald W. 1974. 'Linguistic Significance of the Texts', in A-ABL-BC. Manuscript.

A-L-PC. Langacker, Ronald W. 1966. 'Some Pronominal Constructions of Classical Aztec'. Manuscript.

A-L-PCN. Langacker, Ronald W. 1972. 'Possessives in Classical Nahuatl'. IJAL 38.173-186.

A-L-RC. Langacker, Ronald. W. 1975. 'Relative Clauses in Classical Nahuatl'. IJAL 41.46-68.

A-L-RCCN. Langacker, Ronald W. 1973. 'Relative Clauses in Classical Nahuatl'. Manuscript. [Summary version of A-L-RC.]

A-M-A. Molina, Fray Alonso de. 1571. Arte de la Lengua Mexicana y Castellana, facsimile edition 1945. Madrid: Ediciones Cultura Hispánica. Colección de Incunables Americanos, Siglo XVI, Volume 6.

A-M-GL. Molina, Fray Alonso de. 1975. Grammar of the Mexican (Nahuatl) Language. [English edition of A-M-A, translated by Kenneth C. Hill.] University of Michigan Papers in Linguistics 1.4.

A-M-IN. McQuown, Norman A. 1954. Informal notes on Classical Nahuatl.

A-M-ND. Munro, Pamela. 1973. 'Negative Data'. Informal notes on Aztec negation.

A-M-NM. Munro, Pamela. 1973. 'Aztec Noun Morphology'. Informal notes.

A-M-V1. Molina, Fray Alonso de. 1571. Vocabulario en Lengua Castellana y Mexicana, facsimile edition 1944. Madrid: Ediciones Cultura Hispánica. Colección de Incunables Americanos, Siglo XVI, Volume 4. [Spanish-Nahuatl portion reprinted by Talleres El Escritorio, Puebla, 1910.]

A-M-V2. Molina, Fray Alonso de. 1970. Vocabulario en Lengua Castellana y Mexicana y Mexicana y Castellana. Mexico City: Editorial Porrúa. [Modern edition of A-M-V1.]

A-N-CN. Newman, Stanley. 1967. 'Classical Nahuatl', in UA-M-H, p. 179-199.

A-O-G. Olmos, Andrés de. 1875. Grammaire de la Langue Nahuatl ou Mexicaine. [Composed in 1547 as Arte para Aprender la Lengua Mexicana. Ed. by Rémi Siméon.] Paris: Imprimerie Nationale. [Reprinted as Arte de la Lengua Mexicana, Mexico, Imprenta de Ignacio Escalante, 1885.]

A-P-CR. Paso y Troncoso, Francisco del (trans.) 1902. Comedia de los Reyes, in Biblioteca Náuatl, Volume I, El Teatro, p. 74-127. Florence: Tipografía de Salvador Landi.

A-R-AM. Rincon, Padre Antonio del. 1595. Arte Mexicana. Reprinted by Antonio Peñafiel, Mexico, 1885.

A-R-OP. Rosenthal, Jane M. 1971. 'The Omnipresent Problem of Omnipresent in in Classical Nahuatl'. Chicago: University of Chicago master's paper.

A-R-PO. Rosenthal, Jane M. 1972. 'The Possessives and Other Noun Phrases of Classical Nahuatl--A Different View'. Informal notes.

A-R-RC. Rosenthal, Jane M. 1972. 'On the Relative Clauses of Classical Nahuatl', in UA-P-CWH, p. 246-255.

A-R-TSC. Rosenthal, Jane M. 1973. 'Some Types of Subordinate Clauses in Classical Nahuatl', in UA-C-YTHN, p. 23-32.

A-S-ALM. Sandoval, Rafael. 1965. Arte de la Lengua Mexicana. Mexico City: Universidad Nacional Autónoma de México, Instituto de Investigaciones Históricas. Serie de Cultura Náhuatl, Monografías: 5.

A-S-AS. Schoembs, Jakob. 1949. Aztekische Schriftsprache. Heidelberg: Carl Winter, Universitätsverlag.

A-S-BBC. Steele, Susan. 1975. 'On Being and Becoming a Conjunction in Classical Aztec'. Manuscript.

A-S-CEM. Steele, Susan. 1974. 'Conjunction, Emphasis, and Modality in Classical Aztec'. Manuscript.

A-S-DLN. Siméon, Rémi. 1885. Dictionnaire de la Langue Nahuatl ou Mexicaine. Paris: Imprimerie Nationale. [Reprinted: Akademische Druck, Universität Verlagsanstalt, Graz, Austria, 1963.]

A-S-M. Steele, Susan. 1973. 'Modals in Aztec'. Informal notes.

A-S-WOC. Steele, Susan. 1975. 'A Law of Order: Word Order Change in Classical Aztec'. Manuscript.

A-SS-ME. Swadesh, Morris, and Madalena Sancho. 1966. Los Mil Elementos del Mexicano Clásico. Mexico City: Universidad Nacional Autónoma de México, Instituto de Investigaciones Históricas. Serie de Cultura Náhuatl, Monografías: 9.

A-SZ-SPM. Seiler, Hansjakob, and Günter Zimmermann. 1962. 'Studies in the Phonology and Morphology of Classical Nahuatl: I'. IJAL 28.243-250.

A-T-NL. Troike, Rudolph C. 1961. 'A Nahuatl Loan-Word in Coahuilteco'. IJAL 27.172-175.

A-U-AC. Ulving, Tor. 1953. 'Additions to Croft's Six Decades of Nahuatl'. IJAL 19.245-246.

(Modern) Aztec Dialects

AD-A-NZHS. Anderton, Alice. 1975. 'A Note on the Zacapoaxtla Dialect of Aztec: The Historical Source for t'. Manuscript.

AD-A-PLRI. Aráuz, Próspero. 1960. El Pipil de la Región de los

Itzalcos. San Salvador: Ministerio de Cultura, Departamento Editorial, El Salvador.

AD-B-MVS. Brewer, Forrest. 1969. 'Morelos (Tetelcingo) Nahuatl Verb Stem Constructions', in AD-R-AS1, p. 33-51.

AD-B-PNP. Brockway, Earl. 1963. 'The Phonemes of North Puebla Nahuatl'. AL 5.14-18.

AD-B-SEM. Boas, Franz. 1968. 'Spanish Elements in Modern Nahuatl', in John D. Fitz-Gerald and Pauline Taylor (eds.), Todd Memorial Volumes, Volume I, Philological Studies, p. 85-89. Freeport, New York: Books for Libraries Press. Essay Index Reprint Series. [Original publication: 1930.]

AD-B-VN. Bright, William. 1967. 'Un Vocabulario Náhuatl del Estado de Tlaxcala'. Estudios de Cultura Náhuatl 7.233-253.

AD-BB-VMT. Brewer, Forrest and Jean G. 1962. Vocabulario Mexicano de Tetelcingo, Morelos. Mexico City: Instituto Lingüístico de Verano. Serie de Vocabularios Indígenas, No. 8.

AD-BM-RT. Bartholomew, Doris, and David Mason. 1974. 'The Registration of Transitivity in the Guerrero Aztec Verb'. Manuscript.

AD-BT-H. Bright, William, and Robert A. Thiel. 1965. 'Hispanisms in a Modern Aztec Dialect'. Romance Philology 18.444-452.

AD-C-HA. Campbell, R. Joe. 1973. '/η^w/, or How Abstract Hueyapan, Morelos, Nahuatl Phonology Is!' Informal notes.

AD-C-MA. Croft, Kenneth. 1954. 'Matlapa Nahuatl III: Morpheme Arrangements'. IJAL 20.37-43.

AD-C-MN. Croft, Kenneth. 1953. 'Matlapa Nahuatl II: Affix List and Morphophonemics'. IJAL 19.274-280.

AD-C-POM. Croft, Kenneth. 1951. 'Practical Orthography for Matlapa Nahuatl'. IJAL 17.32-36.

AD-C-UH. Campbell, R. Joe. 1973. 'Underlying /η^w/ in Hueyapan Nahuatl'. Manuscript.

AD-D-PFM. Dakin, Karen. 1973. 'Plural Formations in Morelos Nahuatl'. Manuscript.

AD-F-CRA. Foster, Rand R. 1973. 'Cyclic Rule Application in Chiconcuac Nahuatl'. Informal notes.

AD-F-MT. Feldman, Lawrence H. 1973. 'Mixco Text'. Manuscript.

AD-G-CI. González Casanova, Pablo. 1965. Cuentos Indígenas (second edition). Mexico City: Universidad Nacional Autónoma de México, Instituto de Investigaciones Históricas. [First edition 1946.]

AD-GGW-PO. Goller, Theodore R., Patricia L. Goller, and Viola G. Waterhouse. 1974. 'The Phonemes of Orizaba Nahuatl'. IJAL 40.126-131.

AD-H-CDL. Hasler, Juan A. 1955. 'Los Cuatro Dialectos de la Lengua Nahua'. Revista Mexicana de Estudios Antropológicos 14.145-149.

AD-H-PDP. Hasler, Juan A. 1958. 'La Posición Dialectológica del
Pipil como Parte del Nahua del Este'. América Indígena 18.333-339.

AD-H-TN. Hasler, Juan A. 1961. 'Tetradialectología Nahua', in AD-
XXX-WCT, p. 455-464.

AD-K-SCA. Key, Harold. 1960. 'Stem Construction and Affixation of
Sierra Nahuat Verbs'. IJAL 26.130-145.

AD-KK-PSN. Key, Harold, and Mary Key. 1953. 'The Phonemes
of Sierra Nahuat'. IJAL 19.53-56.

AD-KK-VZ. Key, Harold, and Mary Key. 1953. Vocabulario
Mejicano de la Sierra de Zacapoaxtla, Puebla. Mexico City: Summer
Institute of Linguistics.

AD-KL-SI. Karttunen, Frances, and James Lockhart. 1975. 'The
Spanish Incursion into Colonial Nahuatl: A Working Paper'. Manuscript.

AD-L-LA. Law, Howard W. 1961. 'Linguistic Acculturation in Isthmus
Nahuat', in AD-XXX-WCT, p. 555-561.

AD-L-MS. Law, Howard W. 1958. 'Morphological Structure of Isthmus
Nahuat'. IJAL 24.108-129.

AD-L-NAK. Law, Joan A. 1969. 'Nahua Affinal Kinship: A Comparative
Study'. Ethnology 8.103-121.

AD-L-OC. Law, Howard W. 1966. Obligatory Constructions of Isthmus
Nahuat Grammar. The Hague: Mouton. Janua Linguarum Series
Practica, 29.

AD-L-RR. Law, Howard W. 1971. Review of Dow F. Robinson (ed.),
Aztec Studies I. Language 47.737-742.

AD-M-GNP. Mark, Saint. 1970. In Yancuic Tlahtoli Ica Jesucristo Quen
Oquihcuilui In San Marcos. [Northern Puebla Nahuatl edition of the
Gospel according to Mark, translated by Earl and Gertrude Brockway.]
Mexico City: La Biblioteca Mexicana del Hogar.

AD-M-GSN. Mark, Saint. 1954. In Cuali Tajtoltzin Ten Quijtoj San
Marcos. [Sierra Nahuat edition of the Gospel according to Mark, translated by Harold and Mary Key.] Mexico City: American Bible Society.

AD-M-GT. Mark, Saint. 1960. Cuali Machilistilistli Tli Oquijcuilo San
Marcos. [Tetelcingo Nahuatl edition of the Gospel according to Mark,
translated by Forrest Brewer.] Mexico City: American Bible Society.

AD-M-IN. McQuown, Norman A. No date. 'El Nahuatl Moderno de Milpa
Alta'. Informal notes.

AD-P-GTN. Pittman, Richard S. 1954. A Grammar of Tetelcingo
(Morelos) Nahuatl. Supplement to Language 30. Language Dissertation
No. 50.

AD-P-NH. Pittman, Richard S. 1948. 'Nahuatl Honorifics'. IJAL
14.236-239.

AD-P-PTN. Pittman, Richard S. 1961. 'The Phonemes of Tetelcingo
(Morelos) Nahuatl', in AD-XXX-WCT, p. 643-651.

AD-R-AS1. Robinson, Dow F. (ed.) 1969. Aztec Studies I, Phonological and Grammatical Studies in Modern Nahuatl Dialects. Norman, Oklahoma: Summer Institute of Linguistics, Publications in Linguistics and Related Fields, 19.

AD-R-AS2. Robinson, Dow F. 1970. Aztec Studies II, Sierra Nahuat Word Structure. Norman, Oklahoma: Summer Institute of Linguistics, Publications in Linguistics and Related Fields, 22.

AD-R-CST. Rosenthal, Jane M. 1975. Informal notes on complex sentences in Tlaxcaltec.

AD-R-PCT. Rosenthal, Jane M. 1973. 'The Persistent Characteristics of Tlaxcalan Nahuatl'. Informal notes.

AD-R-PNP. Robinson, Dow F. 1969. 'Puebla (Sierra) Nahuat Prosodies', in AD-R-AS1, p. 15-32.

AD-RS-MCS. Robinson, Dow F., and William R. Sischo. 1969. 'Michoacán (Pómaro) Nahual Clause Structure', in AD-R-AS1, p. 53-74.

AD-S-MPL. Schultze Jena, Leonhard. 1935. Indiana II: Mythen in der Muttersprache der Pipil von Izalco in El Salvador. Jena: Verlag von Gustav Fischer.

AD-W-IVL. Wolgemuth, Carl. 1969. 'Isthmus Veracruz (Mecayapan) Nahuat Laryngeals', in AD-R-AS1, p. 1-14.

AD-W-MA. Whorf, B. L. 1946. 'The Milpa Alta Dialect of Aztec', in ATN-H-LSNA, p. 367-397.

AD-XXX-WCT. XXX. 1961. A William Cameron Townsend en el Vigésimoquinto Aniversario del Instituto Lingüístico de Verano. Mexico City.

Acaxee

AX-B-MT. Beals, Ralph L. 1933. The Acaxee, A Mountain Tribe of Durango and Sinaloa. Berkeley: University of California Press. Ibero-Americana 6.

Bannock

B-L-BP. Liljeblad, Sven. 1950. 'Bannack I: Phonemes'. IJAL 16.126-131.

Cahuilla

CA-B-HC. Bright, William. 1965. 'The History of the Cahuilla Sound System'. IJAL 31.241-244.

CA-B-IN. Bright, William. No date. Informal notes on Cahuilla.

CA-B-MP. Bean, Lowell. 1972. Mukat's People, The Cahuilla Indians of

Southern California. Berkeley: University of California Press.

CA-BL-ISC. Bean, Lowell, and Harry Lawton. 1965. The Cahuilla
Indians of Southern California. Banning, California: Malki Museum
Press. Malki Museum Brochure No. 1.

CA-BS-T. Bean, Lowell, and Katherine Siva Saubel. 1972. Temalpakh,
Cahuilla Indian Knowledge and Usage of Plants. Banning, California:
Malki Museum Press.

CA-D-RF. Davis, John F. 1973. Review of Anna Fuchs, Morphologie
des Verbs im Cahuilla. Language 49.510-514.

CA-F-MV. Fuchs, Anna. 1970. Morphologie des Verbs im Cahuilla. The
Hague: Mouton. Janua Linguarum Series Practica, 87.

CA-H-BSK. Hioki, Kojiro. 1971. 'Zur Beschreibung des Systems der
Klitika im Cahuilla (Uto-Aztekisch, Süd-Kalifornien)'. Manuscript.

CA-H-K. Hioki, Kojiro. 1973. Die Klitika im Cahuilla (Uto-Aztekisch,
Süd-Kalifornien). Köln: University of Köln doctoral dissertation.

CA-J-I. James, Harry C. 1969. The Cahuilla Indians. Banning,
California: Malki Museum Press. [Original publication by Westernlore
Press, 1960.]

CA-J-RF. Jacobs, Roderick A. 1972. Review of Anna Fuchs,
Morphologie des Verbs im Cahuilla. Manuscript.

CA-L-AMM. Lawton, Harry W. 1974. 'Agricultural Motifs in Southern
California Indian Mythology'. JCA 1.55-79.

CA-L-RSF. Liljeblad, Sven. 1973. Review of Hansjakob Seiler, Cahuilla
Texts with an Introduction, and Anna Fuchs, Morphologie des Verbs im
Cahuilla. IJAL 39.110-121.

CA-S-AM. Seiler, Hansjakob. 1965. 'Accent and Morphophonemics in
Cahuilla and in Uto-Aztecan'. IJAL 31.50-59.

CA-S-G. Seiler, Hansjakob. 1971. Grammar of the Cahuilla Language.
[Part I: Semantics.] Manuscript.

CA-S-IN. Seiler, Hansjakob. 1966. Informal notes on Cahuilla.

CA-S-PC. Seiler, Hansjakob. 1974. 'The Principle of Concomitance in
Uto-Aztecan', in Hansjakob Seiler (ed.), Linguistic Workshop II, p. 56-
68. Munich: Wilhelm Fink Verlag. Structura 8, Arbeiten des Kölner
Universalienprojekts.

CA-S-T. Seiler, Hansjakob. 1970. Cahuilla Texts with an Introduction.
The Hague: Mouton. Indiana University Publications, Language Science
Monographs, 6.

CA-S-ZAW. Seiler, Hansjakob. 1958. 'Zur Aufstellung der Wortklassen
des Cahuilla (Uto-Aztekisch, Süd-Kalifornien)'. Münchener Studien zur
Sprachwissenschaft 12.61-79.

Chemehuevi

CH-H-HC.   Hill, Kenneth C. (ed.)   1969.   'J. P. Harrington's Chemehuevi Noun List'.   Manuscript.

CH-L-BF.   Laird, Carobeth.   1974.   'The Buffalo in Chemehuevi Folklore'. JCA 1.220-224.

CH-L-RBP.   Laird, Carobeth.   1974.   'Chemehuevi Religious Beliefs and Practices'.   JCA 1.19-25.

CH-M-B.   Munro, Pamela (ed.)   1974.   'Boyfriend', Chemehuevi text by Pearl Eddy.   Manuscript.

CH-M-IN.   Munro, Pamela.   1974.   Informal notes on Chemehuevi.

CH-M-IO.   Munro, Pamela.   1974.   'Imperative Objects in Chemehuevi'. Manuscript.

CH-M-IPP.   Munro, Pamela.   1974.   'Imperatives, Passives, and Perfectives in Chemehuevi'.   Manuscript.

CH-M-PC.   Munro, Pamela.   Personal communication.

CH-MM-ISC.   Miller, Ronald Dean, and Peggy Jeanne Miller.   1967.   The Chemehuevi Indians of Southern California.   Banning, California: Malki Museum Press.   Malki Museum Brochure No. 3.

CH-P-D.   Press, Margaret L.   1973.   'English-Chemehuevi Dictionary'. Computer print-out.

CH-P-G.   Press, Margaret L.   1975.   A Grammar of Chemehuevi.   Los Angeles: UCLA doctoral dissertation.

Comanche

CM-C-BL.   Casagrande, Joseph B.   1948.   'Comanche Baby Language'. IJAL 14.11-14.   [Reprinted in ATN-H-LCS, p. 245-250.]

CM-C-LA1.   Casagrande, Joseph B.   1954.   'Comanche Linguistic Acculturation: I'.   IJAL 20.140-151.

CM-C-LA2.   Casagrande, Joseph B.   1954.   'Comanche Linguistic Acculturation II'.   IJAL 20.217-237.

CM-C-LA3.   Casagrande, Joseph B.   1955.   'Comanche Linguistic Acculturation III'.   IJAL 21.8-25.

CM-C-T.   Canonge, Elliott.   1958.   Comanche Texts.   Norman, Oklahoma: Summer Institute of Linguistics.

CM-C-VV.   Canonge, Elliott.   1957.   'Voiceless Vowels in Comanche' IJAL 23.63-67.

CM-M-G.   Mark, Saint.   1958.   Mark-ha Tsaatü Narümu'ipü.   [Comanche edition of the Gospel according to Mark, translated by Elliott and Viola Canonge.]   New York: American Bible Society.

CM-M-HP.   Miller, Wick R.   1973.   'Comanche Historical Phonology'.

Informal notes.

CM-OS-F. Osborn, Henry, and William A. Smalley. 1949. 'Formulae for Comanche Stem and Word Formation'. IJAL 15.93-99.

CM-R-APA. Riggs, Venda. 1949. 'Alternate Phonemic Analyses of Comanche'. IJAL 15.229-231.

CM-S-PR. Smalley, William A. 1953. 'Phonemic Rhythm in Comanche'. IJAL 19.297-301.

Cora

CR-C-LDD. Casad, Eugene H. 1975. 'Location and Direction in Cora Discourse'. Manuscript.

CR-C-PC. Casad, Eugene H. Personal communication.

CR-CLZCC-C. Celestino Lauriano, Juan; Anselmo López Cánare; Eusebio Zeferino Enríquez; Eugene H. Casad; and Betty Davis Casad. 1974. Cartilla Cora. Mexico City: Instituto Lingüístico de Verano. [Two parts.]

CR-CLZCC-CT. Celestino Lauriano, Juan; Anselmo López Cánare; Eusebio Zeferino Enríquez; Eugene H. Casad; and Betty Davis Casad. 1974. Cuaderno de Trabajo Cora. Mexico City: Instituto Lingüístico de Verano. [Two parts. Workbook for CR-CLZCC-C.]

CR-M-PPU. McMahon, Ambrose. 1967. 'Phonemes and Phonemic Units of Cora (Mexico)'. IJAL 33.128-134.

CR-MM-CE. McMahon, Ambrose, and María Aiton de McMahon. 1959. Cora y Español. Mexico City: Instituto Lingüístico de Verano. Serie de Vocabularios Indígenas, No. 2.

CR-P-G. Preuss, Konrad-Theodor. 1932. 'Grammatik der Cora-Sprache'. IJAL 7.1-84.

CR-P-NE. Preuss, Konrad-Theodor. 1912. Die Nayarit-Expedition, Text-Aufnahmen und Beobachtungen unter Mexikanischen-Indianern, Volume I. Leipzig.

CR-P-V. Preuss, Konrad-Theodor. 1912. 'Das Verbum in der Sprache der Cora-Indianer', in Proceedings of the XVIII International Congress of Americanists, p. 105-106. London.

CR-P-W. Preuss, Konrad-Theodor. 1935. 'Wörterbuch Deutsch-Cora'. IJAL 8.81-102.

Cupeno

CU-H-CL. Hill, Jane H. 1972. 'Cupeño Lexicalization and Language History'. IJAL 38.161-172.

CU-H-G. Hill, Jane H. 1966. A Grammar of the Cupeño Language. Los Angeles: UCLA doctoral dissertation.

CU-H-PR. Hill, Jane H. 1970. 'A Peeking Rule in Cupeño'. Linguistic Inquiry 1.534-539.

CU-H-VN. Hill, Jane H. 1969. 'Volitional and Non-Volitional Verbs in Cupeño'. CLS 5.348-356.

CU-HN-M. Hill, Jane H., and Rosinda Nolasquez (eds.) 1973. Mulu'wetam: The First People (Cupeño Oral History and Language). Banning, California: Malki Museum Press.

CU-J-PR. Jacobs, Roderick A. 1971. ' "Peeking" Rules and Cupeño Phonology'. Manuscript.

CU-N-CK. Nolasquez, Rosinda. 1971. 'Cheme-sh Kuupa-ngax-wicham', as told to Roderick A. Jacobs. Manuscript.

Gabrielino

GA-BB-AL. Bright, William, and Marcia Bright. No date. 'Archaeology and Linguistics in Prehistoric Southern California'.

GA-H-EE. Hale, Horatio. 1846. Ethnography and Philology. United States Exploring Expedition, 1838-1842. [Reprinted: The Gregg Press, Ridgewood, N. J., 1968.]

Hopi

H-B-GC. Black, Robert A. 1967. 'Hopi Grievance Chants: A Mechanism of Social Control', in ATN-H-SSE, p. 54-67.

H-C-LTR. Carroll, John B. (ed.) 1956. Language, Thought, and Reality (Selected Writings of Benjamin Lee Whorf). Cambridge, Mass.: M.I.T. Press.

H-D-SL. Dockstader, Frederick J. 1955. 'Spanish Loanwords in Hopi; a Preliminary Checklist'. IJAL 21.157-159.

H-EE-HRW. Ekstrom, M. A. and J. O. 1973. How to Read and Write Hopi. Oraibi, Arizona: Hopi Action Program.

H-F-GPA. Freeze, Ray. 1974. 'Hopi Genitive and Possessive Affixation'. Manuscript.

H-F-NIR. Freeze, Ray. 1974. 'Naturalness and Hopi Internal Reconstruction'. Manuscript.

H-H-IN. Hale, Kenneth. 1974. Informal notes on Hopi.

H-J-NC. Jeanne, LaVerne Masayesva. 1975. 'A Note on the Hopi Causatives'. Manuscript.

H-J-RC. Jeanne, LaVerne Masayesva. 1974. 'The Relative Clause in Hopi'. Manuscript.

H-J-RCH. Jeanne, LaVerne Masayesva. 1974. 'The Relative Clause in Hopi'. Informal notes. [Summary of H-J-RC.]

H-J-RTN. Jeanne, LaVerne Masayesva. 1974. 'Reduplication and Tone in Hopi Nouns'. Manuscript.

H-K-FMGW. Kennard, Edward. 1944. Field Mouse Goes to War (Tusan Homichi Tuwvöta). Education Division, United States Indian Service.

H-K-IN. Kalectaca, Milo. 1975. Informal notes on Hopi.

H-K-LA. Kennard, Edward. 1963. 'Linguistic Acculturation in Hopi'. IJAL 29.36-41.

H-K-PC. Kennard, Edward. Personal communication.

H-K-SN. Kennard, Edward. 1974. 'Hopi Syntax in Narratives'. Informal notes.

H-K-T. Kennard, Edward. 1975. Hopi texts. Manuscript.

H-KM-MV. Kluckhohn, Clyde, and Kenneth MacLeish. 1955. 'Moencopi Variations from Whorf's Second Mesa Hopi'. IJAL 21.150-156.

H-KY-H. Kennard, Edward, and Albert Yava. 1948. Hopihoya (Little Hopi). Phoenix: United States Indian Service.

H-L-EN. Langacker, Ronald W. 1975. Hopi elicitation notes.

H-M-IN. Munro, Pamela. 1975. Informal notes on Hopi.

H-M-INO. Malotki, Ekkehart. 1975. Informal notes on Hopi.

H-M-NT. Matthew, Saint, et al. 1972. God Lavayiyat Añ Puhuvasiwni. [Hopi translation of the New Testament.] New York: American Bible Society.

H-M-PC. Munro, Pamela. Personal communication.

H-M-PCO. Malotki, Ekkehart. Personal communication.

H-S-IN. Sekaquaptewa, Emory. No date. Informal notes on Hopi.

H-T-SFS. Titiev, Mischa. 1946. 'Suggestions for the Further Study of Hopi'. IJAL 12.89-91.

H-V-PDS. Voegelin, C. F. 1956. 'Phonemicizing for Dialect Study, with Reference to Hopi'. Language 32.116-135.

H-V-PN. Voth, H. R. 1905. 'Hopi Proper Names'. Field Museum Anthropological Series 6.63-113.

H-VV-AL. Voegelin, C. F. and F. M. 1971. 'The Autonomy of Linguistics and the Dependence of Cognitive Culture', in Jesse Sawyer (ed.), Studies in American Indian Languages, p. 303-317. Berkeley and Los Angeles: University of California Press. UCPL 65.

H-VV-D. Voegelin, C. F. and F. M. 1957. Hopi Domains, A Lexical Approach to the Problem of Selection. Indiana University Publications in Anthropology and Linguistics, IJAL Memoir 14.

H-VV-H. Voegelin, C. F. and F. M. 1969. 'Hopi /ʔas/'. IJAL 35.192-202.

H-VV-HN. Voegelin, C. F. and F. M. 1970. 'Hopi Names and No Names', in UA-S-LCWN, p. 47-53.

H-VV-IN. Voegelin, C. F. and F. M. 1973. Informal notes on Hopi.

H-VV-ISNL. Voegelin, C. F. and F. M. 1974. 'Some Recent (and Not so Recent) Attempts to Interpret Semantics of Native Languages in North America'. Manuscript.

H-VV-PT. Voegelin, C. F. and F. M. 1967. 'Passive Transformations from Non-Transitive Bases in Hopi'. IJAL 33.276-281.

H-VV-Q. Voegelin, C. F. and F. M. 1975. 'Hopi /-qa/'. To appear in IJAL.

H-VVJ-S. Voegelin, C. F. and F. M., and LaVerne Masayesva Jeanne. 1975. 'Hopi Semantics'. Manuscript. [Written for Smithsonian Handbook of American Indians.]

H-W-AIMU. Whorf, B. L. 1950. 'An American Indian Model of the Universe'. IJAL 16.67-72. [Reprinted in H-C-LTR, p. 57-64.]

H-W-DHL. Whorf, B. L. 1956. 'Discussion of Hopi Linguistics', in H-C-LTR, p. 102-111. [Manuscript date: 1937.]

H-W-L. Whorf, B. L. 1956. The Hopi Language. Chicago: Microfilm Collection of Manuscripts on Middle American Cultural Anthropology, No. 48. University of Chicago Library. [Manuscript date: 1935.]

H-W-LF. Whorf, B. L. 1953. 'Linguistic Factors in the Terminology of Hopi Architecture'. IJAL 19.141-145. [Reprinted in H-C-LTR, p. 199-206.]

H-W-PSA. Whorf, B. L. 1936. 'The Punctual and Segmentative Aspects of Verbs in Hopi'. Language 12.127-131. [Reprinted in H-C-LTR, p. 51-56.]

H-W-RHTB. Whorf, B. L. 1941. 'The Relation of Habitual Thought and Behavior to Language', in UA-S-LCP, p. 75-93. [Reprinted in H-C-LTR, p. 134-159.]

H-W-TD. Whorf, B. L. 1946. 'The Hopi Language, Toreva Dialect', in ATN-H-LSNA, p. 158-183.

H-W-VC. Whorf, B. L. 1938. 'Some Verbal Categories of Hopi'. Language 14.275-286. [Reprinted in H-C-LTR, p. 112-124.]

H-W-VCL. Whorf, B. L. 1934. 'Hopi Verb Classes'. Informal notes. American Philosophical Society Library manuscript, No. 1570.

Huichol

HU-D-I. Diguet, Léon. 1911. 'Idiome Huichol, Contribution à l'Étude des Langues Mexicaines'. JSAP 8.23-54.

HU-F-RG. Foster, Mary L. 1966. Review of Joseph E. Grimes, Huichol Syntax. IJAL 32.290-291.

HU-G-HTI. Grimes, Joseph E. 1959. 'Huichol Tone and Intonation'. IJAL 25.221-232.

HU-G-PC. Grimes, Joseph E. Personal communication.

HU-G-S. Grimes, Joseph E. 1964. Huichol Syntax. The Hague: Mouton. Janua Linguarum Series Practica, 11.

HU-G-SHS. Grimes, Joseph E. 1955. 'Style in Huichol Structure'. Language 31.31-35.

HU-G-SNH. Grimes, Joseph E. 1960. 'Spanish-Nahuatl-Huichol Monetary Terms'. IJAL 26.162-165.

HU-GG-SDK. Grimes, Joseph E. and Barbara F. 1962. 'Semantic Distinctions in Huichol (Uto-Aztecan) Kinship'. AA 64.104-114.

HU-H-SMA. Hamp, Eric P. 1957. 'Stylistically Modified Allophones in Huichol'. Language 33.139-142.

HU-L-SP. Landar, Herbert. 1967. 'Syntactic Patterns in Navaho and Huichol'. IJAL 33.121-127.

HU-M-HP. McIntosh, John B. 1945. 'Huichol Phonemes'. IJAL 11.31-35.

HU-MG-V. McIntosh, John B., and Joseph E. Grimes. 1954. Niuqui ʔɨquisicayari: Vocabulario Huichol-Castellano Castellano-Huichol. Mexico City: Summer Institute of Linguistics.

HU-P-TTT. Price, P. David. 1967. 'Two Types of Taxonomy: A Huichol Ethnobotanical Example'. AL 9.1-28.

Kawaiisu

K-M-PC. Munro, Pamela. Personal communication.

K-M-SPO. Munro, Pamela. 1974. 'Some Preliminary Observations on Kawaiisu'. Manuscript.

K-Z-D. Zigmond, Maurice L. 1972. A Kawaiisu Dictionary. Manuscript.

K-Z-MSAE. Zigmond, Maurice L. 1972. 'Some Mythological and Supernatural Aspects of Kawaiisu Ethnography and Ethnobiology', in NUM-F-GBCE, p. 129-134.

Kitanemuk

KT-A-CS. Anderton, Alice. 1975. 'Complex Sentences in Kitanemuk'. Informal notes.

KT-A-PR. Anderton, Alice. 1974. 'A Progress Report on Research into Kitanemuk'. Manuscript.

KT-A-PRR. Anderton, Alice. 1975. 'Haminawət? III. A Progress Report on Research into Kitanemuk'. Manuscript.

Luiseno

L-A-IPRV. Anderson, Stephen R. 1975. 'On the Interaction of

Phonological Rules of Various Types'. Journal of Linguistics 11.39-62. [P. 45-48.]

L-B-D. Bright, William. 1968. A Luiseño Dictionary. Berkeley and Los Angeles: University of California Press. UCPL 51.

L-B-LP. Bright, William. 1965. 'Luiseño Phonemics'. IJAL 31.342-345.

L-B-RH. Bright, William. 1971. Review of Villiana Hyde, An Introduction to Luiseño [pre-publication version of L-H-I]. The Indian Historian 4.22.

L-C-PC. Chung, Sandra. Personal communication.

L-C-RPT. Chung, Sandra. 1974. 'Remarks on Pablo Tac's La Lingua degli Indi Luiseños'. IJAL 40.292-307.

L-D-PG. Davis, John F. 1973. A Partial Grammar of Simplex and Complex Sentences in Luiseño. Los Angeles: UCLA doctoral dissertation.

L-H-I. Hyde, Villiana. 1971. An Introduction to the Luiseño Language, ed. by Ronald W. Langacker et al. Banning, California: Malki Museum Press.

L-H-RH. Heath, Jeffrey. 1973. Review of Villiana Hyde, An Introduction to the Luiseño Language. IJAL 39.59.

L-KG-SG. Kroeber, A. L., and George William Grace. 1960. The Sparkman Grammar of Luiseño. Berkeley and Los Angeles: University of California Press. UCPL 16.

L-L-FN. Langacker, Ronald W. 1970. Luiseno field notes.

L-M-PC. Munro, Pamela. Personal communication.

L-M-RKG. Miller, Wick R. 1961. Review of A. L. Kroeber and George William Grace, The Sparkman Grammar of Luiseño. Language 37.186-189.

L-M-RS. Malécot, André. 1961. Review of A. L. Kroeber and George William Grace, The Sparkman Grammar of Luiseño. IJAL 27.64-71.

L-M-SA. Malécot, André. 1964. Luiseño: A Structural Analysis. Philadelphia: University of Pennsylvania. [Collected reprints of L-M-SA1, L-M-SA2, L-M-SA3, and L-M-SA4.]

L-M-SA1. Malécot, André. 1963. 'Luiseño, A Structural Analysis I: Phonology'. IJAL 29.89-95.

L-M-SA2. Malécot, André. 1963. 'Luiseño, A Structural Analysis II: Morpho-Syntax'. IJAL 29.196-210.

L-M-SA3. Malécot, André. 1964. 'Luiseño, A Structural Analysis III: Texts and Lexicon'. IJAL 30.14-31.

L-M-SA4. Malécot, André. 1964. 'Luiseño, A Structural Analysis IV: Appendices'. IJAL 30.243-250.

L-MB-RRO. Munro, Pamela, and Peter Benson. 1973. 'Reduplication and Rule Ordering in Luiseño'. IJAL 39.15-21.

L-S-CLI. Sparkman, P. S. 1908. 'The Culture of the Luiseño Indians'. UCPAAE 8.187-234. [Reprinted: Ramona, California, Ballena Press.]

L-S-OCO. Steele, Susan. 1975. 'On the Count of One'. Manuscript.

L-S-SG. Sparkman, P. S. 1905. 'Sketch of the Grammar of the Luiseño Language of California'. AA 7.656-662.

L-T-FD. Tagliavini, Carlo. 1930. 'Frammento d'un Dizionarietto Luiseño-Spagnuolo Scritto da un Indigeno'. Proceedings of the XXIII International Congress of Americanists, p. 905-917.

L-T-LIL. Tagliavini, Carlo. 1926. La Lingua degli Indi Luiseños. Bologna: Cooperativa Tipografica Azzoguidi. [Edition of a grammar by Pablo Tac.]

L-W-PR. Wilbur, Ronnie Bring. 1973. 'The Phonology of Reduplication'. Bloomington: Indiana University Linguistics Club. [P. 18-24, 45-46, 60-62, 73-74.]

Mono

M-L-FILL. Liljeblad, Sven. 1964. 'Fort Independence Mono Lexical List'. Manuscript.

M-L-G. Lamb, Sydney M. 1958. Mono Grammar. Berkeley: University of California doctoral dissertation.

M-L-PTP. Lamb, Sydney M. 1966. 'Prolegomena to a Theory of Phonology'. Language 42.536-573.

Mayo

MA-C-ES. Crumrine, Lynne S. 1968. 'An Ethnography of Mayo Speaking'. AL 10.19-31.

MA-CC-CM. Collard, Howard, and Elizabeth Collard. 1962. Castellano-Mayo, Mayo-Castellano. Mexico City: Instituto Lingüístico de Verano. Serie de Vocabularios Indígenas, No. 6.

MA-M-G. Mark, Saint. 1963. San Márcosta Jí'ojteri. [Mayo edition of the Gospel according to Mark, translated by Howard and Elizabeth Collard.] Mexico City: American Bible Society.

Northern Paiute

NP-AA-AS. Anderson, John and Joy. 1972. 'Alternate Solutions to Paiute Phonology'. Manuscript.

NP-AA-S. Anderson, John and Joy. 1975. 'Northern Paiute Subordination'. Informal notes.

NP-AF-N. Angulo, Jaime de, and L. S. Freeland. 1929. 'Notes on the Northern Paiute of California'. JSAP 21.313-335.

NP-FL-NC. Fowler, Catherine S., and Joy Leland. 1967. 'Some Northern Paiute Native Categories'. Ethnology 6.381-404.

NP-L-M. Liljeblad, Sven. 1967. Northern Paiute Manual. [Course notes, University of Nevada, 1966-67.]

NP-L-PL. Liljeblad, Sven. 1971. 'A Primitive Language?', in Charlton Laird and Robert M. Gorrell (eds.), Reading about Language, p. 67-76. New York: Harcourt Brace Jovanovich.

NP-M-LO. Marsden, W. L. 1923. 'The Northern Paiute Language of Oregon'. UCPAAE 20.175-191.

NP-N-HG. Nichols, Michael J. P. 1974. Northern Paiute Historical Grammar. Berkeley: University of California doctoral dissertation.

NP-N-IN. Nichols, Michael J. P. 1971. Informal notes on Northern Paiute.

NP-N-V. Natches, Gilbert. 1923. 'Northern Paiute Verbs'. UCPAAE 20.245-259.

NP-W-PE. Waterman, T. T. 1911. 'The Phonetic Elements of the Northern Paiute Language'. UCPAAE 10.13-44.

Northern Tepehuan

NT-B-T. Bascom, Burton. 1959. 'Tonomechanics of Northern Tepehuan'. Phonetica 4.71-88.

NT-M-G. Mark, Saint. 1962. Marcos Ojai Gocʌʌcaidájʌdʌ Susicrísto Vʌtárʌ. [Northern Tepehuan edition of the Gospel according to Mark, translated by Burton Bascom.] Mexico City: American Bible Society.

NT-MNR-LM. Merrifield, William, Constance M. Naish, and Calvin R. Rensch. 1960. Morphology-Syntax Laboratory Manual. Glendale, California: Summer Institute of Linguistics.

NT-MNRS-LM. Merrifield, William, Constance M. Naish, Calvin R. Rensch, and Gillion Story. 1961. Morphology-Syntax Laboratory Manual, Supplement. Santa Ana, California: Summer Institute of Linguistics.

NT-PBB-IC. Pike, Kenneth L., Ralph P. Barrett, and Burton Bascom. 1959. 'Instrumental Collaboration on a Tepehuan (Uto-Aztecan) Pitch Problem'. Phonetica 3.1-22.

NT-W-TNT. Woo, Nancy. 1970. 'Tone in Northern Tepehuan'. IJAL 36.18-30.

Opata

O-J-ITS. Johnson, Jean B. 1950. The Opata: An Inland Tribe of Sonora. Albuquerque: University of New Mexico Press. University of New Mexico Publications in Anthropology, No. 6.

Papago

P-A-PP.   Alvarez, Albert. 1965. 'Some Papago Puns'. IJAL 31.106-107.

P-AH-TM. Alvarez, Albert, and Kenneth Hale. 1970. 'Toward a Manual of Papago Grammar: Some Phonological Terms'. IJAL 36.83-97.

P-CH-SR. Casagrande, Joseph B., and Kenneth Hale. 1967. 'Semantic Relationships in Papago Folk-Definitions', in ATN-H-SSE, p. 165-193.

P-D-NS.   Dolores, Juan. 1923. 'Papago Nominal Stems'. UCPAAE 20.19-31.

P-D-VS.   Dolores, Juan. 1913. 'Papago Verb Stems'. UCPAAE 10.241-263.

P-G-RM.   Grimes, Joseph E. 1953. Review of J. Alden Mason, The Language of the Papago of Arizona. IJAL 19.313-315.

P-H-D.   Hale, Kenneth. 1975. 'Papago Data'. Informal notes.

P-H-G.   Hale, Kenneth. 1959. A Papago Grammar. Bloomington: Indiana University doctoral dissertation.

P-H-IN.   Hale, Kenneth. 1970, 1974. Informal notes on Papago.

P-H-IWO. Hale, Kenneth. 1975. 'Papago Intonation and Word Order'. Manuscript.

P-H-NP.   Hale, Kenneth. 1969. 'A New Perspective on American Indian Linguistics'. Manuscript.

P-H-P.   Hale, Kenneth. 1969. 'Papago /čɨm/'. IJAL 35.203-212.

P-H-PC.   Hale, Kenneth. Personal communication.

P-H-PL.   Hale, Kenneth. 1970. 'On Papago Laryngeals', in UA-S-LCWN, p. 54-60.

P-H-PO.   Hale, Kenneth. 1965. 'Some Preliminary Observations on Papago Morphophonemics'. IJAL 31.295-305.

P-H-RK.   Halpern, A. M. 1946. Review of William Kurath, A Brief Introduction to Papago, a Language of Arizona. IJAL 12.44-45.

P-H-TTE. Hankamer, Jorge. 1973. 'Why There are Two Than's in English'. CLS 9.179-191. [P. 190.]

P-I-TNT. Ives, Ronald L. 1947. 'Two Nahuatlan Terms from Northwestern Sonora'. IJAL 13.119.

P-KM-MRME. Kroch, Anthony S., and Byron Marshall. 1973. 'Movement Rules and Modal Expressions in Papago'. IJAL 39.80-88.

P-L-FN.   Langacker, Ronald W. 1965. Papago field notes.

P-L-M.   Lynch, Richard. No date. 'Papago Morphophonemics'. Informal notes.

P-M-CSNN. Mathiot, Madeleine. 1967. 'The Cognitive Significance of the Category of Nominal Number in Papago', in ATN-H-SSE, p. 197-237.

P-M-G.   Mark, Saint. 1966. Mark O'ohana ab amjeD g Jiosh Alidag.
[Papago edition of the Gospel according to Mark, translated by Dean and
Lucille Saxton.] New York: American Bible Society.

P-M-LPA.   Mason, J. Alden. 1950. The Language of the Papago of
Arizona. Philadelphia: University of Pennsylvania Museum Monographs.

P-M-NCFT.   Mathiot, Madeleine. 1962. 'Noun Classes and Folk Taxonomy in Papago'. AA 64.340-350. [Reprinted in ATN-H-LCS, p. 154-163.]

P-OD-NCD.   O'Neale, Lila M., and Juan Dolores. 1943. 'Notes on
Papago Color Designations'. AA 45.387-397.

P-S-PP.   Saxton, Dean. 1963. 'Papago Phonemes'. IJAL 29.29-35.

P-SS-D.   Saxton, Dean and Lucille. 1969. Dictionary, Papago & Pima to
English, English to Papago & Pima. Tucson: University of Arizona
Press.

P-SS-LL.   Saxton, Dean and Lucille. 1973. Legends and Lore of the
Papago and Pima Indians. Tucson: University of Arizona Press.

Pima

PI-H-CCL.   Herzog, George. 1941. 'Culture Change and Language:
Shifts in the Pima Vocabulary', in UA-S-LCP, p. 66-74.

Pochutla

PO-B-DMP.   Boas, Franz. 1917. 'El Dialecto Mexicano de Pochutla,
Oaxaca'. IJAL 1.9-44.

PO-B-PML.   Boas, Franz. 1912. 'Phonetics of the Mexican Language',
in Proceedings of the XVIII International Congress of Americanists,
p. 107-108. London.

PO-H-DN.   Hasler, Juan A. 1975. 'El Pochuteco en la Dialectología
Nahua'. Manuscript.

Shoshoni

SH-B-EDG.   Booth, Curtis (ed.) 1975. 'Early Days at Gosiute', Shoshoni
text by Minnie Bonimont, collected by Wick R. Miller. Manuscript.

SH-C-LV.   Crapo, Richley H. 1970. Language Variation among the
Duckwater Shoshoni. Salt Lake City: University of Utah doctoral dissertation.

SH-D-PMS.   Daley, Jon P. 1970. Shoshone Phonology and Morphological
Sketch. Pocatello: Idaho State University master's thesis.

SH-H-RM.   Heath, Jeffrey. 1974. Review of Wick R. Miller, Newe
Natekwinappeh: Shoshoni Stories and Dictionary. IJAL 40.162-164.

SH-HM-EB.   Hage, Per, and Wick R. Miller. 1974. ' "Eagle" = "Bird":

A Note on the Structure and Evolution of Shoshoni Ethnoornithological
Nomenclature'. Manuscript.

SH-M-DL. Miller, Wick R. 1971. 'The Death of Language or Serendipity
among the Shoshoni'. AL 13.114-120.

SH-M-IN. Miller, Wick R. 1968, 1971. Informal notes on Shoshoni.

SH-M-NN. Miller, Wick R. 1972. Newe Natekwinappeh: Shoshoni Stories
and Dictionary. Salt Lake City: University of Utah Press. University
of Utah Anthropological Papers, No. 94.

SH-M-SPR. Miller, Wick R. 1968. 'Shoshoni Phonological Rules'. Informal notes.

SH-M-WSD. Miller, Wick R. 1970. 'Western Shoshoni Dialects', in UA-
S-LCWN, p. 17-36.

SH-MB-LC. Miller, Wick R., and Curtis Booth. 1971-72. Shoshoni
Language Course Materials. Informal notes.

SH-MTF-LSD. Miller, Wick R., James L. Tanner, and Lawrence
Foley. 1971. 'A Lexicostatistic Study of Shoshoni Dialects'. AL
13.142-164.

SH-S-HS. Shaul, David L. 1975. 'A History of the Study of Shoshone'.
Manuscript.

SH-S-LST. Shimkin, D. B. 1949. 'Shoshone, I: Linguistic Sketch and
Text'. IJAL 15.175-188.

SH-S-ML. Shimkin, D. B. 1949. 'Shoshone II: Morpheme List'. IJAL
15.203-212.

SH-S-NPEG. Smith, Janet Hugie. 1972. 'Native Pharmacopoeia of the
Eastern Great Basin: A Report on Work in Progress', in NUM-F-
GBCE, p. 73-86.

SH-S-WRLF. Shimkin, D. B. 1947. 'Wind River Shoshone Literary
Forms: An Introduction'. Journal of the Washington Academy of
Sciences 37.329-352. [Reprinted in ATN-H-LCS, p. 344-355.]

Southern Paiute

SP-B-ESPI. Bye, Robert A., Jr. 1972. 'Ethnobotany of the Southern
Paiute Indians in the 1870's: With a Note on the Early Ethnobotanical
Contributions of Dr. Edward Palmer', in NUM-F-GBCE, p. 87-104.

SP-CH-SPE. Chomsky, Noam, and Morris Halle. 1968. The Sound Pattern of English. New York: Harper and Row. [P. 345-349.]

SP-H-DTUR. Hastings, Ashley J. 1974. 'Howard's Directional Theory
and the Unordered Rule Hypothesis', in Anthony Bruck et al. (eds.),
Papers from the Parasession on Natural Phonology, p. 146-159.
Chicago: Chicago Linguistic Society. [P. 153.]

SP-H-SGP. Heath, Jeffrey. 1968. 'Study of Southern Paiute Grammar,
Part I: Phonology'. Manuscript.

SP-H-SVL. Harms, Robert T. 1966. 'Stress, Voice, and Length in Southern Paiute'. IJAL 32.228-235.

SP-L-SP. Lovins, Julie B. 1972. 'Southern Paiute /s/ and /c/'. IJAL 38.136-142.

SP-M-RCH. McCawley, James D. 1974. Review of Noam Chomsky and Morris Halle, The Sound Pattern of English. IJAL 40.50-88. [P. 80.]

SP-R-ITS. Rogers, Jean H. 1967. 'Some Implications of Two Solutions to a Phonological Problem'. IJAL 33.198-205.

SP-S-D. Sapir, Edward. 1931. 'Southern Paiute Dictionary'. AAASP 65.537-729.

SP-S-G. Sapir, Edward. 1930. 'Southern Paiute, A Shoshonean Language'. AAASP 65.1-296.

SP-S-PRP. Sapir, Edward. 1933. 'La Réalité Psychologique des Phonèmes'. Journal de Psychologie Normale et Pathologique 30.247-265. [Reprinted as 'The Psychological Reality of Phonemes', in David G. Mandelbaum (ed.), Selected Writings of Edward Sapir in Language, Culture and Personality, Berkeley and Los Angeles, University of California Press, 1949, p. 46-60.]

SP-S-T. Sapir, Edward. 1930. 'Texts of the Kaibab Paiutes and Uintah Utes'. AAASP 65.297-535.

SP-S-VM. Statha-Halikas, Hara. 1975. 'Southern Paiute Verb Morphology'. Informal notes.

SP-SS-GC. Sapir, Edward, and Morris Swadesh. 1946. 'American Indian Grammatical Categories'. Word 2.103-112. [Reprinted in ATN-H-LCS, p. 101-111.]

SP-W-CS. Wendell, Marlys. 1967. 'Some Comments on Sapir's The Southern Paiute Language'. Manuscript.

Serrano

SR-C-CAC. Crook, Donald. 1975. 'Complements and Adverbial Clauses in Serrano'. Manuscript.

SR-C-IN. Crook, Donald. 1974, 1975. Informal notes on Serrano.

SR-C-IO. Crook, Donald. 1974. 'Imperative Objects in Serrano'. Manuscript.

SR-C-ME. Crook, Donald. 1974. 'Modal Enclitics in Serrano'. Manuscript.

SR-C-PC. Crook, Donald. Personal communication.

SR-H-C. Hill, Kenneth C. 1969. 'Serrano Clitics'. University of Michigan Phonetics Laboratory Notes 4.27-30.

SR-H-D. Hill, Kenneth C. 1972. A Serrano Dictionary. Computer print-out.

SR-H-D2. Hill, Kenneth C. 1973. A Serrano Dictionary. Computer print-out.

SR-H-G. Hill, Kenneth C. 1967. A Grammar of the Serrano Language. Los Angeles: UCLA doctoral dissertation.

SR-H-ISP. Hill, Kenneth C. 1969. 'Some Implications of Serrano Phonology'. CLS 5.357-365.

SR-J-ISC. Johnston, Francis J. 1965. The Serrano Indians of Southern California. Banning, California: Malki Museum Press. Malki Museum Brochure No. 2.

SR-W-RRO. Wilbur, Ronnie Bring. 1973. 'Reduplication and Rule Ordering'. CLS 9.679-687.

Tarahumara

TA-B-G. Brambila, David, S. J. 1953. Gramática Rarámuri. Mexico: Editorial Buena Prensa.

TA-B-M. Basauri, Carlos. 1929. Monografía de los Tarahumaras. Mexico: Talleres Gráficos de la Nación.

TA-B-TP. Burgess, Don H. 1970. 'Tarahumara Phonology (Rocoroibo Dialect)', in Ralph W. Ewton, Jr. and Jacob Ornstein (eds.), Studies in Language and Linguistics (1969-70), p. 45-65. El Paso: Texas Western Press.

TA-H-PF. Hilton, Kenneth S. 1947. 'Palabras y Frases de las Lenguas Tarahumara y Guarijío'. Anales del Instituto Nacional de Antropología e Historia 2.307-313. [1941-1946.] Mexico City: Secretaria de Educacion Pública.

TA-H-TE. Hilton, Kenneth S. 1959. Tarahumara y Español. Mexico City: Instituto Lingüístico de Verano. Serie de Vocabularios Indígenas, No. 1.

TA-L-SE. Llaguno, José A. 1970. El Tarahumar sin Esfuerzo (third edition). Sisoguichi, Chihuahua.

TA-M-G. Mark, Saint. 1947. We Garabé Raʔíčari Mapurigá Osári Márko. [Tarahumara edition of the Gospel according to Mark, translated by Kenneth S. Hilton.] Mexico City: American Bible Society.

TA-R-CC. Rosenthal, Jane M. 1968. 'Case and Category in Tarahumara Verbs--and Boas, Sapir, and Fillmore'. Informal notes.

TA-T-TED. Thord-Gray, I. 1955. Tarahumara-English English-Tarahumara Dictionary. Coral Gables, Florida: University of Miami Press.

Tepecano

TO-M-PL. Mason, J. Alden. 1916. 'Tepecano, A Piman Language of

Western Mexico'. Annals of the New York Academy of Science 25.309-416.

TO-M-TP. Mason, J. Alden. 1918. 'Tepecano Prayers'. IJAL 1.91-153.

Tubatulabal

TU-A-WSVS. Anderson, Stephen R. 1969. West Scandinavian Vowel Systems and the Ordering of Phonological Rules. Cambridge, Mass.: MIT doctoral dissertation. [P. 118-121.]

TU-B-IN. Bergman, Coral. 1975. Informal notes on Tubatulabal.

TU-H-DTRA. Howard, Irwin. 1972. A Directional Theory of Rule Application in Phonology. Cambridge, Mass.: MIT doctoral dissertation. [P. 38-39, 187-197, 227-232. Printed as University of Hawaii Working Papers in Linguistics 4.7, 1972.]

TU-J-SVP. Jensen, James R. 1973. Stress and the Verbal Phonology of Tubatulabal. Bloomington: Indiana University doctoral dissertation.

TU-KK-UBO. Kenstowicz, Michael J., and Charles W. Kisseberth. 1973. 'Unmarked Bleeding Orders', in Charles W. Kisseberth (ed.), Studies in Generative Phonology, p. 1-12. Papers in Linguistics Monograph Series 3. [P. 4-5.]

TU-L-SVP. Lightner, Theodore M. 1970. 'On Swadesh and Voegelin's "A Problem in Phonological Alternation"'. Papers in Linguistics 3.201-220. [Also in IJAL 37.227-237, 1971.]

TU-M-LV. McCawley, James D. 1969. 'Length and Voicing in Tübatulabal'. CLS 5.407-415.

TU-SV-PPA. Swadesh, Morris, and C. F. Voegelin. 1939. 'A Problem in Phonological Alternation'. Language 15.1-10. [Reprinted in Martin Joos (ed.), Readings in Linguistics, New York, American Council of Learned Societies, 1958, p. 88-92.]

TU-T-RP. Tranel, Bernard. 1971. 'Some Remarks on Tübatulabal Phonology'. Informal notes.

TU-V-G. Voegelin, C. F. 1935. 'Tübatulabal Grammar'. UCPAAE 34.55-189.

TU-V-T. Voegelin, C. F. 1935. 'Tübatulabal Texts'. UCPAAE 34.191-246.

TU-V-WD. Voegelin, C. F. 1958. 'Working Dictionary of Tübatulabal'. IJAL 24.221-228.

TU-W-N. Whorf, B. L. 1936. 'Notes on the Tübatulabal Language'. UCPAAE 38.341-344.

Ute

U-G-BPEM. Goss, James A. 1972. 'A Basin-Plateau Shoshonean Ecological Model', in NUM-F-GBCE, p. 123-128.

U-G-GGSN. Goss, James A. 1974. 'Gumming to Glory: A Ute Socio-
linguistic Note'. Manuscript.

U-G-LKMN. Goss, James A. 1967. 'Ute Language, Kin, Myth, and
Nature: A Demonstration of a Multi-Dimensional Folk Taxonomy'. AL
9.1-11.

U-K-N. Kroeber, A. L. 1908. 'Notes on the Ute Language'. AA 10.74-
87.

U-S-FC. Sapir, Edward. 1910. 'Some Fundamental Characteristics of
the Ute Language'. AA 12.66-69.

Varohio

V-JJ-V. Johnson, Jean B., and Irmgard W. de Johnson. 1947. 'Un
Vocabulario Varohio'. Revista Mexicana de Estudios Antropológicos
9.27-45.

Yaqui

Y-C-PAY. Crumrine, Lynne S. 1961. The Phonology of Arizona Yaqui,
with Texts. Tucson: University of Arizona Press. Anthropological
Papers of the University of Arizona, No. 5.

Y-F-YP. Fraenkel, Gerd. 1959. 'Yaqui Phonemics'. AL 1.7-18.

Y-J-CCLA. Johnson, Jean B. 1943. 'A Clear Case of Linguistic Acculturation'. AA 45.427-434.

Y-J-I. Johnson, Jean B. 1962. El Idioma Yaqui. Mexico City: Instituto
Nacional de Antropología e Historia, Departamento de Investigaciones
Antropológicas, Publicaciones 10.

Y-L-PC. Lindenfeld, Jacqueline. Personal communication.

Y-L-RL. Langacker, Ronald W. 1974. Review of Jacqueline Lindenfeld,
Yaqui Syntax. To appear in IJAL.

Y-L-S. Lindenfeld, Jacqueline. 1973. Yaqui Syntax. Berkeley and Los
Angeles: University of California Press. UCPL 76.

Y-L-SC. Lindenfeld, Jacqueline. 1971. 'Semantic Categorization as a
Deterrent to Grammatical Borrowing: A Yaqui Example'. IJAL 37.6-
14.

Y-L-SIS. Lindenfeld, Jacqueline. 1975. 'Spanish Influences in Yaqui
Syntax'. Manuscript.

Y-L-TG. Lindenfeld, Jacqueline. 1969. A Transformational Grammar of
Yaqui. Los Angeles: UCLA doctoral dissertation.

Y- M- PS.   Mason, J. Alden.   1923.   'A Preliminary Sketch of the Yaqui Language'.   <u>UCPAAE</u> 20. 195-2 12.

Y- S- LAA.   Spicer, Edward H.   1943.   'Linguistic Aspects of Yaqui Accul-turation'.   <u>AA</u> 45. 410-426.

ISBN: 0-520-09539-1